PHILIP'S

NEW SCHOOL ATLAS

FIRST EDITION

CONTENTS

Note: Each section is colour-coded on this contents page and on the heading of each page for ease of reference.

Published in Great Britain in 1999
by George Philip Limited,
a division of Octopus Publishing Group Limited,
2–4 Heron Quays, London E14 4JP

© 1999 George Philip Limited

Cartography by Philip's

This edition produced for
The Book People Limited,
Hall Wood Avenue,
Haydock,
St Helens WA11 9UL

ISBN 1–85613–574–8

BRITISH ISLES MAPS

A separate map key is provided on the first page of the World Maps section.

SETTLEMENTS

▣ **LONDON** ▣ **GLASGOW** ▣ **BRADFORD** ▣ **Brighton** ● Gateshead

◉ *Aylesbury* ◎ *Sligo* ⊙ *Selkirk* ○ *Burford* ○ *Lampeter*

Settlement symbols and type styles vary according to the population and importance of towns

⬡ Built up areas ▫ London Boroughs

ADMINISTRATION

——	International boundaries	**W A L E S**	Country names
——	National boundaries	KENT	Administrative area names
·—·—·	Administrative boundaries	*EXMOOR*	National park names

COMMUNICATIONS

══	Motorways	——	Main passenger railways
===:	*under construction*	——·—	*under construction*
		⌐----⌐	*in tunnels*
——	Major roads		
——·—	*under construction*	——	Other passenger railways
⌐----⌐	*in tunnels*	——·—	*under construction*
		⌐----⌐	*in tunnels*
——	Other important roads		
——·—	*under construction*	—⊢—⊢—	Canals
⌐----⌐	*in tunnels*	·····—·····	*in tunnels*

⊕ Major airports ⊕ Other airports

PHYSICAL FEATURES

⌒	Perennial rivers	▲ 444	Elevations in metres
⌒	Tidal flats	▼ 38	Depths below sea level in metres
⬭	Lakes or reservoirs		
⌐¯⌐	Reservoirs under construction		

ELEVATION AND DEPTH TINTS

Height of Land above Sea Level   Land below Sea Level   Depth of Sea

in metres	1000	750	500	400	200	100	0							
								150	300	600	1500	3000	6000	in feet
in feet	3000	2250	1500	1200	600	300								
							0	20	50	100	200	500	1000	2000
														in metres

SHETLAND ISLANDS
on same scale

Projection: Conical with two standard parallels

West from Greenwich

ORKNEY ISLANDS on same scale

CARTOGRAPHY BY PHILIP'S.

1:1 000 000

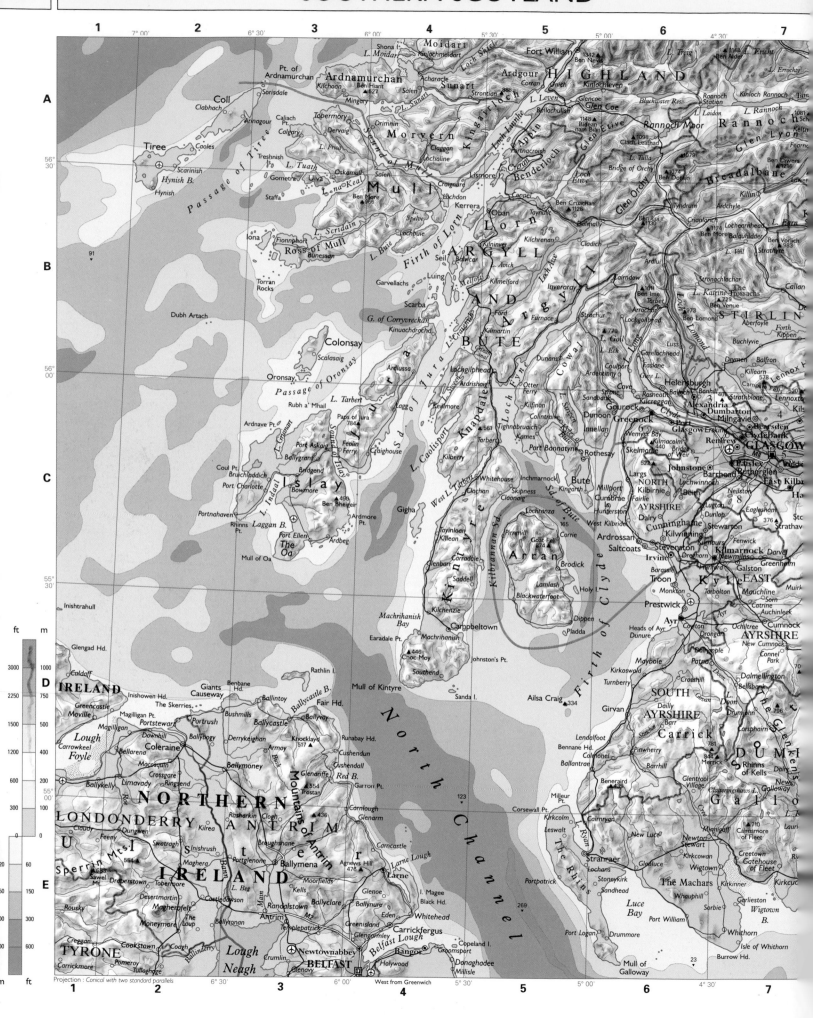

CARTOGRAPHY BY PHILIP'S.

1:1 000 000

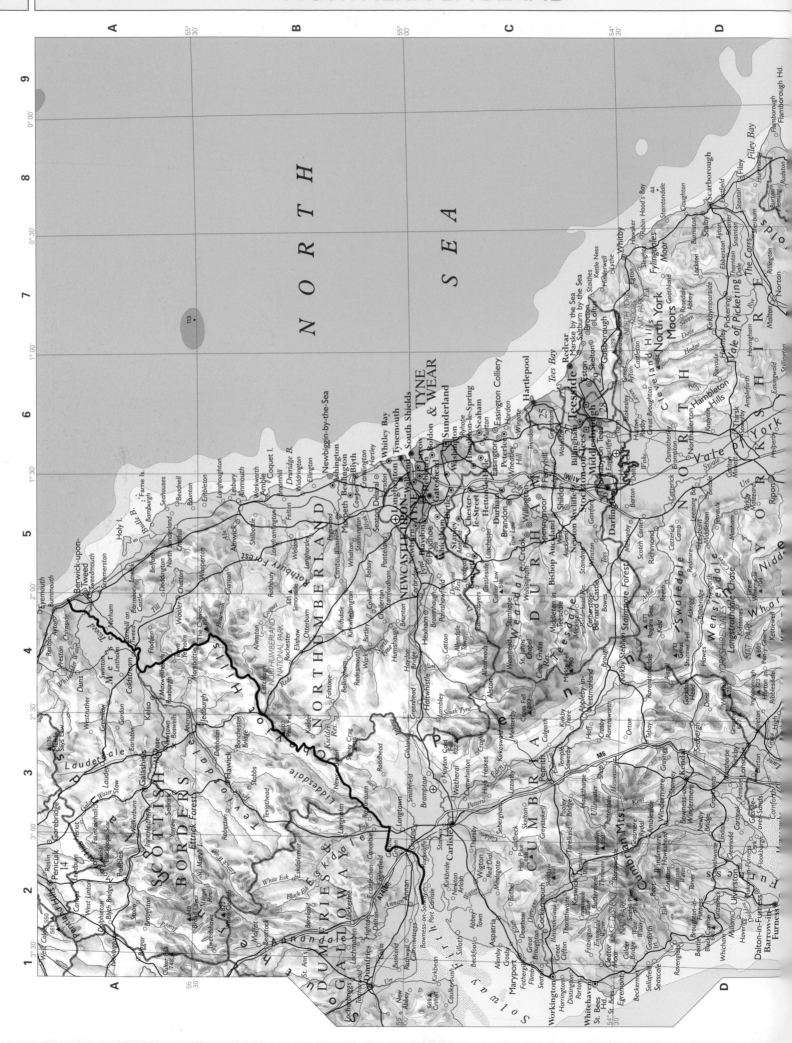

CARTOGRAPHY BY PHILIP'S

1:1 000 000

Projection : Conical with two standard parallels

West from Greenwich

SOUTH AND SOUTH-EAST ENGLAND

Projection : Conical with two standard parallels

West from Greenwich

7 8 9 10 11 12

LINCOLNSHIRE

NORFOLK

CAMBRIDGESHIRE

SUFFOLK

NORTHAMPTONSHIRE

BEDFORDSHIRE

HERTFORDSHIRE

ESSEX

GREATER LONDON

LONDON

SURREY

KENT

WEST SUSSEX

EAST SUSSEX

The Wash

The Fens

Breckland

NORFOLK BROADS NAT. PARK

North Downs

The Weald

Thames Estuary

Strait of Dover

FRANCE

Norwich · Great Yarmouth · Lowestoft · King's Lynn · Cromer · Peterborough · Cambridge · Ipswich · Colchester · Chelmsford · Southend-on-Sea · Bedford · Luton · Stevenage · St. Albans · London · Guildford · Brighton · Eastbourne · Hastings · Dover · Folkestone · Margate · Ramsgate · Canterbury · Maidstone · Rochester · Gillingham · Gravesend · Watford · Harlow · Harwich · Felixstowe · Clacton-on-Sea · Bury St. Edmunds · Newmarket · Ely · Northampton · Milton Keynes · Worthing · Crawley · Tunbridge Wells · Ashford · Calais · Boulogne-sur-Mer

52° 30'
52° 00'
51° 30'
51° 00'

0° 30' 0° 00' 0° 30' 1° 00'

A B C D

East from Greenwich

CARTOGRAPHY BY PHILIP'S.

1:1 000 000

10   10   20 miles
10   20   30 km

WALES AND

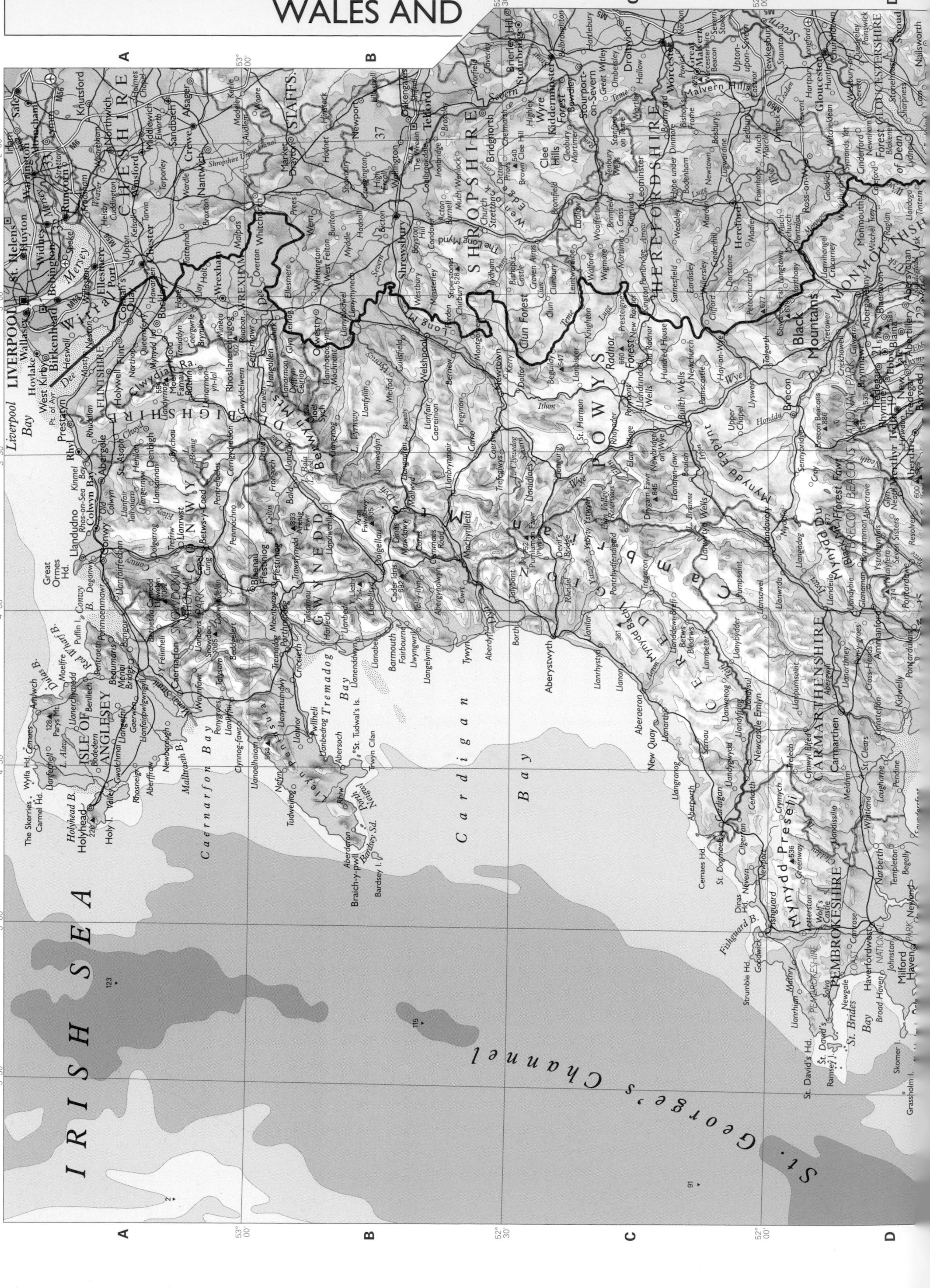

IRISH SEA

St. George's Channel

Cardigan Bay

Caernarfon Bay

Tremadog Bay

Liverpool Bay

CHESHIRE

SHROPSHIRE

HEREFORDSHIRE

GLOUCESTERSHIRE

MONMOUTHSHIRE

POWYS

GWYNEDD

CONWY

DENBIGHSHIRE

FLINTSHIRE

ISLE OF ANGLESEY

SNOWDONIA NATIONAL PARK

CEREDIGION

CARMARTHENSHIRE

PEMBROKESHIRE

BRECON BEACONS NATIONAL PARK

STAFFS.

Black Mountains

Malvern Hills

LIVERPOOL

Chester

Shrewsbury

Wrexham

Hereford

Aberystwyth

Cardigan

Milford Haven

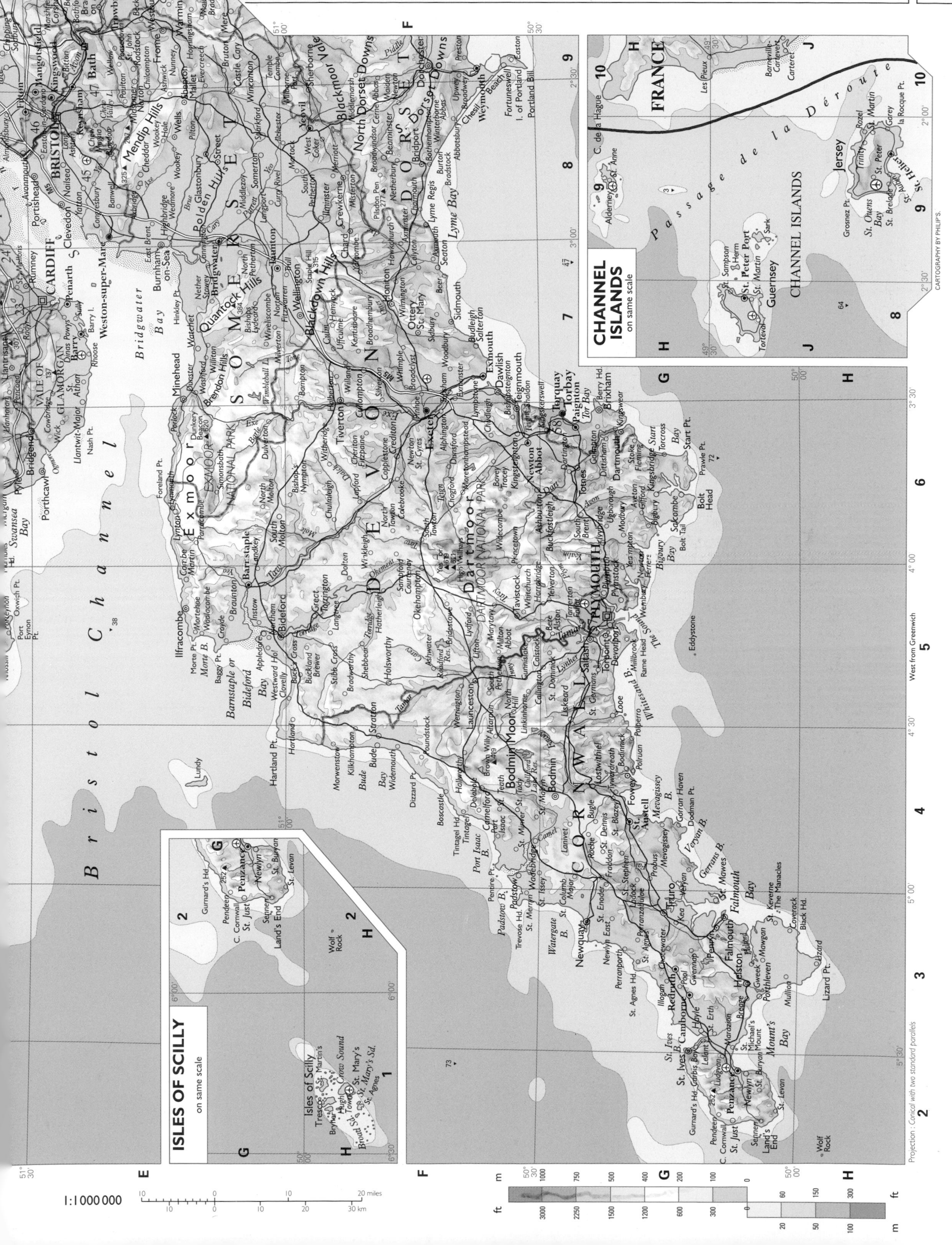

CHANNEL ISLANDS
on same scale

FRANCE

C. de la Hague
St. Anne
Alderney
Les Pieux
Barneville-Carteret
Carteret

Passage de la Déroute

Jersey
Rozel
Trinity
St. Martin
Grosnez Pt.
St. Peter
St. Ouens Bay
St. Martin
St. Helier
St. Brelade
la Rocque Pt.

Sampson
St. Sampson
Herm
Peter Port
St. Martin
Guernsey
Jethou
Sark
Torteval

CHANNEL ISLANDS

CARTOGRAPHY BY PHILIP'S.

ISLES OF SCILLY
on same scale

Gurnard's Hd.
Pendeen
C. Cornwall
St. Just
Penzance
Newlyn
Seqnen
St. Buryan
St. Levan
Land's End
Wolf Rock

Isles of Scilly
Tresco
St. Martin's
Bryher
St. Mary's
St. Mary's Sd.
Hugh Town
Crow Sound
Broad Sd.
St. Agnes

SOMERSET

DORSET

DEVON

CORNWALL

DARTMOOR NATIONAL PARK

EXMOOR NATIONAL PARK

Bristol Channel

Bridgwater Bay

Lyme Bay

Barnstaple or Bideford Bay

Mount's Bay

BRISTOL
CARDIF
Bath
Frome
Weston-super-Mare
Bridgwater
Taunton
Tiverton
Exeter
Exmouth
Dawlish
Teignmouth
Torquay
Torbay
Paignton
Brixham
Dartmouth
PLYMOUTH
Saltash
Looe
Fowey
St. Austell
Truro
Falmouth
Helston
Penzance
St. Ives
Newquay
Padstow
Bude
Barnstaple
Bideford
Ilfracombe
Minehead
Weymouth
Dorchester
Yeovil
Sherborne
Glastonbury
Wells

Projection: Conical with two standard parallels

1:1 000 000

West from Greenwich

ATLANTIC

OCEAN

A

55° 00'

B

54° 30'

C

54° 00'

D

53° 30'

E

ft   m

2250   750

1500   500

1200   400

600   200

300   100

0

20   60

50   150

100   300

200   600

500   1500

1000   3000

2000   6000

m   ft

Projection : Conical with two standard parallels   West from Greenwich

DONEGAL

Malin

Tory I.

Bloody Foreland

GLENVEAGH NAT. PARK

Errigal   752

Aran I.

The Rosses   683

Letterkenny

Londonderry

NORTH

Crohy Hd.

Dawros Hd.

Loughros More B.

Slieve Tobey   444   676

Glencolumbkille   Lavagh More

Rossan Pt.

Slieve League   601

Carrick

Carrigan Hd.

Muckros Hd.

Killybegs

Mc Swyne's B.   St. John's Pt.   Inver B.

Donegal Harbour

Donegal Bay   Ballyshannon

FERMANAGH

Inishmurray I.   Bundoran   Lough Melvin   Lough Erne

Enniskillen

Sligo Bay   Sligo   LEITRIM

Erris Hd.   Broad Haven   Benwee Hd.   Portacloy   Downpatrick Hd.

Belderg   Maumakeogh   380

Lenadoon Pt.   38

Killala B.

Killala   Inishcrone   Easky   Rosses Point   Strandhill   L. Gill   Lackagh Hills

Annagh Hd.   Belmullet   Glenamoy   Carrowmore

Dromore West

Knocklalong   544   Beltra   Ballysadare   Colloney   L. Allen

An Geata Mór (Binghamstown)   Crossmolina   Ballina   Coolaney   Drumkeeran

Inishkea North   Bellacorick   L. Conn   Moy   Tobercurry   Corry Mt.   591   Slieve Anierin   587

Inishkea South   Fallmore   Nephin Beg Range   722   Lahardaun   806   Nephin   Bunnyconnellan   Ballymote   Bunnanaddan   L. Arrow

Blacksod Pt.   Ridge Pt.   Ballycroy   627   Castlehill   Foxford   Cloonacool   Aclare   L. Key   Boyle

Saddle Hd.   Slievemore   672   L. Cullin   Callow   Curlew Mts.   Drumshanbo

Achill Hd.   Keel   714   Feeagh   Beltra   Strade Friary   Charlestown   L. Gara   Carrick-on-Shannon

Achill I.   Dooega Hd.   Corraun Pen.   Mallaranny   Beltra L.   Swinford   Tawnyinah   Frenchpark   Croghan   Drumsna

Achillbeg I.   Newport B.   Newport   Castlebar   Kiltamagh   Kilkelly   Ballaghaderreen   Ballinameen   Elphin   Mohill

Clare I.   Clew Bay   Westport B.   Westport   MAYO   Manulla   Knock   ROSCOMMON   Bellanagare   Strokestown   Drumlish   Corn Hill   279

Louisburgh   765   Croagh Patrick   Balla   Ballyhaunis   Ballinlough   Castlerea   Ballinfull   Scramoge   Newtown Forbes   LONGFORD

Inishturk   Caher I.   Cregganbaun   CONNACHT   Claremorris   Cloonfad   Ballymoe   Oran   Ballintober   Roscommon   Killashee   Edgeworthstown Cast.

Killadoon   Sheeffry Hills   392   Kilvally   Mayo   Ballindine   Williamstown   Keenagh   Carrickboy

Inishbofin   763   Mweelrea   Partry Mts.   Ballinrobe   Hollymount   Dunmore   Glennamaddy   Fuerty   Athleague   Lough Ree

Inishshark   Killary Harbour   683   Leenaun   Lough Mask   Kilmaine   Milltown   Ballymurray

Cleggan   Letterfrack   Joyce Country   Maum   Shrule   Kilbennan Church   Barnaderg   Mount Bellew Bridge   Ballinamore Bridge   Ballygar   Ballymahon   Tang

CONNEMARA NAT. PARK   Maumturk Mts.   Clonbur   Clare   Tuam   Mayough   Thomas Street   Rathconrath   WESTMEATH

Clifden B.   Benbaun   730   Recess   660   Maam Cross   Lough Corrib   Belclare   Headford   Abbert   Castleblakeney   Glantane   Mount Talbot   Athlone   Moate

Clifden   Derryrush   Screeb   Oughterard   Rosscahill   GALWAY   Moylough   Ballinamore Bridge   Ahascragh   Ballyhaunish

Slyne Hd.   Toombeola   Roundstone   Glinsk   Moycullen   Monivea   Kilconnell   Ballinasloe   Moore   Horseleap

Ballyconneely B.   Carna   Kilkieran   Lettermore   Costelloe   Claregalway   Athenry   Attymon   Aughrim   Suck   Shannonbridge   Clara

Bertraghboy Bay   Kilkieran Bay   Galway   Killtullagh   Killconnell

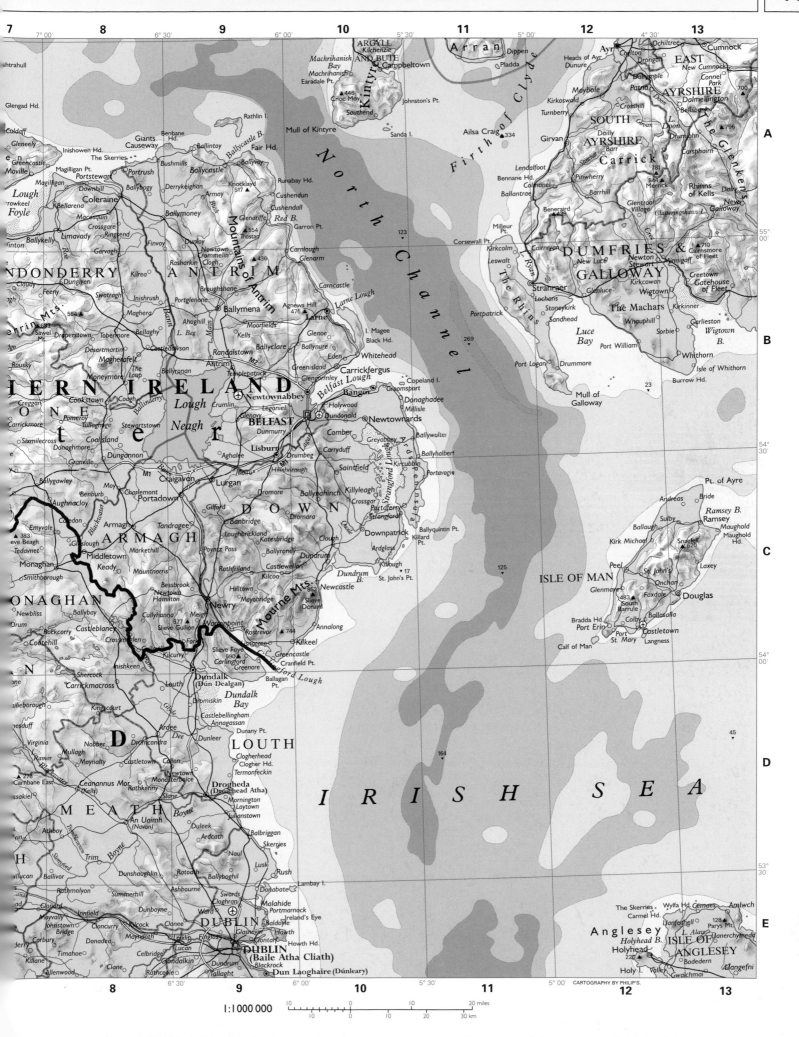

1:1 000 000

CARTOGRAPHY BY PHILIP'S.

IRELAND – SOUTH

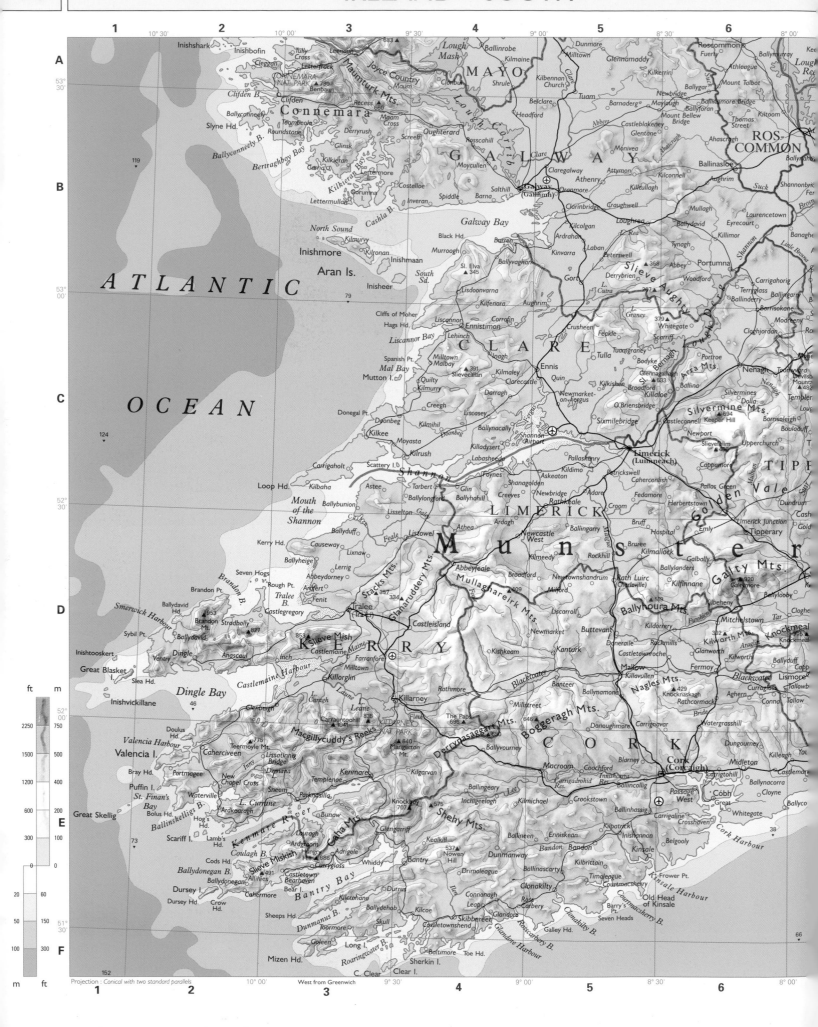

West from Greenwich

CARTOGRAPHY BY PHILIP'S

1:1 000 000

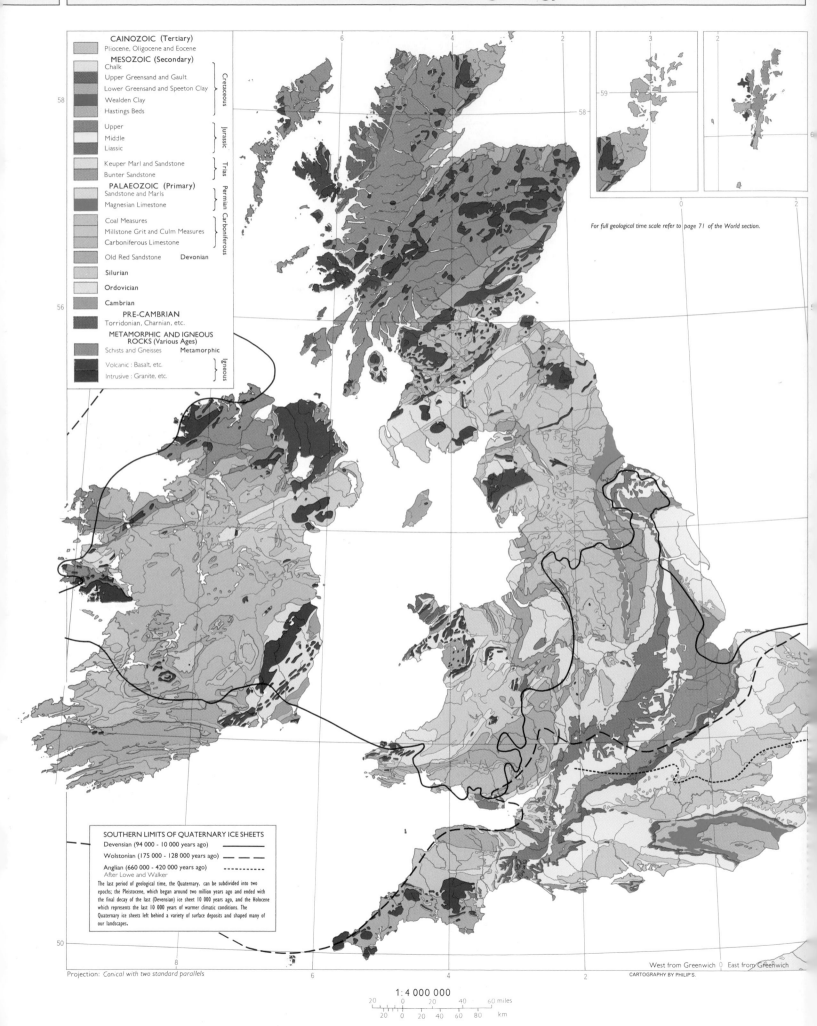

CAINOZOIC (Tertiary)
Pliocene, Oligocene and Eocene

MESOZOIC (Secondary)
Chalk
Upper Greensand and Gault
Lower Greensand and Speeton Clay — Cretaceous
Wealden Clay
Hastings Beds

Upper
Middle — Jurassic
Liassic

Keuper Marl and Sandstone — Trias
Bunter Sandstone

PALAEOZOIC (Primary)
Sandstone and Marls — Permian
Magnesian Limestone

Coal Measures
Millstone Grit and Culm Measures — Carboniferous
Carboniferous Limestone

Old Red Sandstone — Devonian
Silurian
Ordovician
Cambrian

PRE-CAMBRIAN
Torridonian, Charnian, etc.

METAMORPHIC AND IGNEOUS ROCKS (Various Ages)
Schists and Gneisses — Metamorphic
Volcanic : Basalt, etc. — Igneous
Intrusive : Granite, etc.

For full geological time scale refer to page 71 of the World section.

SOUTHERN LIMITS OF QUATERNARY ICE SHEETS
Devensian (94 000 - 10 000 years ago) ———
Wolstonian (175 000 - 128 000 years ago) – – –
Anglian (660 000 - 420 000 years ago) ·········
After Lowe and Walker

The last period of geological time, the Quaternary, can be subdivided into two epochs; the Pleistocene, which began around two million years ago and ended with the final decay of the last (Devensian) ice sheet 10 000 years ago, and the Holocene which represents the last 10 000 years of warmer climatic conditions. The Quaternary ice sheets left behind a variety of surface deposits and shaped many of our landscapes.

Projection: *Conical with two standard parallels*

West from Greenwich 0 East from Greenwich

CARTOGRAPHY BY PHILIP'S.

1:4 000 000

20 0 20 40 60 miles

20 0 20 40 60 80 km

Projection: Conical with two standard parallels

1 : 4 000 000

CARTOGRAPHY BY PHILIP'S.

20   0   20   40   60   80 Miles

20 0 20 40 60 80 100 120 Km

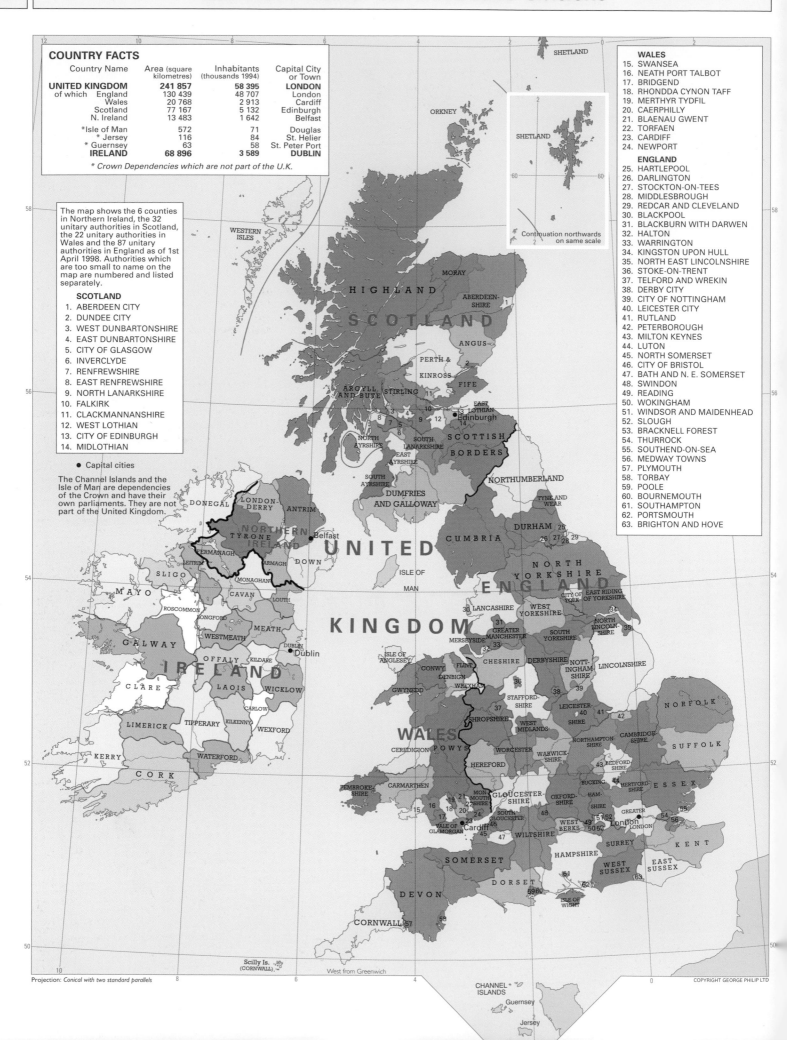

COUNTRY FACTS

Country Name	Area (square kilometres)	Inhabitants (thousands 1994)	Capital City or Town
UNITED KINGDOM	**241 857**	**58 395**	**LONDON**
of which England	130 439	48 707	London
Wales	20 768	2 913	Cardiff
Scotland	77 167	5 132	Edinburgh
N. Ireland	13 483	1 642	Belfast
*Isle of Man	572	71	Douglas
* Jersey	116	84	St. Helier
* Guernsey	63	58	St. Peter Port
IRELAND	**68 896**	**3 589**	**DUBLIN**

* Crown Dependencies which are not part of the U.K.

The map shows the 6 counties in Northern Ireland, the 32 unitary authorities in Scotland, the 22 unitary authorities in Wales and the 87 unitary authorities in England as of 1st April 1998. Authorities which are too small to name on the map are numbered and listed separately.

SCOTLAND
1. ABERDEEN CITY
2. DUNDEE CITY
3. WEST DUNBARTONSHIRE
4. EAST DUNBARTONSHIRE
5. CITY OF GLASGOW
6. INVERCLYDE
7. RENFREWSHIRE
8. EAST RENFREWSHIRE
9. NORTH LANARKSHIRE
10. FALKIRK
11. CLACKMANNANSHIRE
12. WEST LOTHIAN
13. CITY OF EDINBURGH
14. MIDLOTHIAN

● Capital cities

The Channel Islands and the Isle of Man are dependencies of the Crown and have their own parliaments. They are not part of the United Kingdom.

WALES
15. SWANSEA
16. NEATH PORT TALBOT
17. BRIDGEND
18. RHONDDA CYNON TAFF
19. MERTHYR TYDFIL
20. CAERPHILLY
21. BLAENAU GWENT
22. TORFAEN
23. CARDIFF
24. NEWPORT

ENGLAND
25. HARTLEPOOL
26. DARLINGTON
27. STOCKTON-ON-TEES
28. MIDDLESBROUGH
29. REDCAR AND CLEVELAND
30. BLACKPOOL
31. BLACKBURN WITH DARWEN
32. HALTON
33. WARRINGTON
34. KINGSTON UPON HULL
35. NORTH EAST LINCOLNSHIRE
36. STOKE-ON-TRENT
37. TELFORD AND WREKIN
38. DERBY CITY
39. CITY OF NOTTINGHAM
40. LEICESTER CITY
41. RUTLAND
42. PETERBOROUGH
43. MILTON KEYNES
44. LUTON
45. NORTH SOMERSET
46. CITY OF BRISTOL
47. BATH AND N. E. SOMERSET
48. SWINDON
49. READING
50. WOKINGHAM
51. WINDSOR AND MAIDENHEAD
52. SLOUGH
53. BRACKNELL FOREST
54. THURROCK
55. SOUTHEND-ON-SEA
56. MEDWAY TOWNS
57. PLYMOUTH
58. TORBAY
59. POOLE
60. BOURNEMOUTH
61. SOUTHAMPTON
62. PORTSMOUTH
63. BRIGHTON AND HOVE

Continuation northwards on same scale

Projection: Conical with two standard parallels

West from Greenwich

COPYRIGHT GEORGE PHILIP LTD

INDEX TO BRITISH ISLES MAPS

This index lists the major placenames which appear on the large-scale maps of the British Isles (pages *2–15* with the yellow band). Placenames for the rest of the world can be found in the World Index, with the turquoise band.

The first number beside each name in the index gives the map page on which that feature or place will be found. The letter and figure immediately after the page number give the grid square within which the feature is situated. The letter represents the latitude and the figure the longitude. In some cases the feature may fall within the specified square, while the name is outside. This is usually the case only with very large features. Rivers are indexed to their mouths or confluence.

The 'geographical co-ordinates' which follow the letter-figure references give the latitude and longitude of each place. The first co-ordinate indicates latitude – the distance north of the Equator. The second co-ordinate indicates longitude – the distance east or west of the Greenwich Meridian. Both latitude and longitude are measured in degrees and minutes (there are 60 minutes in a degree).

Thus the entry in the index for Runcorn reads:

Runcorn............ **7 F3** 53 20N 2 44W

This indicates that Runcorn appears on map page 7 in grid square F3 at latitude 53 degrees, 20 minutes north and at longitude 2 degrees, 44 minutes west. To find Runcorn by using the geographical co-ordinates, look at the edges of the map. The degrees of latitude are indicated by blue figures on the left-hand edge of the map and the degrees of longitude are marked on the bottom edge of the map. Runcorn will be found where lines extended from the two points on the map edge would cross on the map.

An open square □ indicates that the name refers to an administrative unit such as a county or region; rivers are indicated by an arrow →. Names composed of a proper name (Wight) and a description (Isle of) are positioned alphabetically by the proper name. All names beginning St. are alphabetized under Saint. A list of abbreviations used can be found in the World Index at the end of the atlas.

A

Abberton Res. **9 C10** 51 50N 0 52 E
Abbeyfeale **14 D4** 52 23N 9 20W
Aberaeron **10 C5** 52 15N 4 16W
Aberayron = Aberaeron **10 C5** 52 15N 4 16W
Abercarn **10 D7** 51 39N 3 9W
Aberchirder **3 G12** 57 34N 2 40W
Aberdare **10 D7** 51 43N 3 27W
Aberdeen **3 H13** 57 9N 2 6W
Aberdeenshire □ **3 H12** 57 17N 2 36W
Aberdovey = Aberdyfi **10 B5** 52 33N 4 3W
Aberdyfi **10 B5** 52 33N 4 3W
Aberfeldy **5 A8** 56 37N 3 50W
Abergavenny **10 D7** 51 49N 3 1W
Abergele **10 A6** 53 17N 3 35W
Abersychan **10 D7** 51 44N 3 3W
Abertillery **10 D7** 51 44N 3 9W
Aberystwyth **10 C5** 52 25N 4 6W
Abingdon **8 C6** 51 40N 1 17W
Aboyne **3 H12** 57 4N 2 48W
Accrington **7 E4** 53 46N 2 22W
Achill Hd. **12 D1** 53 59N 10 15W
Achill I. **12 D1** 53 58N 10 5W
A'Chralaig **2 H7** 57 11N 5 10W
Adlington **7 E3** 53 36N 2 36W
Adwick le Street **7 E6** 53 35N 1 12W
Agnews Hill **13 B10** 54 51N 5 55W
Ailsa Craig **4 D5** 55 15N 5 7W
Ainsdale **7 E2** 53 37N 3 2W
Aird Brenish **2 F3** 58 8N 7 8W
Airdrie **5 C8** 55 53N 3 57W
Aire → **7 E7** 53 42N 0 55W
Alcester **8 B5** 52 13N 1 52W
Aldbrough **7 E8** 53 50N 0 7W
Aldeburgh **9 B12** 52 9N 1 35 E
Alderley Edge **7 F4** 53 18N 2 15W
Alderney **11 H9** 49 42N 2 12W
Aldershot **9 D7** 51 15N 0 43W
Aldridge **7 G5** 52 36N 1 55W
Alexandria **4 C6** 55 59N 4 40W
Alford, *Aberds.* **3 H12** 57 13N 2 42W
Alford, *Lincs.* **7 F9** 53 16N 0 10 E
Alfreton **7 F6** 53 6N 1 22W
Allen, Bog of **15 B9** 53 15N 7 0W
Allen, L. **12 C5** 54 12N 8 5W
Alloa **5 B8** 56 7N 3 49W
Alness **3 G9** 57 41N 4 15W
Alnmouth **6 B5** 55 24N 1 37W
Alnwick **6 B5** 55 25N 1 42W
Alsager **7 F4** 53 7N 2 20W
Alsh, L. **2 H6** 57 15N 5 39W
Alston **6 C4** 54 48N 2 26W
Alton **9 D7** 51 8N 0 59W
Altrincham **7 F4** 53 25N 2 21W
Alva **5 B8** 56 9N 3 49W
Alyth **5 A9** 56 38N 3 15W
Amble **6 B5** 55 20N 1 36W
Ambleside **6 D3** 54 26N 2 58W
Amersham **9 C7** 51 40N 0 38W
Amesbury **8 D5** 51 10N 1 46W
Amlwch **10 A5** 53 24N 4 21W
Ammanford **10 D5** 51 48N 4 0W
Ampthill **9 B8** 52 3N 0 30W
An Teallach **2 G7** 57 49N 5 18W
An Uaimh **13 D8** 53 39N 6 40W
Andover **8 D6** 51 13N 1 29W
Anglesey, Isle of □ **10 A5** 53 16N 4 18W
Angus □ **5 A10** 56 46N 2 56W
Angus, Braes of **3 J11** 56 51N 3 10W
Annagh Hd. **12 C1** 54 15N 10 5W
Annalee → **13 C7** 54 3N 7 15W
Annan **5 E9** 54 57N 3 17W
Annan → **5 E9** 54 58N 3 18W
Annandale **5 D9** 55 10N 3 25W
Anstey **7 G6** 52 41N 1 14W
Anstruther **5 B10** 56 14N 2 40W
Antrim **13 B9** 54 43N 6 13W
Antrim □ **13 B9** 54 55N 6 20W
Antrim, Mts. of **13 B9** 54 57N 6 8W
Appin **4 A5** 56 37N 5 20W
Appleby-in-Westmorland **6 C4** 54 35N 2 29W
Appledore **11 E5** 51 3N 4 12W
Aran Fawddwy **10 B6** 52 48N 3 40W
Aran I. **12 B4** 55 0N 8 30W
Aran Is. **14 B3** 53 5N 9 42W
Arbroath **5 A10** 56 34N 2 35W
Arbury Hill **8 B6** 52 13N 1 12W
Ardee **13 D8** 53 51N 6 32W
Arderin **15 B7** 53 3N 7 40W
Ardgour **4 A5** 56 45N 5 25W
Ardivachar Pt. **2 H3** 57 23N 7 25W
Ardmore Hd. **15 E7** 51 58N 7 43W
Ardmore Pt. **4 C3** 55 40N 6 2W
Ardnamurchan **4 A4** 56 43N 6 0W
Ardnamurchan, Pt. of **4 A3** 56 44N 6 14W
Ardnave Pt. **4 C3** 55 54N 6 20W
Ardrossan **4 C6** 55 39N 4 50W
Ards Pen. **13 B10** 54 30N 5 30W
Arenig Fawr **10 B6** 52 56N 3 45W
Argyll **4 B5** 56 14N 5 10W
Argyll & Bute □ **4 B5** 56 13N 5 28W
Arisaig **2 J6** 56 55N 5 50W
Arisaig, Sd. of **2 J6** 56 50N 5 50W
Arkaig, L. **2 J7** 56 58N 5 10W
Arklow **15 C10** 52 48N 6 10W
Arklow Hd. **15 C10** 52 46N 6 10W
Armadale **5 C8** 55 54N 3 42W
Armagh **13 C8** 54 22N 6 40W
Armagh □ **13 C8** 54 18N 6 37W
Armthorpe **7 E6** 53 32N 1 3W
Arnold **7 F6** 53 2N 1 8W
Arran **4 C5** 55 34N 5 12W
Arrow, L. **12 C5** 54 3N 8 20W
Arun → **9 E7** 50 48N 0 33W
Arundel **9 E7** 50 52N 0 32W
Ascot **9 D7** 51 24N 0 41W
Ash **9 D7** 51 14N 0 43W
Ashbourne **7 F5** 53 2N 1 44W
Ashburton **11 F6** 50 31N 3 45W
Ashby de la Zouch **7 G6** 52 45N 1 29W
Ashdown Forest **9 D9** 51 4N 0 2 E
Ashford **9 D10** 51 8N 0 53 E
Ashington **6 B5** 55 12N 1 35W
Ashton-in-Makerfield **7 F3** 53 29N 2 39W
Ashton under Lyne **7 F4** 53 30N 2 8W
Aspatria **6 C2** 54 45N 3 20W
Assynt **2 F7** 58 20N 5 10W
Athboy **13 D8** 53 37N 6 55W
Athenry **14 B5** 53 18N 8 45W
Atherstone **7 G5** 52 35N 1 32W
Atherton **7 E3** 53 32N 2 30W
Athlone **14 B7** 53 26N 7 57W
Atholl, Forest of **3 J10** 56 51N 3 50W
Athy **15 C9** 53 0N 7 0W
Attleborough **9 A11** 52 32N 1 1 E
Auchterarder **5 B8** 56 18N 3 43W
Auchtermuchty **5 B9** 56 18N 3 15W
Aughnacloy **13 C8** 54 25N 6 58W
Aviemore **3 H10** 57 11N 3 50W
Avoca **15 C10** 52 52N 6 13W
Avoca → **15 C10** 52 48N 6 9W
Avon →, *Bristol* **8 D3** 51 30N 2 43W
Avon →, *Hants.* **8 E5** 50 44N 1 45W
Avon →, *Warks.* **8 C4** 51 57N 2 9W
Avonmouth **8 C3** 51 30N 2 42W
Awe, L. **4 B5** 56 15N 5 15W
Axe Edge **7 F5** 53 14N 1 59W
Axminster **11 F7** 50 47N 3 1W
Aylesbury **9 C7** 51 48N 0 49W
Aylsham **9 A11** 52 48N 1 16 E
Ayr **4 D6** 55 28N 4 37W
Ayr → **4 D6** 55 29N 4 40W
Ayr, Heads of **4 D6** 55 25N 4 43W
Ayr, Pt. of **10 A7** 53 21N 3 19W
Ayre, Pt. of **3 E12** 58 55N 2 43W

B

Bacton **9 A11** 52 50N 1 29 E
Bacup **7 E4** 53 42N 2 12W
Badenoch **3 J9** 56 59N 4 15W
Bagenalstown = Muine Bheag **15 C9** 52 42N 6 57W
Baggy Pt. **11 E5** 51 11N 4 12W
Bagh nam Faoileann **2 H3** 57 22N 7 13W
Baginbun Hd. **15 D9** 52 10N 6 50W
Bagshot **9 D7** 51 22N 0 41W
Baildon **7 E5** 53 52N 1 46W
Baile Atha Cliath = Dublin **15 B10** 53 20N 6 18W
Bakewell **7 F5** 53 13N 1 40W
Bala **10 B6** 52 54N 3 36W
Bala, L. **10 B6** 52 53N 3 38W
Balbriggan **13 D9** 53 35N 6 10W
Baldock **9 C8** 51 59N 0 11W
Ballachulish **4 A5** 56 40N 5 10W
Ballagan Pt. **13 D9** 54 0N 6 6W
Ballaghaderreen **12 D4** 53 55N 8 35W
Ballater **3 H11** 57 2N 3 2W
Ballina, *Mayo,* **12 C3** 54 7N 9 10W
Ballina, *Tipp.,* **14 C6** 52 49N 8 27W
Ballinasloe **14 B6** 53 20N 8 12W
Ballinderry → **13 B8** 54 40N 6 32W
Ballinrobe **12 D3** 53 36N 9 13W
Ballinskelligs B. **14 E2** 51 46N 10 11W
Ballybunion **14 C3** 52 30N 9 40W
Ballycastle **13 A9** 55 12N 6 15W
Ballyclare **13 B10** 54 46N 6 0W
Ballyconneely B. **14 B2** 53 23N 10 8W
Ballydavid Hd. **14 D2** 52 15N 10 20W
Ballydonegan B. **14 E2** 51 38N 10 6W
Ballyhaunis **12 D4** 53 47N 8 47W
Ballyhoura Mts. **14 D5** 52 18N 8 33W
Ballymena **13 B9** 54 53N 6 18W
Ballymoney **13 A8** 55 5N 6 30W
Ballymote **12 C4** 54 5N 8 31W
Ballynahinch **13 C10** 54 24N 5 55W
Ballyquintin Pt. **13 C11** 54 20N 5 30W
Ballyshannon **12 B5** 54 30N 8 10W
Balmoral Forest **3 J11** 57 0N 3 15W
Baltimore **14 F4** 51 29N 9 22W
Bamber Bridge **7 E3** 53 44N 2 39W
Bamburgh **6 A5** 55 36N 1 42W
Banbridge **13 C9** 54 21N 6 17W
Banbury **8 B6** 52 4N 1 21W
Banchory **3 H13** 57 3N 2 30W
Bandon **14 E5** 51 44N 8 45W
Bandon → **14 E5** 51 40N 8 41W
Banff **3 G12** 57 40N 2 32W
Bangor, *Down* **13 B10** 54 40N 5 40W
Bangor, *Gwynedd* **10 A5** 53 13N 4 9W
Bann →, *Down* **13 C8** 54 30N 6 31W
Bann →, *L'derry.* **13 A8** 55 10N 6 40W
Bannockburn **5 B8** 56 5N 3 55W
Bannow B. **15 D9** 52 13N 6 48W
Banstead **9 D8** 51 19N 0 10W
Bantry **14 E4** 51 40N 9 28W
Bantry B. **14 E3** 51 35N 9 50W
Bard Hd. **2 B15** 60 6N 1 5W
Bardsey Sd. **10 B4** 52 47N 4 46W
Bargoed **10 D7** 51 42N 3 22W
Barking and Dagenham **9 C9** 51 31N 0 10 E
Barmouth **10 B5** 52 44N 4 3W
Barnard Castle **6 C5** 54 33N 1 55W
Barnet **9 C8** 51 37N 0 15W
Barnoldswick **7 E4** 53 55N 2 11W
Barns Ness **5 C11** 55 59N 2 27W
Barnsley **7 E6** 53 33N 1 29W
Barnstaple **11 E5** 51 5N 4 3W
Barnstaple B. **11 E5** 51 5N 4 20W
Barra **2 J3** 57 0N 7 30W
Barra Hd. **2 J2** 56 47N 7 40W
Barrhead **4 C7** 55 48N 4 23W
Barrow → **15 D9** 52 14N 6 58W
Barrow-in-Furness **6 D2** 54 8N 3 15W
Barrow upon Humber **7 E8** 53 41N 0 22W
Barrowford **7 E4** 53 51N 2 14W
Barry **11 E7** 51 23N 3 19W
Barry I. **11 E7** 51 23N 3 17W
Barry's Pt. **14 E5** 51 36N 8 40W
Barton upon Humber **7 E8** 53 41N 0 27W
Basildon **9 C9** 51 34N 0 29 E
Basingstoke **8 D6** 51 15N 1 5W
Bass Rock **5 B10** 56 5N 2 40W
Bath **8 D4** 51 22N 2 22W
Bathgate **5 C8** 55 54N 3 38W
Batley **7 E5** 53 43N 1 38W
Battle **9 E9** 50 55N 0 30 E
Beachy Hd. **9 E9** 50 44N 0 16 E
Beaconsfield **9 C7** 51 36N 0 39W
Beaminster **8 E3** 50 48N 2 44W
Bearsden **4 C7** 55 55N 4 21W
Beauly **3 H9** 57 29N 4 27W
Beauly → **3 H9** 57 26N 4 28W
Beauly Firth **3 H9** 57 30N 4 20W
Beaumaris **10 A5** 53 16N 4 7W
Bebington **7 F2** 53 23N 3 1W
Beccles **9 B12** 52 27N 1 33 E
Bedford **9 B8** 52 8N 0 29W
Bedford Level **9 A8** 52 35N 0 15W
Bedfordshire □ **9 B8** 52 4N 0 28W
Bedlington **6 B5** 55 8N 1 35W
Bedwas **11 D7** 51 36N 3 10W
Bedworth **8 B6** 52 28N 1 29W
Bee, L. **2 H3** 57 22N 7 21W
Beeston **7 G6** 52 55N 1 11W
Beighton **7 F6** 53 21N 1 21W
Beinn a' Ghlo **3 J10** 56 51N 3 42W
Beinn Mhor **2 G4** 57 59N 6 39W
Beith **4 C6** 55 45N 4 38W
Belfast **13 B10** 54 35N 5 56W
Belfast L. **13 B10** 54 40N 5 50W
Belmullet **12 C2** 54 13N 9 58W
Belper **7 F6** 53 2N 1 29W
Belturbet **12 C7** 54 6N 7 28W
Bembridge **8 E6** 50 41N 1 4W
Ben Alder **3 J9** 56 50N 4 30W
Ben Avon **3 H11** 57 6N 3 28W
Ben Bheigeir **4 C3** 55 43N 6 6W
Ben Chonzie **5 B8** 56 27N 4 0W
Ben Cruachan **4 B5** 56 26N 5 8W
Ben Dearg, *Highl.* **3 G8** 57 47N 4 58W
Ben Dearg, *Perth & Kinr.* **3 J10** 56 52N 3 52W
Ben Dhorain **3 F10** 58 7N 3 50W
Ben Dorain **4 A6** 56 32N 4 42W
Ben Eighie **2 G7** 57 37N 5 30W
Ben Hee **3 F8** 58 16N 4 43W
Ben Hiant **4 A3** 56 42N 6 1W
Ben Hope **3 F8** 58 24N 4 36W
Ben Ime **4 B6** 56 14N 4 49W

Place names on the turquoise-coded World Map section are to be found in the index at the rear of the book.

Place names on the turquoise-coded World Map section are to be found in the index at the rear of the book.

Place names on the turquoise-coded World Map section are to be found in the index at the rear of the book.

Narrows   **Slieve Elva**

Place names on the turquoise-coded World Map section are to be found in the index at the rear of the book.

WORLD MAPS

EUROPE 4-15, ASIA 16-25, AFRICA 26-33, AUSTRALIA AND OCEANIA 34-37,
NORTH AMERICA 38-45, SOUTH AMERICA 46-47

SETTLEMENTS

⬭ PARIS ■ Berne ◉ Livorno ◉ Brugge ◎ Algeciras ⊙ Frejus ○ Oberammergau ○ Thira

Settlement symbols and type styles vary according to the scale of each map and indicate the importance
of towns on the map rather than specific population figures

∴ Ruins or Archæological Sites   ᵛ Wells in Desert

ADMINISTRATION

─── International Boundaries

─ ─ ─ International Boundaries (Undefined or Disputed)

······· Internal Boundaries

National Parks

Country Names

NICARAGUA

Administrative Area Names

KENT

CALABRIA

International boundaries show the *de facto* situation where there are rival claims to territory

COMMUNICATIONS

─── Principal Roads

⌢ Other Roads

····· Trails and Seasonal Roads

⤨ Passes

✧ Airfields

⌢ Principal Railways

···· Railways Under Construction

⌢ Other Railways

⊐---⊏ Railway Tunnels

········ Principal Canals

PHYSICAL FEATURES

⌐ Perennial Streams

····· Intermittent Streams

◯ Perennial Lakes

⬭ Intermittent Lakes

Swamps and Marshes

Permanent Ice and Glaciers

▲ 8848 Elevations in metres

▼ 8050 Sea Depths in metres

1134 Height of Lake Surface Above Sea Level in metres

ELEVATION AND DEPTH TINTS

Height of Land Above Sea Level

in metres 6000 4000 3000 2000 1500 1000 400 200 0

in feet 18 000 12 000 9000 6000 4500 3000 1200 600

Land Below Sea Level

6000 12 000 15 000 18 000 24 000 in feet

0 200 2000 4000 5000 6000 8000 in metres

Depth of Sea

Some of the maps have different contours to highlight and clarify the principal relief features

Projection: Hammer Equal Area

A R C T I C   O C E A N

Barents Sea Novaya Zemlya Kara Sea Severnaya Zemlya New Siberian Is. East Siberian Sea Wrangel I. Arctic Circle

SWEDEN FINLAND Murmansk Arkhangelsk Salekhard Norilsk Verkhoyansk Laptev Sea

Helsinki ST.PETERSBURG Perm Yekaterinburg Tomsk Krasnoyarsk Irkutsk Yakutsk Magadan Bering Sea

Stockholm EST. LATVIA LITH. MOSCOW Kazan Chelyabinsk Omsk Novosibirsk L. Baikal Ulan Ude Sea of Okhotsk Petropavlovsk-Kamchatskiy

penhagen Berlin POLAND BELARUS Minsk Volga Samara Saratov Aqmola Barnaul Irtysh Okhotsk Komsomolsk Sakhalin

Warsaw UKRAINE Volgograd KAZAKSTAN L. Balkhash Ulan Bator Harbin Khabarovsk Kuril Is. International Date Line

Prague CZECH Kiev Odessa Astrakhan Aral Sea MONGOLIA Changchun Vladivostok Sapporo

AUSTRIA Budapest ROMANIA Bucharest GEORGIA Tbilisi Baku Bishkek Alma Ata Ürümqi SHENYANG NORTH KOREA Pyŏngyang

Milan YUG. BULGARIA Black Sea ARM. AZER. UZBEKISTAN Samarkand Tashkent KYRGYZSTAN BEIJING TIANJIN SEOUL JAPAN

Rome ITALY Sofia GREECE Ankara Yerevan TURKMENISTAN Dushanbe TAJIKISTAN CHINA Lanzhou Taiyuan Dalian SOUTH KOREA Osaka TŌKYŌ

Naples Athens Izmir TURKEY ISTANBUL Tabriz Ashkhabad Kābul Lhasa Xi'an Hwang Ho Kitakyūshū PACIFIC

MALTA Crete CYPRUS SYRIA TEHRĀN Mashhad AFGHANISTAN JAMMU & KASHMIR TIBET Chengdu Nanjing OCEAN

TUNISIA Sea Beirut Damascus Baghdād Eşfahān Islamabad Lahore Katmandu CHONGQING Wuhan SHANGHAI East China Sea

Tripoli Benghazi Alexandria Amman IRAQ IRAN DELHI NEPAL Fuzhou Ryukyus Volcano Is. (Japan) Bonin Is. (Japan)

Jerusalem ISR. JORDAN Shīrāz New Delhi Kanpur Ganges BANGLA- Kunming GUANGZHOU Taipei Marcus I. (Japan) Tropic of Cancer

CAIRO KUWAIT The Gulf Abu Dhabi Kābul PAKISTAN DESH DACCA TAIWAN Wake I. (U.S.A.)

LIBYA EGYPT Aswân Riyadh BAHRAIN QATAR U.A.E. KARACHI INDIA CALCUTTA BURMA HONG KONG

NIGER Mecca SAUDI Muscat Ahmadabad Nagpur MYANMAR Hanoi Hainan NORTHERN MARIANAS (U.S.A.)

CHAD Omdurmân ARABIA OMAN Arabian MUMBAI Bay of Bengal Rangoon South China Sea

Kano Khartoum Asmara ERITREA YEMEN Sea (Bombay) Hyderabad THAILAND VIET- MANILA

NIGERIA Abuja L.Chad Ndjamena SUDAN Sana Aden Socotra (Yemen) Bangalore CHENNAI BANGKOK NAM PHILIPPINES GUAM (U.S.A.) MARSHALL IS.

CAMEROON DJIBOUTI G. of Aden Lakshadweep Is. (India) (Madras) Andaman Is. (India) CAMBODIA Phnom Yap FEDERATED STATES Truk Pohnpei

Douala CENTRAL AFRICAN REP. Addis Ababa SOMALI SRI LANKA Nicobar Is. (India) Penh Ho Chi Minh City PALAU Caroline Is. OF MICRONESIA

Yaounde Bangui ETHIOPIA REP. Colombo MALDIVES MALAYSIA Kuala Lumpur SABAH Gilbert Is.

GABON Kisangani UGANDA Mogadishu PEN. MALAYSIA BRUNEI NAURU KIRIBATI

Libreville CONGO Kampala KENYA Equator Medan SINGAPORE Borneo

CONGO (ZAÏRE) Kigali RWANDA L. Turkana Sumatra IRIAN

Brazzaville Kinshasa Kananga BURUNDI Dodoma Nairobi SEYCHELLES INDONESIA JAYA PAPUA

CABINDA (Angola) Bujumbura Lake Victoria Mombasa Palembang Banjarmasin New Ireland NEW GUINEA

Luanda Lubumbashi TANZANIA Zanzibar Dar es Salaam Amirante Is. Chagos Arch. (U.K.) JAKARTA Ujung Pandang Port Moresby New Britain

ANGOLA Kasai ZAMBIA L. Tanganyika Aldabra Is. Diego Garcia INDIAN Bandung Surabaya Java SOLOMON IS.

Benguela Lusaka Lilongwe Malawi COMOROS Mayotte OCEAN Timor Arafura Sea York

NAMIBIA ZIMBABWE MOZAMBIQUE MADAGASCAR Cargados Carajos Cocos Is. (Austral.) Christmas I. (Austral.) Darwin VANUATU

Windhoek Harare Bulawayo Mozambique Channel Antananarivo RÉUNION (Fr.) MAURITIUS Cairns NEW CALEDONIA (Fr.) FIJI

BOTSWANA Gaborone Pretoria SWAZILAND Rodriguez Townsville Suva

Johannesburg SOUTH Maputo LESOTHO Tropic of Capricorn Port Hedland Alice Springs Rockhampton NEW (Austral.)

AFRICA Durban Amsterdam I. (Fr.) AUSTRALIA Lord Howe I. (Austral.)

Cape Town Port Elizabeth St.Paul (Fr.) Geraldton Kalgoorlie-Boulder Brisbane Norfolk I. (Austral.)

C. of Good Hope Perth Fremantle Adelaide Darling Newcastle Sydney Auckland North I.

Great Australian Bight Melbourne Canberra Tasman NEW ZEALAND

Prince Edward Is. (S.Africa) Crozet Is. (Fr.) Kerguelen (Fr.) Tasmania Sea Wellington

McDonald Is. (Austral.) Heard I. (Austral.) Hobart South I. Christchurch

OUTHERN OCEAN Campbell I. (N.Z.) Auckland Is. (N.Z.) Stewart I. Dunedin Bounty Is. (N.Z.) Antipodes Is. (N.Z.)

c t i c a Macquarie Is. (Austral.)

Antarctic Circle

Greenwich

Ross Sea

Hanoi ● Capital Cities

CARTOGRAPHY BY PHILIP'S.

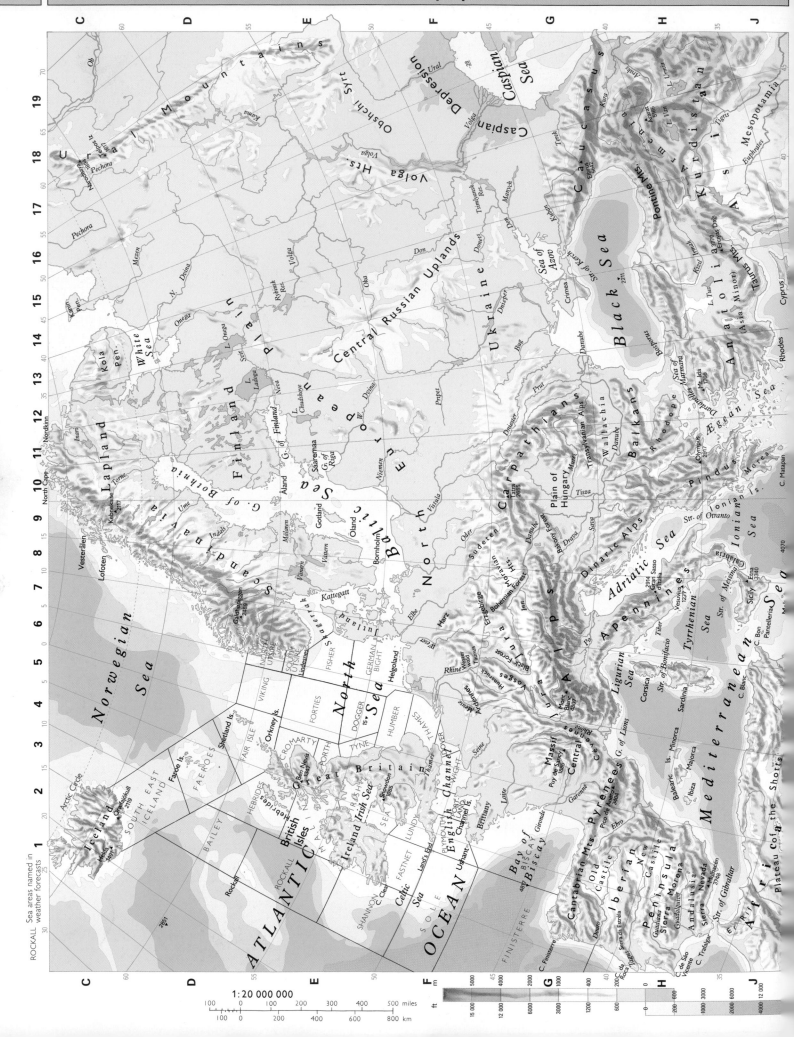

ROCKALL Sea areas named in weather forecasts

1:20 000 000

100   0   100   200   300   400   500 miles

100   0   200   400   600   800 km

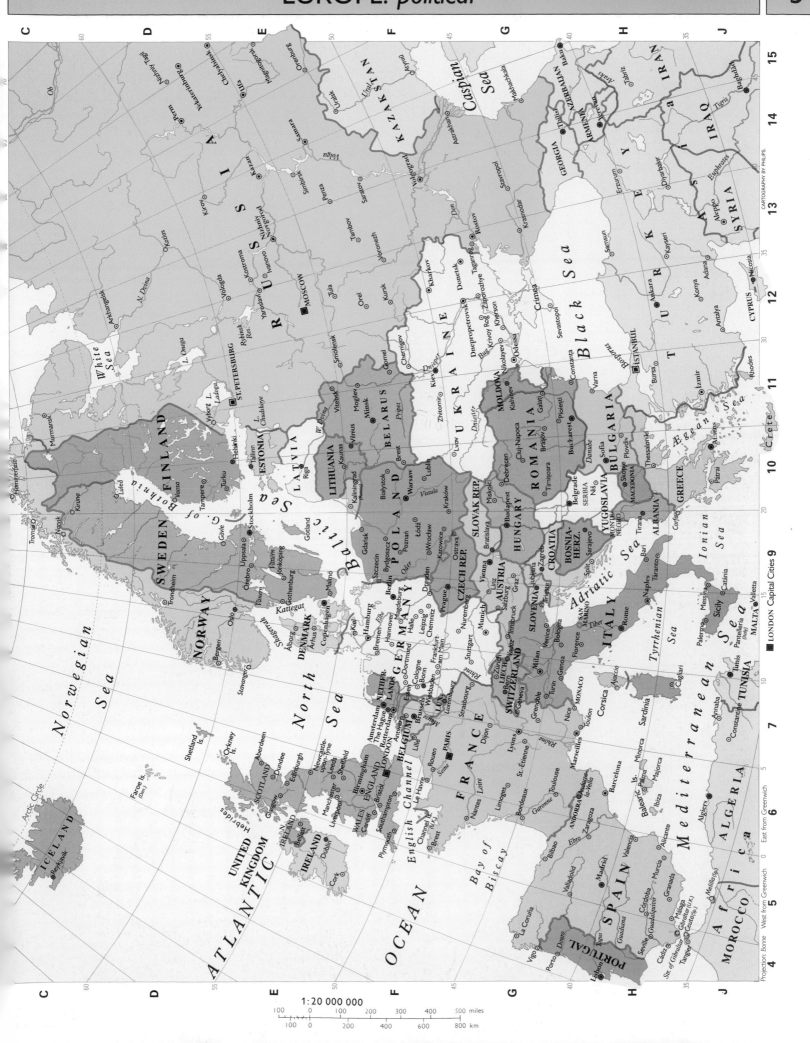

1:20 000 000

100   0   100   200   300   400   500 miles
100   0   200   400   600   800 km

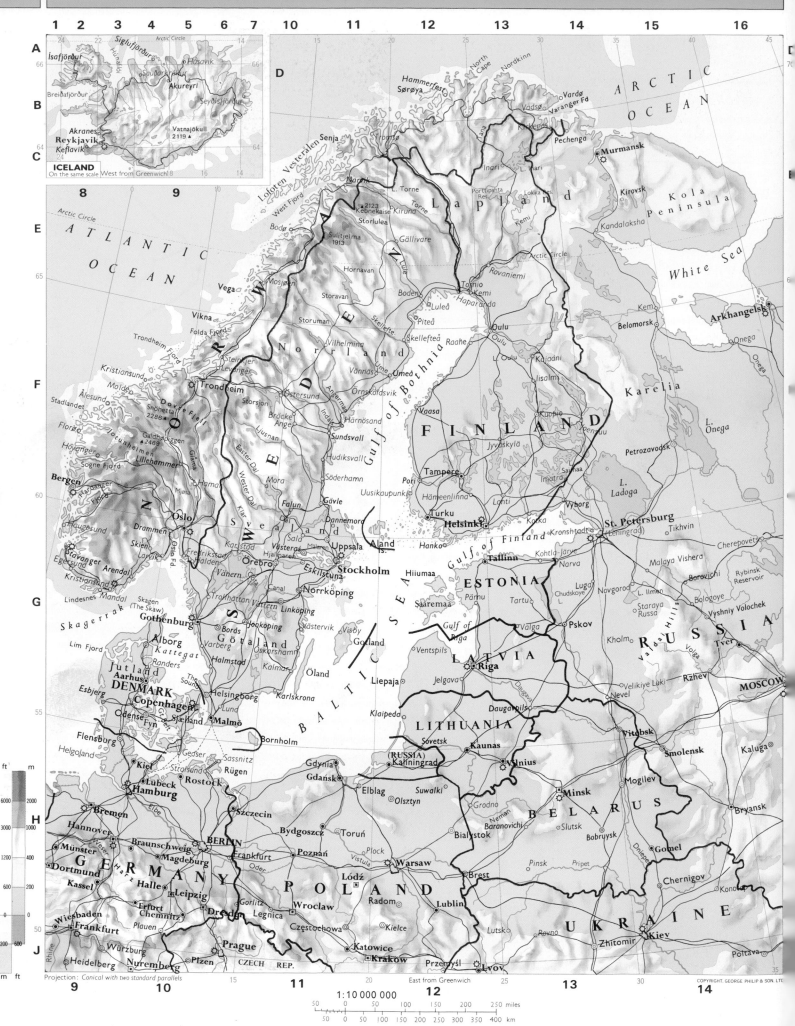

ICELAND
On the same scale West from Greenwich

Projection: Conical with two standard parallels

1:10 000 000

East from Greenwich

COPYRIGHT. GEORGE PHILIP & SON LTD.

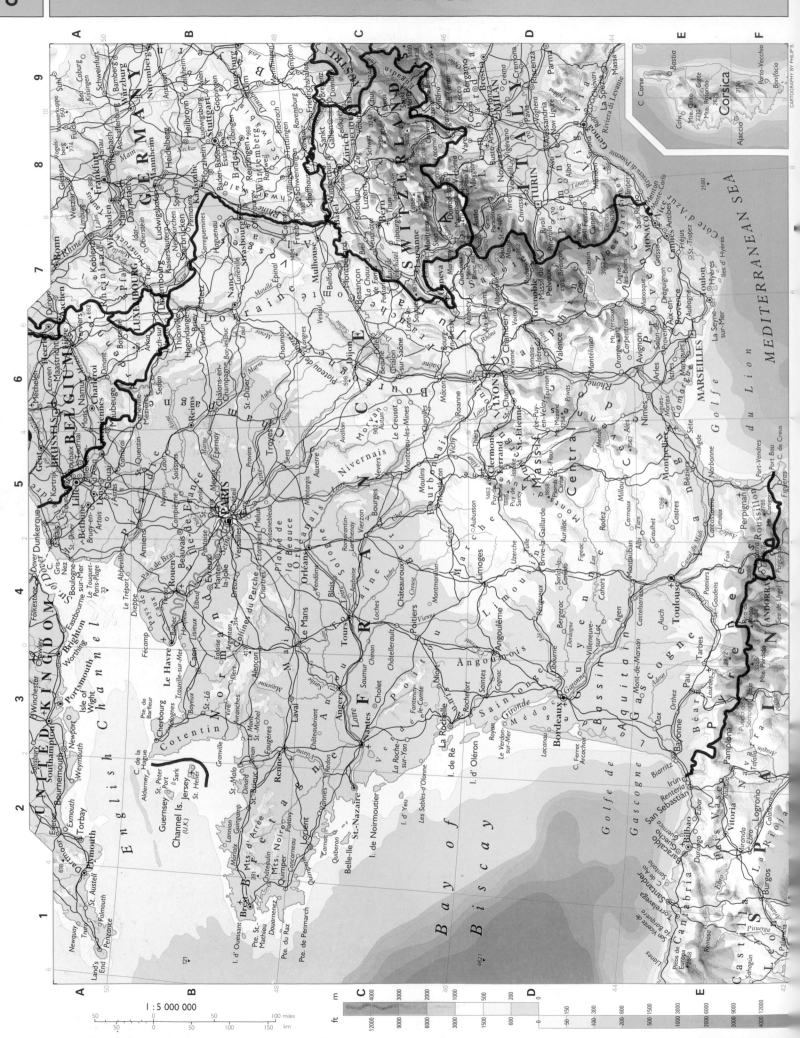

1 : 5 000 000

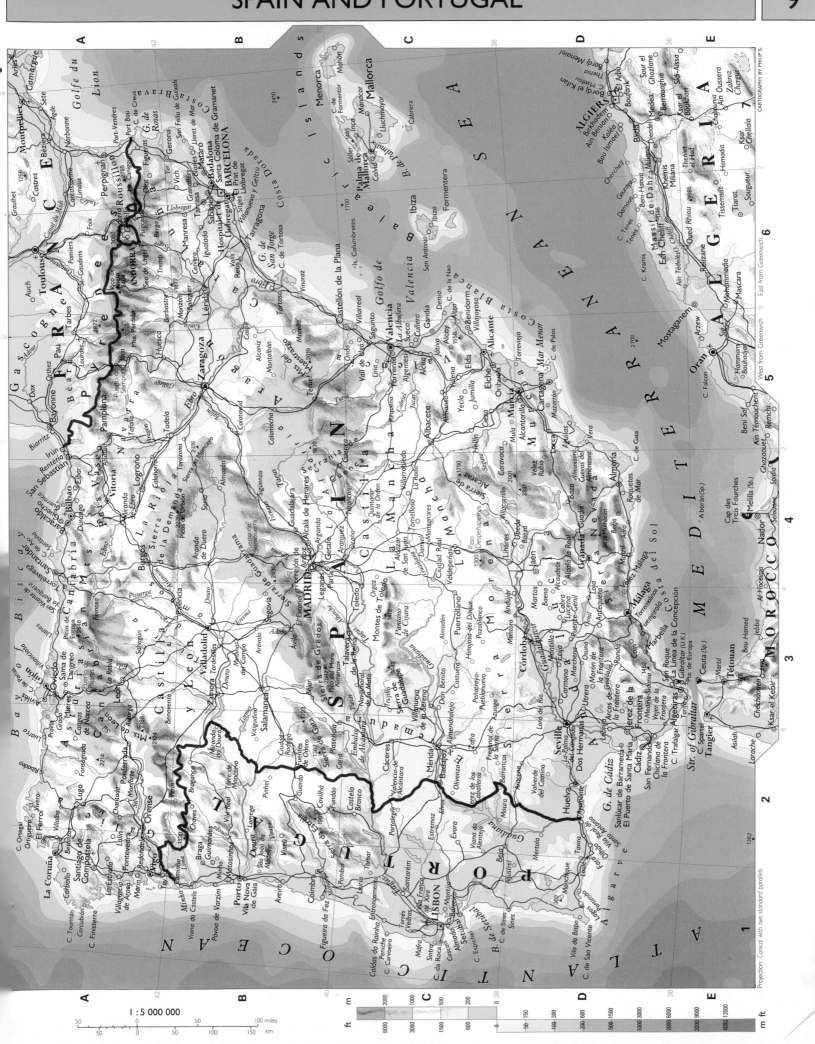

CARTOGRAPHY BY PHILIP'S.

Projection: Conical with two standard parallels

1 : 5 000 000

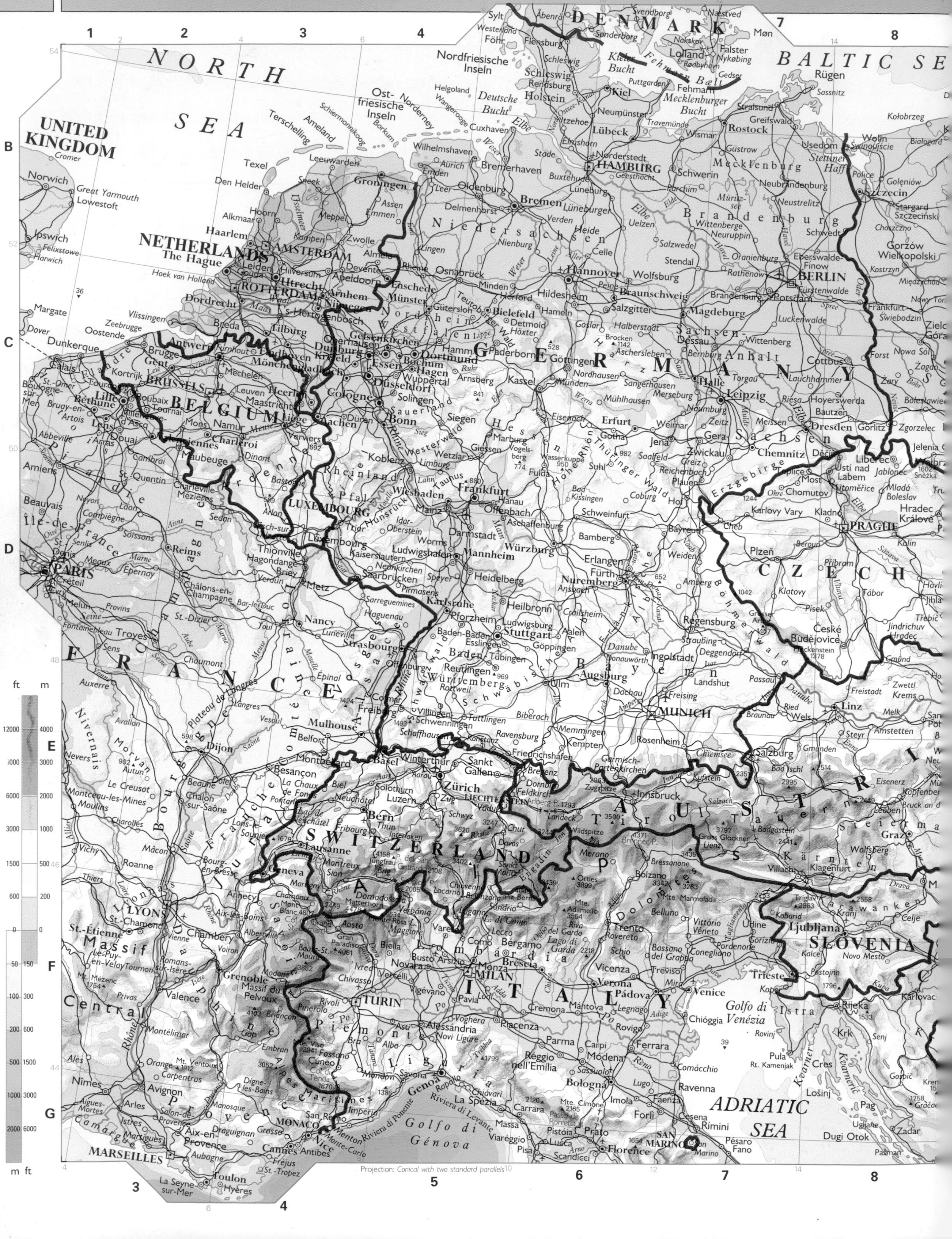
NORTH SEA
BALTIC SEA
UNITED KINGDOM
DENMARK
NETHERLANDS
BELGIUM
LUXEMBOURG
GERMANY
FRANCE
SWITZERLAND
LIECHTENSTEIN
AUSTRIA
CZECH
SLOVENIA
ITALY
MONACO
SAN MARINO
ADRIATIC SEA
Golfo di Génova
Golfo di Venézia
AMSTERDAM
The Hague
ROTTERDAM
BRUSSELS
PARIS
LYONS
MARSEILLES
HAMBURG
BERLIN
PRAGUE
MUNICH
MILAN
TURIN
Frankfurt
Cologne
Nuremberg
Stuttgart
Zürich
Bern
Venice
Genoa
Florence
Ljubljana
Innsbruck
Salzburg
Leipzig
Dresden
Hannover
Bremen
Projection: Conical with two standard parallels
ft m
12000 4000
9000 3000
6000 2000
3000 1000
1500 500
600 200
0 0
50 150
100 300
200 600
500 1500
1000 3000
2000 6000
m ft

1 2 3 4 5 6 7

SWITZERLAND

AUSTRIA

Rhine Chur Wildspitze 3797 Badgastein 2441 Graz Steiermark

Davos 3224 Brenner P. Gross Glockner Lienz Wolfsberg Klagenfurt

Domodossola Merano Bolzano 3263 Villach Celje Varaždin Nagyk

Locarno Sondrio Trento Belluno Udine Ljubljana **SLOVENIA** Novo Mesto **Zagreb**

Como Bérgamo Brescia Verona Vicenza Treviso Trieste Koper Rijeka **CROA**

MILAN Pádova Venice Golfo di Venézia Pula Cres Karlovac

Novara Lodi Cremona Mantova Rovigo Chióggia Rovinj Krk Senj

TURIN Piacenza Parma Carpi Ferrara Comácchio Lošinj Pag

Asti Alessandria Modena Bologna Ravenna Cres Zadar

FRANCE Cuneo Savona Génoa La Spézia Rímini Fano Pésaro Dugi Otok

Grenoble Imola Faenza Forlì San Marino Senigállia Ancona Šibenik

Monaco Nice La Spezia Massa Carrara Pisa Livorno Ascoli Piceno Split

MARSEILLES Toulon Hyères **LIGURIAN SEA** Volterra **Toscana** Perúgia Macerata Fermo Brač Hva

C. Corse Capraia Siena Arezzo Assisi Térni Teramo Pescara Vis

Calvi Bastia Elba Grosseto Orvieto Spoleto Chieti Lanciano Korčula

Corsica Ajaccio Montecristo Viterbo Rieti L'Aquila Vasto Térmoli

Bonifácio Civitavecchia **ROME** Tívoli San Severo Foggia Barletta

Sardinia Sássari Olbia Vatican City Frosinone Isérnia Campobasso Manfredónia Trani

Alghero Nuoro Latina Cassino Benevento Andria Corato

Oristano **Cágliari** Fórmia Caserta **NAPLES** Avellino Potenza Matera

San Pietro Iglésias Terracina Salerno

Sant' Antíoco Capri Castellammare di Stábia

C. Spartivento **TYRRHENIAN SEA** 3580

Ustica (Italy) Ísole Eólie Strómboli Vibo Valéntia

Salina Lipari Vulcano Cosenza Nicastro

Palermo Bagheria Cefalù Milazzo Messina Réggio di Calábria

Ísole Égadi Trápani Érice Términi Imerese Barcellona Pozzo di Gotto

Marsala Alcamo Partinico Monti Nébrodi Etna Giarre Catánia

ALGERIA Mazara del Vallo Castelvetrano Caltanissetta Enna Adrano Acireale

Annaba Collo Skikda Bizerte Menzel-Bourguiba Sciacca Porto Empédocle Agrigento Fávara Calcagirone Lentini Augusta

Constantine Tunis Ariana La Marsa Kélibia Licata Gela Vittória Ragusa Siracusa Módica Avola

TUNISIA Nabeul Hammamet Pantelleria (Italy) Ísole Pelágie (Italy) Gozo Valletta **MALTA**

Kairouan Sousse Monastir Mahdia El Djem Lampedusa **MEDITE**

Projection: Conical with two standard parallels

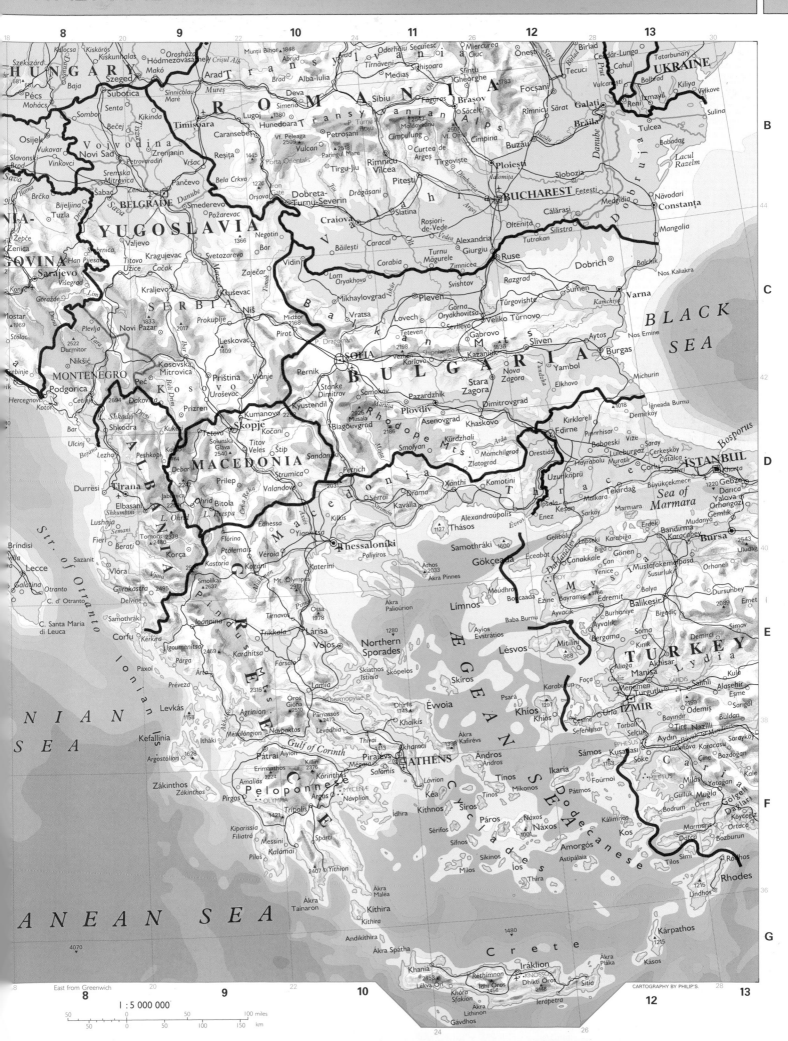

9

1. Crimea (Ukr.)
2. Adygea-Cherkessia (Russ.)
3. Karachey-Balkana (Russ.)
4. Kabardino-Balkana (Russ.)
5. North Ossetia (Russ.)
6. Ingushetia (Russ.)
7. Chechenia (Russ.)
8. Nakhichevan (Azer.)

Karagiye Depression

Kara
Bogaz
Gol

C A S P I A N   S E A

8

7

6

5

Division between Greeks and Turks
in Cyprus, Turks to the North

4

Projection: Conical with two standard parallels

East from Greenwich

1:10 000 000

50   0   50   100   150   200   250 miles

50   0   50   100   150   200   250   300   350   400 km

COPYRIGHT GEORGE PHILIP & SON LTD.

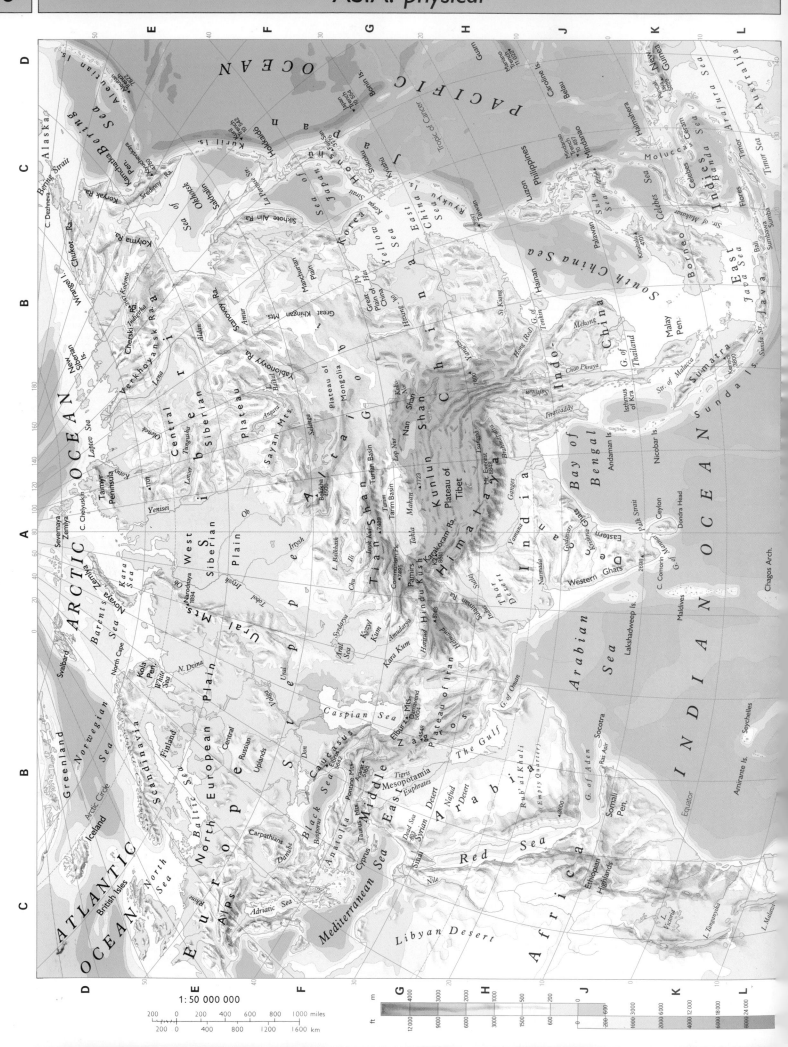

1 : 50 000 000

200 0 200 400 600 800 1000 miles

200 0 400 800 1200 1600 km

ft m
12000 4000
9000 3000
6000 2000
3000 1000
1500 500
600 200
0
200 600
3000
6000
12000
18000
24000

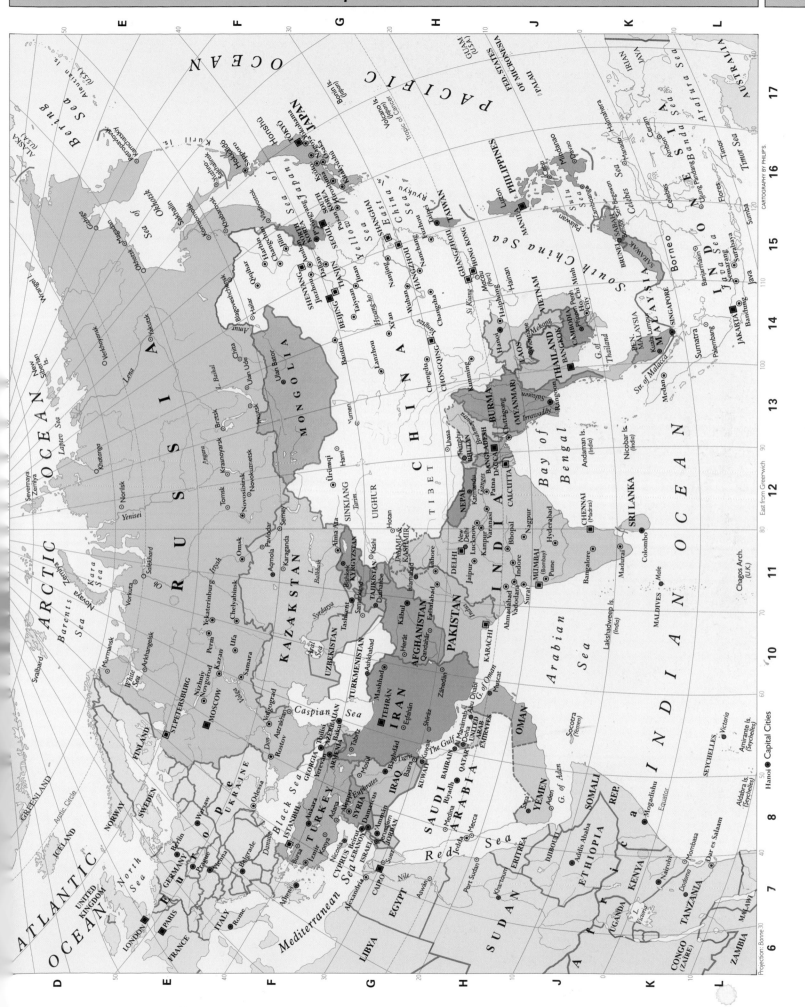

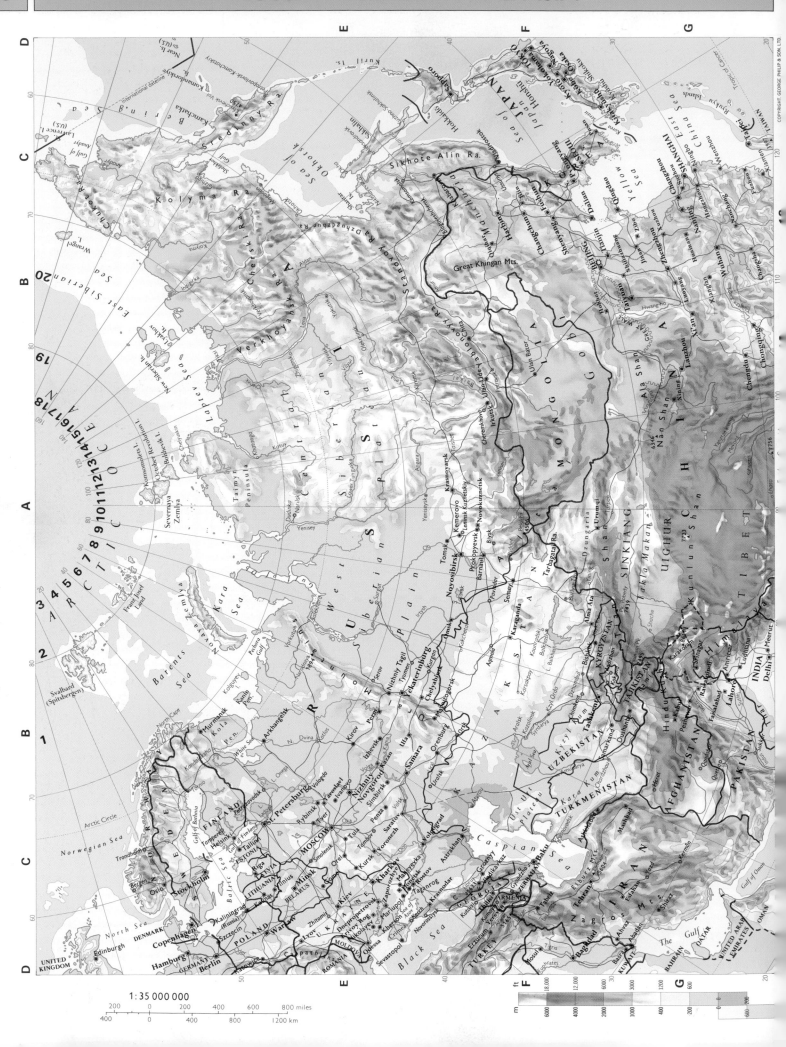

1:35 000 000

200   0   200   400   600   800 miles
400   0   400   800   1200 km

**SOUTHERN HONSHU,
KYUSHU AND SHIKOKU**

SEA OF JAPAN

PACIFIC OCEAN

SEA OF JAPAN

EAST CHINA SEA

Sea of Okhotsk

1:5 000 000
Projection: Conical with two standard parallels

1:10 000 000

East from Greenwich

Projection: Bonne

JAPAN

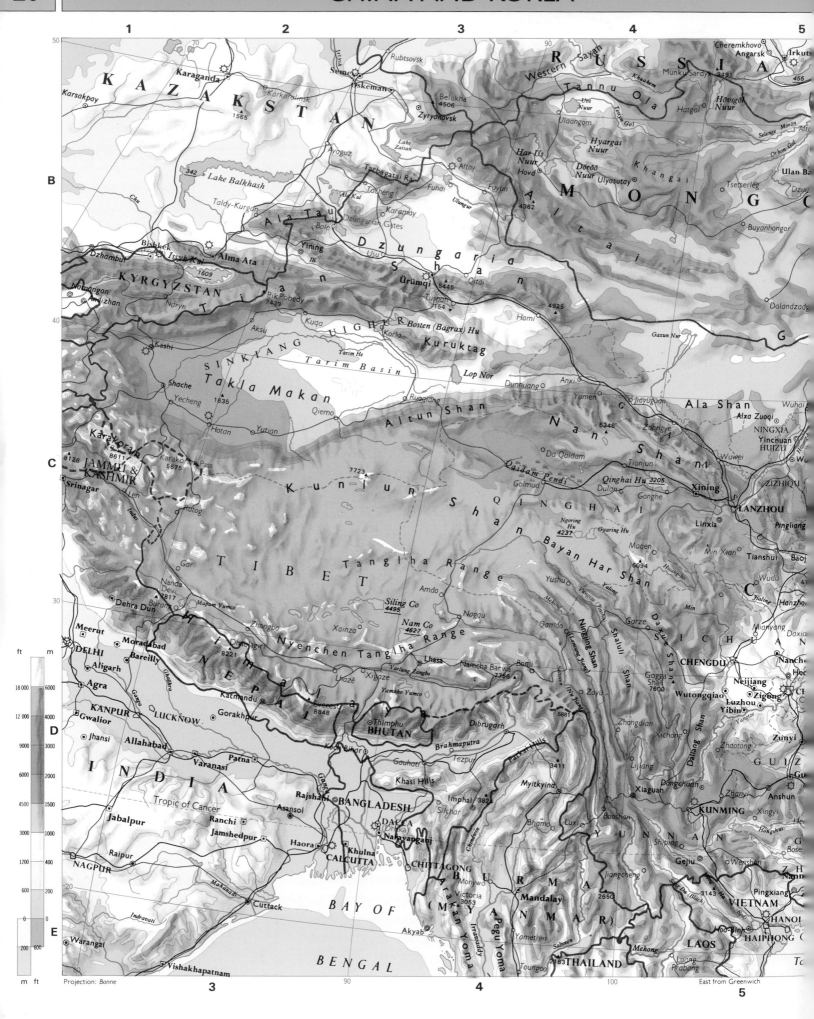

1:15 000 000

100   0   100   200   300   400 miles

100   0   100   200   300   400   500   600 km

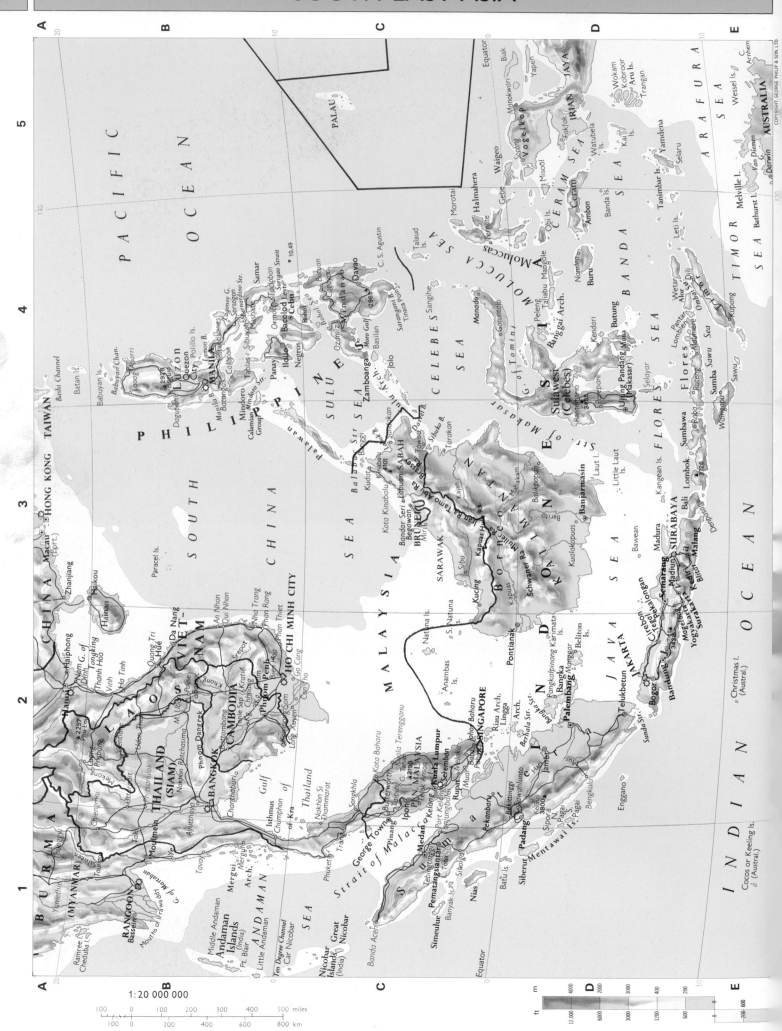

1:20 000 000

100 0 100 200 300 400 500 miles
100 0 200 400 600 800 km

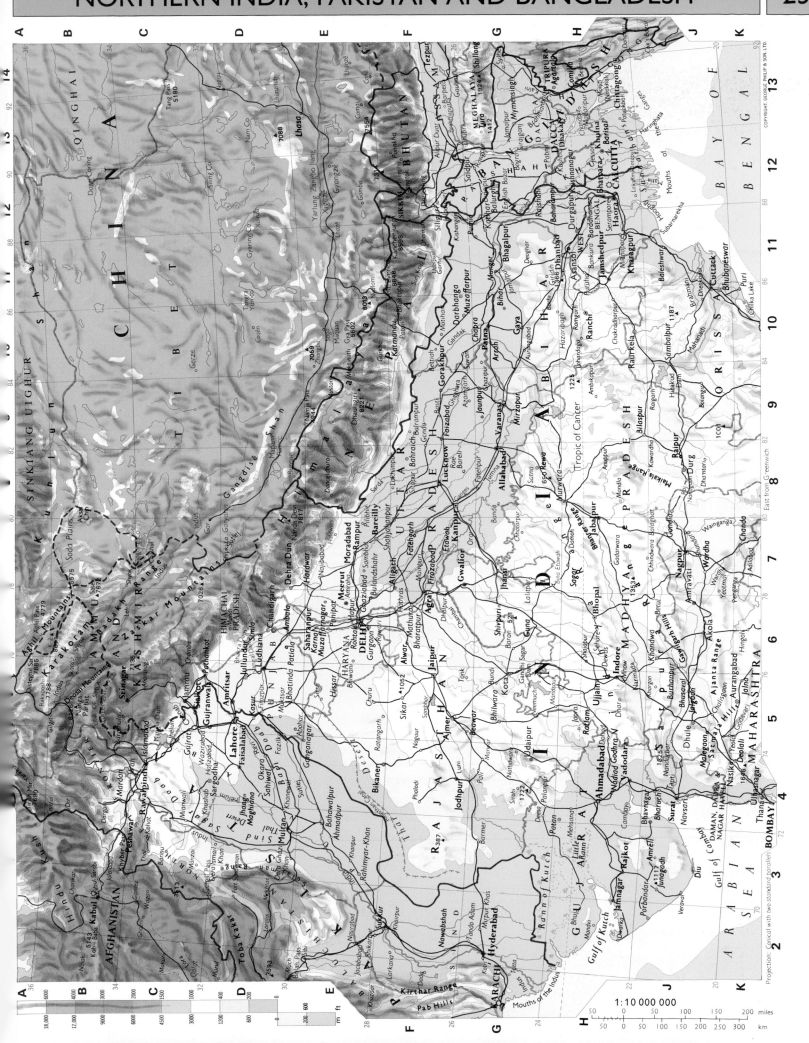

Projection: Conical with two standard parallels

1:10 000 000

Projection : Alber's Equal Area with two standard parallels

East from Greenwich

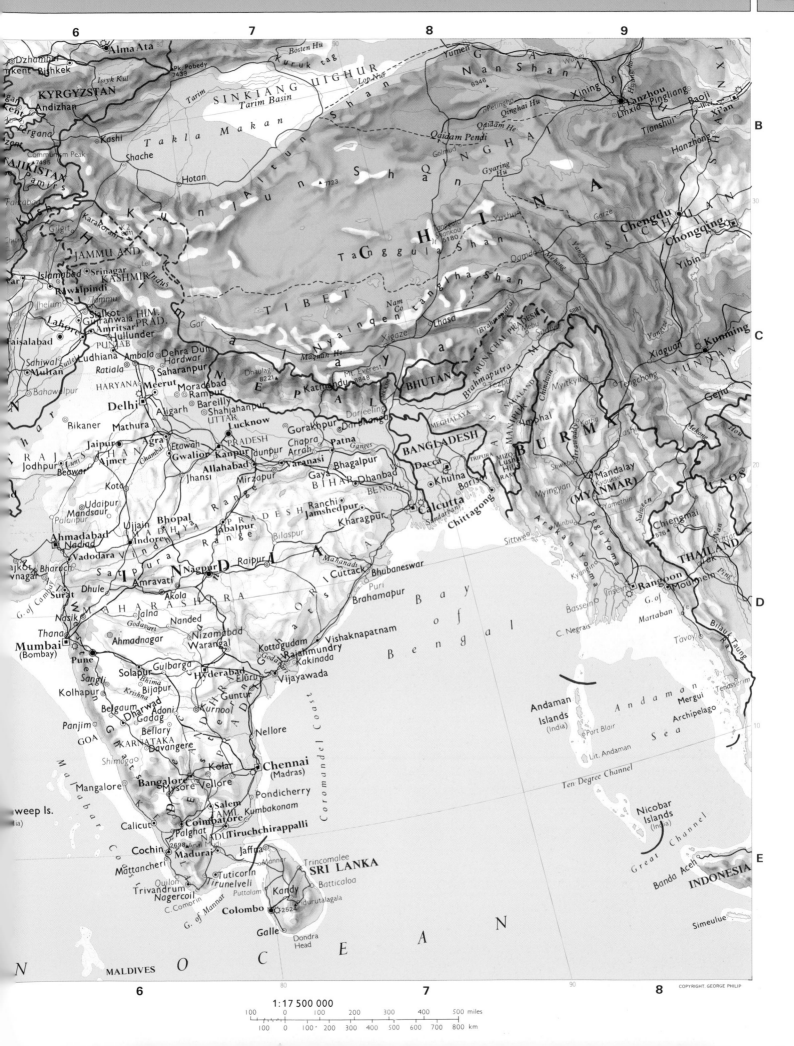

1:17 500 000

AFRICA : *physical*

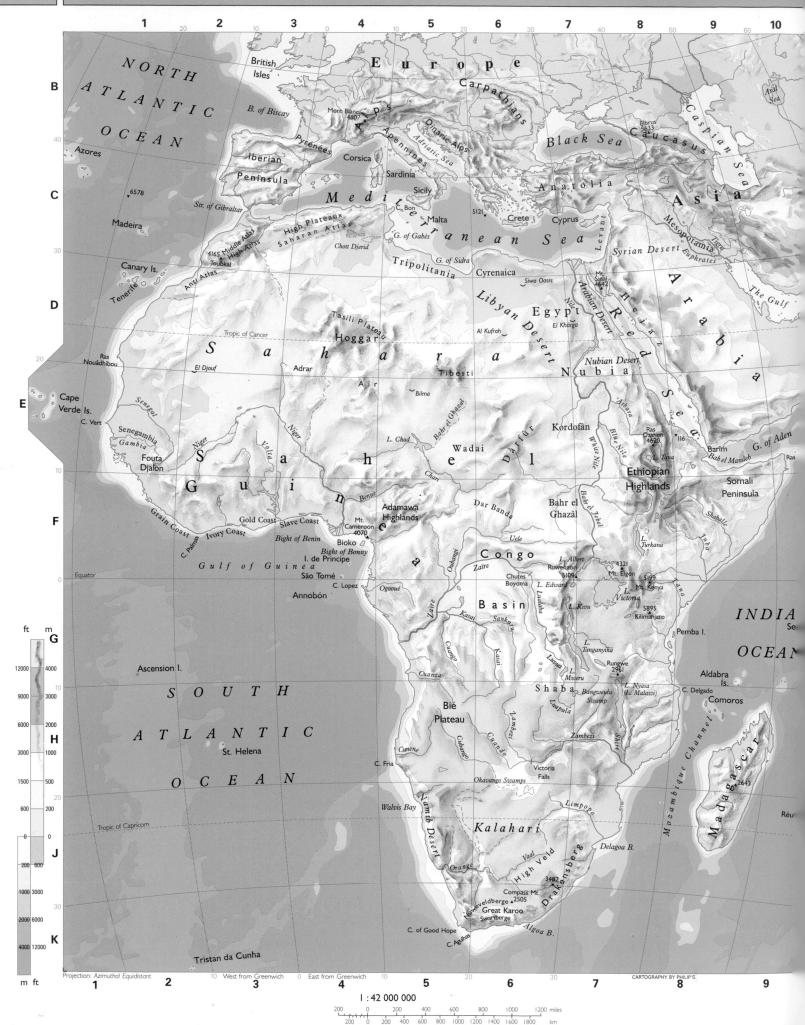

NORTH ATLANTIC OCEAN

Azores

Madeira

Canary Is.
Tenerife

British Isles

Europe

B. of Biscay

Mont Blanc
4807

Alps

Carpathians

Pyrénées

Iberian
Peninsula

Corsica

Str. of Gibraltar

6578

High Plateaux
Saharan Atlas

Apennines

Dinaric Alps

Adriatic Sea

Black Sea

Caucasus

Elbrus
5633

Aral
Sea

Caspian Sea

Anatolia

Asia

4165 Middle Atlas
High Atlas
Toubkal

Anti Atlas

Sardinia

Sicily

C. Bon
Malta

Mediterranean Sea

5121

Crete

Cyprus

Levant

Mesopotamia

Tigris
Euphrates

The Gulf

Chott Djerid

G. of Gabès

G. of Sidra

Tripolitania

Cyrenaica

Siwa Oasis

Mt. Sinai
4642

Syrian Desert

Tropic of Cancer

Ras
Nouâdhibou

El Djouf

Tasili Plateau

Hoggar

Adrar

Aïr

Libyan Desert

Al Kufrah

El Khârga

Egypt

Nile

Arabian Desert

Arabia

Hejaz

Red Sea

Cape
Verde Is.

C. Vert

Senegambia
Gambia

Senegal

Niger

Fouta
Djalon

Grain Coast

Sahara

Tibesti

Bilma

L. Chad

Bahr el Ghazal

Wadai

Darfûr

Sahel

Kordofân

Nubian Desert

Nubia

White Nile

Atbara

Blue Nile

Ras
Dashen
4620

L. Tana

116

Barïm
Bab el Mandeb

G. of Aden

Ras

Volta

Niger

Chari

Guinea

Ivory Coast

C. Palmas

Gold Coast

Slave Coast

Bight of Benin

Benue

Mt.
Cameroon
4070

Adamawa
Highlands

Dar Banda

Uele

Bahr el
Ghazâl

Bahr el Jebel

Ethiopian
Highlands

Somali
Peninsula

Shabelle

Juba

Bioko

Bight of Bonny

I. de Principe

Oubangi

Congo

L. Albert
Ruwenzori
5109

4321

Mt. Elgon

L. Turkana

5199
Mt. Kenya

São Tomé

Equator

Gulf of Guinea

C. Lopez

Annobón

Ogooué

Zaïre

Zaïre

Kasai

Basin

Chutes
Boyoma

Lualaba

L. Edward

L. Kivu

L. Victoria

5895
Kilimanjaro

Tana

INDIA

Se

OCEAN

Ascension I.

SOUTH ATLANTIC OCEAN

St. Helena

Sankuru

Kasai

Cuango

Cuanza

L. Mweru

L. Tanganyika

Lwewu

Luapula

L. Mweru

Rungwe
2961

Shaba

Bangweulu
Swamp

L. Nyasa
(L. Malawi)

Pemba I.

Aldabra
Is.

C. Delgado

Comoros

Bié
Plateau

Cunene

Cubango

Cuando

Zambezi

Zambezi

Luangwa

Shire

Mozambique Channel

Madagascar

Réu

C. Fria

Victoria
Falls

2643

Walvis Bay

Okavango Swamps

Namib Desert

Kalahari

Limpopo

Tropic of Capricorn

Orange

Vaal

High Veld

Drakensberg

Delagoa B.

3482
Compass Mt.
Nuweveldberge 2505
Great Karoo
Swartberge

Algoa B.

C. of Good Hope

C. Agulhas

Tristan da Cunha

ft m

12000 4000

9000 3000

6000 2000

3000 1000

1500 500

600 200

0 0

200 600

1000 3000

2000 6000

4000 12000

m ft

1 : 42 000 000

200 0 200 400 600 800 1000 1200 miles

200 0 200 400 600 800 1000 1200 1400 1600 1800 km

West from Greenwich 0 East from Greenwich

CARTOGRAPHY BY PHILIP'S.

1 : 42 000 000

● Dakar Capital Cities

CARTOGRAPHY BY PHILIP'S.

Projection: Azimuthal Equidistant

West from Greenwich | East from Greenwich

| 200 | 0 | 200 | 400 | 600 | 800 | 1000 | 1200 miles |
| 200 | 0 | 200 | 400 | 600 | 800 | 1000 | 1200 | 1400 | 1600 | 1800 | km |

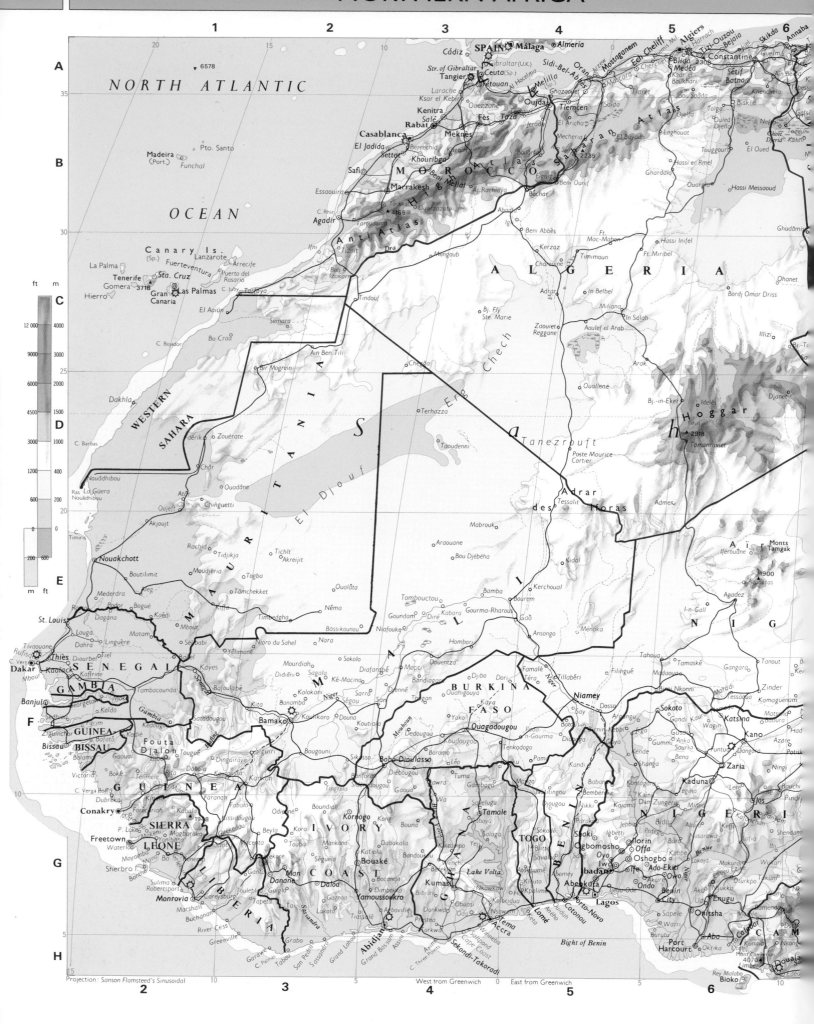

Projection : Sanson Flamsteed's Sinusoidal

West from Greenwich   East from Greenwich

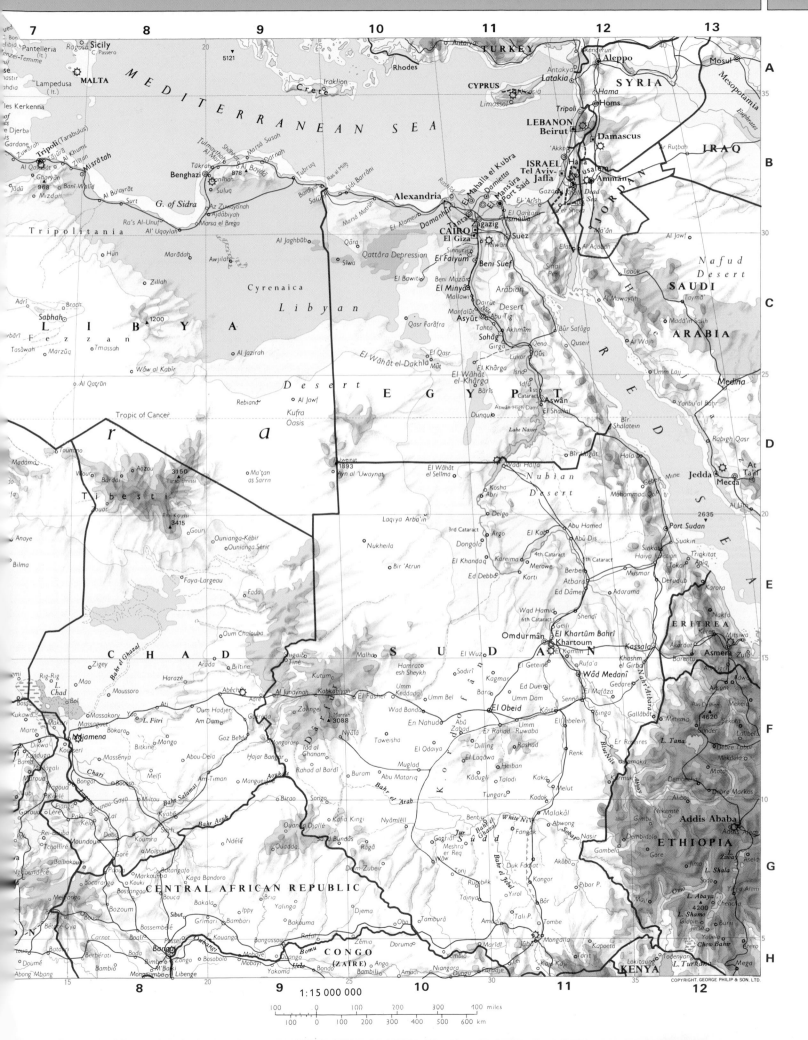

1:15 000 000

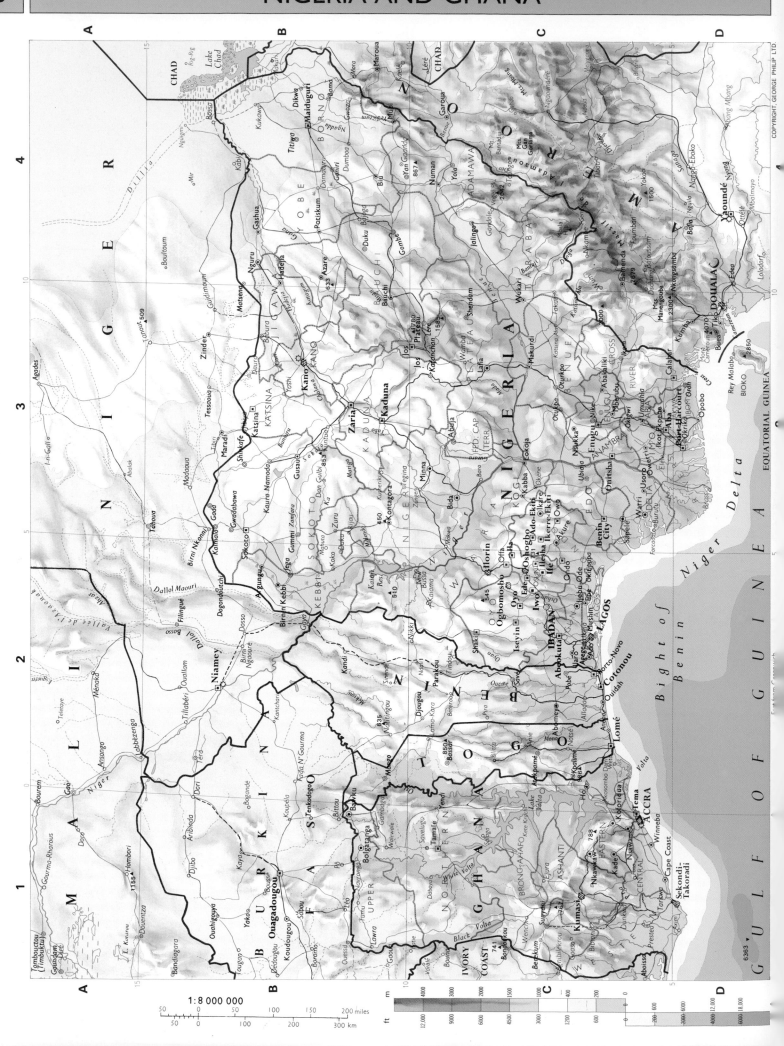

1 : 8 000 000

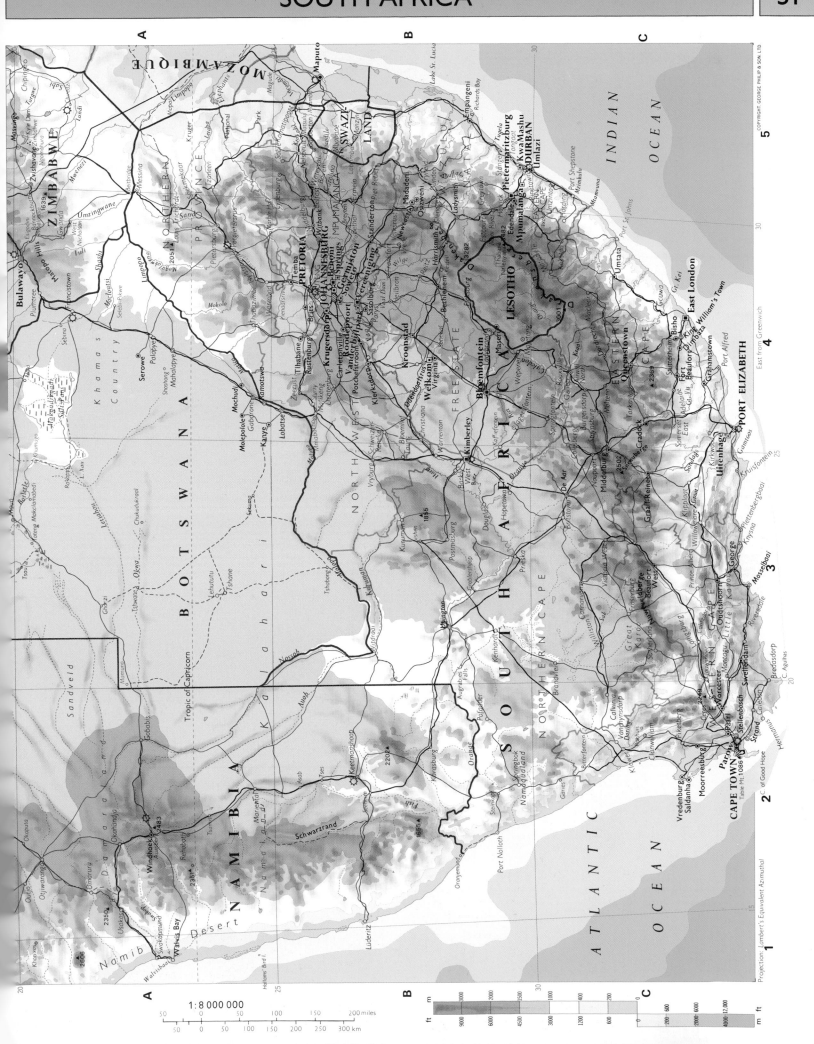

1 : 8 000 000

Projection: Lambert's Equivalent Azimuthal

East from Greenwich

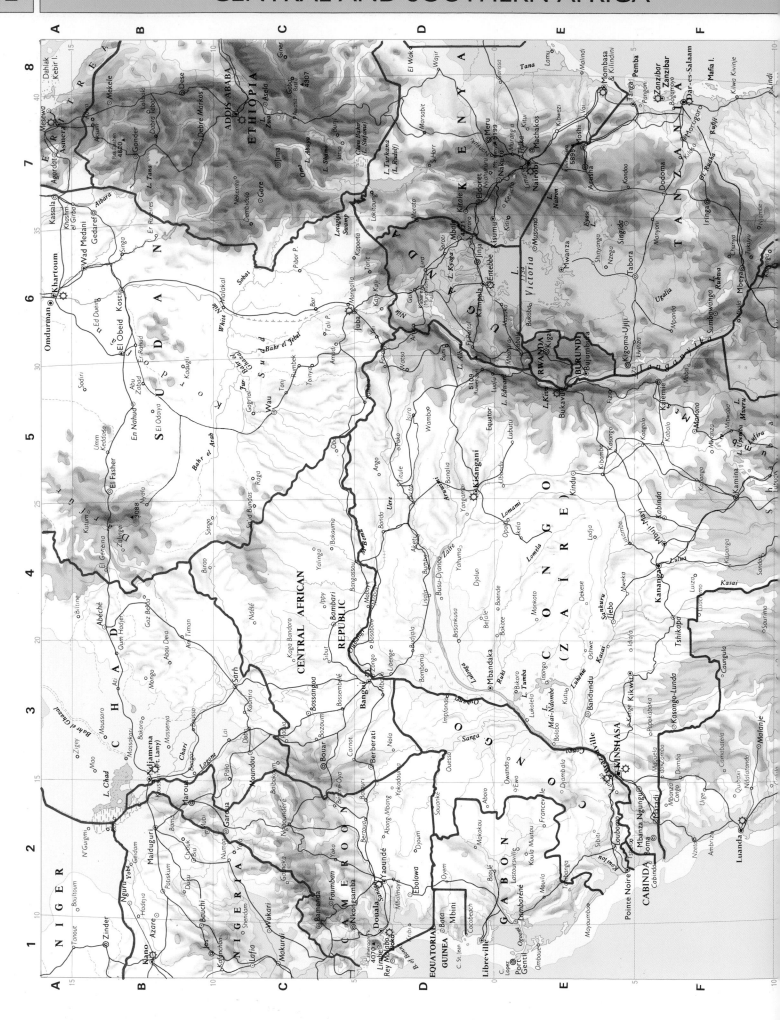

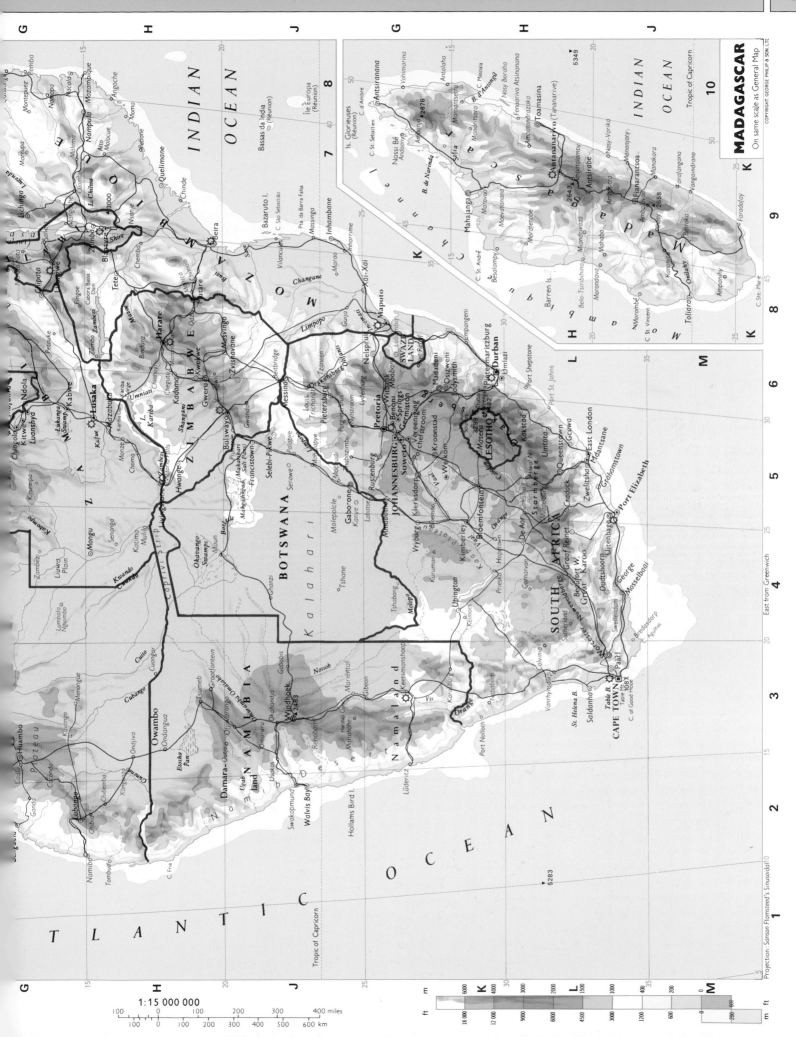

MADAGASCAR

On same scale as General Map

COPYRIGHT GEORGE PHILIP & SON LTD

INDIAN OCEAN

INDIAN OCEAN

Tropic of Capricorn

Antsiranana
C. St. Sébastien
Vohémar
Antalaha
C. d'Ambre
B.d'Antongil
C. Masoala
Nosy Boraha
Nosy Bé Ambilobe
Andoany
Sofia Bealanana
Mandritsara
Fenoarivo Atsinanana
Imbotondrazoka
Toamasina
(Tamatave)
Mahajanga Antananarivo (Tananarive)
Maevatanana
Marovoay Ambohimahasoa
Fianarantsoa
Besalampy
Maintirano
Miandrivazo
Manakara
Mahabo
Farafangana
Morondava
Vangaindrano
Belo-Tsiribihina
Barren Is.
N.Morombe
C. St. Vincent
Toliara
(Tuléar)
Ampanihy
Betroka
Ambovombe
Ankazoabo
C. Ste.-Marie

Is. Glorieuses (Réunion)
5349

2876

2643

2658

INDIAN OCEAN

Ile Europa (Réunion)
Bassas da India (Réunion)
Ile de la Réunion

L. Chilwa
Tembe
Nacala
Nampula
Mozambique
Montepuez
Angoche
Moma
Alto Molocue
Pebane
Quelimane
Chinde
Blantyre
Shire
Zomba
Beira
Bazaruto I.
C. São Sebastião
Vilanculos
Inhambane
Massinga
Pta. da Barra Falsa
Harrisme
Xai-Xai
Inhassoro

INDIAN OCEAN

Lichinga
Mandimba
Fíngoe
Tete
Zumbo
Cabora Bassa Dam
Cahora Bassa
Changara
Messina
Chicualacuala
Harare
Bindura
Mutare
Chimoio
Chegutu
Kadoma
Marondera
Kwekwe
Gweru
Masvingo
Zvishavane
Beitbridge
Messina
Changane
Limpopo
Guija
Maputo
Nelspruit
Mbabane
SWAZI LAND
Lobamba

Louis Trichardt
Pietersburg
Potgietersrus
Tzaneen
Phalaborwa
Lydenburg
Witbank
Middelburg
Pretoria
Benoni
Springs
Germiston
JOHANNESBURG
Soweto
Krugersdorp
Klerksdorp
Carletonville
Vereeniging
Vanderbijlpark
Welkom
Kroonstad
Bethlehem
Madadeni
Osizweni
Ladysmith
Pietermaritzburg
Durban
Umlazi
Port Shepstone
Port St. Johns
Umtata
Kokstad

Ndola
Kitwe
Luanshya
Chingola
Mufulira
Kabwe
Kafue
LUSAKA
ZAMBIA
Kariba Dam
L. Kariba
Monze
Choma
Hwange
Kariba
Bulawayo
Francistown
Gwanda
Gwai
Victoria Falls
Kazungula

ZIMBABWE

Selebi-Pikwe
Serowe
Palapye
Mahalapye
Gaborone
Kanye
Lobatse
Mafikeng
Zeerust
Rustenburg
Mmabatho
Ventersdorp
Vryburg
Kuruman
Kimberley
Bloemfontein
Kroonstad

LESOTHO
Maseru
3239
Matatiele

SOUTH AFRICA

Mongu
Senanga
Katima Mulilo
Caprivi Strip
Kwando
Liuwa Plain
Kaboinpo
Lumbala N'guimbo

Kalahari

Ghanzi
Maun
Makgadikgadi Salt Pans
Mahalapye
Molepolole

BOTSWANA

Tshane
Tshabong
Molopo
Nossob
Upington
Keimoes
Kakamas
Kenhardt
Prieska
De Aar
Carnarvon
Victoria West
Beaufort W.
Graaff Reinet
Cradock
Middelburg
Queenstown
Cathcart
Stutterheim
King William's Town
East London
Grahamstown
Port Alfred
Port Elizabeth
Uitenhage
Humansdorp

Namib Desert

Namibe
Tombua
C. Fria

Huambo
Caála
Menongue
Cuíto Cuanavale
Mavinga
Cuando
Cubango
Cuito
Cuangar
Rundu
Owambo
Ondangua
Ondjiva
Oshakati

NAMIBIA

Etosha Pan
Tsumeb
Grootfontein
Otjiwarongo
Omaruru
Okahandja
Windhoek
2483
Gobabis
Rehoboth
Mariental
Keetmanshoop
Gibeon
Karasburg
Lüderitz
Oranjemund
Port Nolloth
Alexander Bay

Orange
Springbok
Calvinia
Clanwilliam
Vanrhynsdorp
Sutherland
Ceres
Worcester
CAPE TOWN
Paarl
Table B.
Table M. 1087
C. of Good Hope
Saldanha
St. Helena B.
Vredenburg
Malmesbury
Stellenbosch
Somerset West
Caledon
Bredasdorp
C. Agulhas
Swellendam
Mossel Bay
George
Oudtshoorn
Knysna
Great Karoo
Graaff-Reinet

ATLANTIC OCEAN

Tropic of Capricorn

East from Greenwich

Projection: Sanson Flamsteed's Sinusoidal

1:15 000 000

100   0   100   200   300   400 miles
100   0   100 200 300 400 500   600 km

m   ft
6000   18 000   K
4000   12 000
3000   9000
2000   6000
1500   4500   L
1000   3000
400   1200
200   600
0   0   M
200   600

AUSTRALIA AND OCEANIA

Indonesia
Sulawesi (Celebes)
Ujung Pandang (Makasar)
Kendari
Butung
Buru
Ambon
Ceram
Misool
Sorong
Vogelkop
Fakfak
Kai Is.
Aru Is.
Banda Sea
5300
7260
3350
Sumbawa
Raba
Flores
Ende
Alor
Wetar
Leti
Babar
Tanimbar Is.
3310
Flores Sea
Sumba
6204
Timor
Kupang
Dili
Timor Sea
Biak
Jayapura
Irian Jaya
Pegunungan Maoke
Puncak Jaya 5029
New Guinea
Wewak
Madang
Mount Hagen
Mt. Wilhelm 4508
Lae
PAPUA NEW GUINEA
Bismarck Archipelago
Rabaul
New Ireland
New Britain
Solomon Sea
D'Entrecasteaux
Port Moresby
Gulf of Papua
Owen Stanley Range
Fly
Louisiade Archipelago
Torres Strait
C. York
Pulau Yos Sudarso
Arafura Sea
Melville I.
C. Croker
C. Arnhem
Darwin
Arnhem Land
Gulf of Carpenteria
Wellesley I.
Weipa
Cape York Peninsula
Coral Sea
C. Londonderry
Cambridge G.
Wyndham
Kimberley Plateau
Derby
Daly Waters
Larrimah
Cooktown
Mitchell
Cairns
1611 Bartle Frere
Broome
Tanami Desert
Tennant Creek
NORTHERN
Barkly Tableland
Normanton
Forsayth
Flinders
Townsville
Charters Towers
Coral Sea
Great Sandy Desert
TERRITORY
Kajaabi
Mount Isa
Hughenden
Mackay
Territory
L. Mackay
Macdonnell Ranges
1510 Mt. Ziel
Alice Springs
QUEENSLAND
Winton
Longreach
Rockhampton
Gladstone
Port Hedland
Dampier
N.W. Cape
Lake Disappointment
Gibson Desert
Ayers Rock
Mt. Woodroffe 1440
Simpson Desert
Diamantina
Yaraka
Maryborough
Bundaberg
Mt. Bruce 1226
Hamersley Range
Newman
AUSTRALIA
Mt.
Musgrave Ranges
SOUTH
Cooper Creek
Grey Range
Charleville
Roma
Gympie
Carnarvon
WESTERN
L. Carnegie
Great Victoria Desert
AUSTRALIA
Lake Eyre
Quilpie
Thargomindah
Cunnamulla
Dirrabandi
BRISBANE
Toowoomba
Meekatharra
Leonora
Marree
AUSTRALIA
Bourke
Walgett
161
Round Mt.
Tarcoola
Flinders Range
Broken Hill
Cobar
Tamworth
NEW SOUTH
Geraldton
Lake Barlee
Kalgoorlie-Boulder
Deakin
Penong
Port Augusta
Darling
Dubbo
Orange
Bathurst
WALES
Newcastle
Murchison
Norseman
Nullarbor Plain
Whyalla
Port Pirie
Murray
Mildura
Wagga Wagga
Goulburn
SYDNEY
Wollongong
Shellharbour
Northam
Great Australian Bight
Port Lincoln
Spencer Gulf
Adelaide
Murray
Albury
Canberra
CAPITAL TERRITORY
Perth
Darling Range
Esperance
5632
Kangaroo I.
Encounter B.
Shepparton
Horsham
Mt. Kosciuszko 2237
Australian Alps
Bombala
Bunbury
Port Gambier
VICTORIA
Bendigo
Ballarat
MELBOURNE
Geelong
C. Howe
C. Leeuwin
Augusta
Albany
Warrnambool
Mount Gambier
Bass Strait
King I.
Furneaux Group
INDIAN OCEAN
Burnie
Launceston
1617 Mt. Ossa
TASMANIA
Hobart
S.E. Cape

ft   m
6000   2000
4500   1500
3000   1000
1200   400
600   200
0   0
200   600
2000   6000
4000   12,000
6000   18,000
m   ft

PACIFIC OCEAN

SOLOMON ISLANDS

NAURU

KIRIBATI

Bougainville
Choiseul
Santa Isabel
New Georgia
Malaita
Honiara ▲2331
Guadalcanal
San Cristóbal
Rennell
▼7223

Melanesia

Tamana
Namumea
Abariringa
▼6195
Phoenix Is.
Carondelet

TUVALU
(Ellice Is.) Funafuti
○Funafuti
Nukulaelae

Tokelau Is.
(N.Z.)

Santa Cruz Is.
Fataka

Rotuma

Banks Is.

Espíritu Santo
▲1880
VANUATU
(New Hebrides)
Malakula
Port-Vila ○ Efate

Mata-Utu ○ Uvea
Wallis & Futuna
Horn (Fr.)

WESTERN SAMOA
Savai'i
Upolu ○ Apia

American Samoa
Tutuila

Vanua Levu
Viti Levu
▲1324 **FIJI**
Suva

Niuafo'ou

Loyalty Is.
▲1628 ▼7569

New Caledonia
(Fr.)
Noumea

Ceve-i-Ra
Matthew

Lau Is.

Vavau Is.

Ha'apai Is.
TONGA

Niue
(N.Z.)

hesterfield Is.

Nuku'Alofa
Tongatapu Is.

PACIFIC
▼5303

10882▼ Tonga Trench

Cook Is.
(N.Z.)

OCEAN

Tropic of Capricorn

Norfolk
(Austr.)

Raoul
Kermadec Is.
(N.Z.)

Lord Howe
(Austr.)
▼734

Kermadec Trench

10047▼

asman Sea

North C.
Kaitaia
Whangarei
Auckland
Hamilton
Bay of Plenty
North Island
New Plymouth
Rotorua
Raupehu
2797
Gisborne
NEW ZEALAND
Wanganui
Napier
Palmerston North
Nelson
Cook Strait
Wellington
Greymouth
Blenheim
Southern Alps
South Island
Mt.Cook
3753
Christchurch
Wakatipu
Timaru
Invercargill
Dunedin
Stewart

International Date Line

Chatham
(N.Z.)

▼5267

West from Greenwich

1:20 000 000

100 0 100 200 300 400 500 miles

100 0 200 400 600 800 km

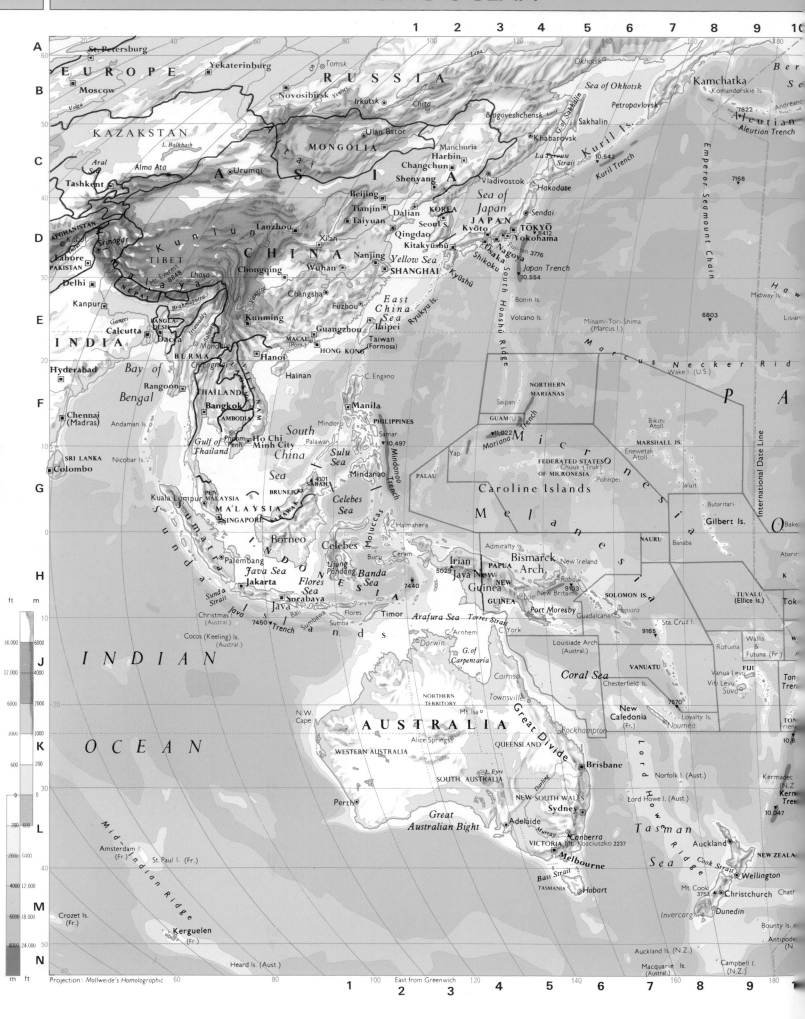

A

St. Petersburg

EUROPE
Moscow   Yekaterinburg   RUSSIA   Tomsk
B   Novosibirsk   Yenisey   Irkutsk   Chita   Okhotsk   Kamchatka
        Volga   Sea of Okhotsk   Komandorskie Is.
                        Ulan Bator   Blagoveshchensk   Amur   Petropavlovsk   7822
KAZAKSTAN   MONGOLIA   G. of Sakhalin   Aleutian
        L. Balkhash   A   Manchuria   Khabarovsk   Sakhalin   Aleutian Trench
C   Aral   Alma Ata   Urumqi   S   Harbin   La Perouse   Kuril Is.   7168
        Sea   Changchun   Strait   10,542
Tashkent   I   Shenyang   Vladivostok   Hakodate   Kuril Trench
                        Beijing   A   Sea of   Emperor Seamount Chain
                Lanzhou   Tianjin   Dalian   KOREA   Japan
AFGHANISTAN   Srinagar   Taiyuan   Seoul S.   Kyōto   Sendai
Kabul   Xi'an   Qingdao   TOKYO   7412
D   Lahore   TIBET   Osaka   Nagoya   Yokohama
PAKISTAN   CHINA   Nanjing   Yellow Sea   Shikoku   Fuji-san 3776
Delhi   Chongqing   Wuhan   SHANGHAI   Kyūshū   Japan Trench   6603
        Kanpur   NEPAL   Mt. Everest   Lhasa   South Honshū Ridge   10,554
                        8848   Changsha   East   Bonin Is.   Midway Is.   Hawai
        Ganges   BANGLA-   Brahmaputra   Fuzhou   China   Ryukyu Is.   Volcano Is.   Minami-Tori-Shima   Lisian
E   Calcutta   DESH   Kunming   Guangzhou   Sea   Taipei   (Marcus I.)
INDIA   Dacca   Mandalay   MACAU   Taiwan   Marcus   Necker Ridge
Hyderabad   BURMA   Chengdu   (Port.)   HONG KONG   (Formosa)   Wake I. (U.S.)
                        VIETNAM   Hanoi   Hainan   C. Engano   NORTHERN   P   A
Bay of   Rangoon   THAILAND   MARIANAS
F   Bengal   Chennai   Andaman Is.   Bangkok   Manila   Saipan   GUAM (U.S.)   Bikini
(Madras)   CAMBODIA   Mindoro   PHILIPPINES   Atoll
        SRI LANKA   Nicobar Is.   Phnom   Ho Chi   Palawan   Samar   11,022   Micronesia   MARSHALL IS.   Enewetak
        Colombo   Penh   Minh City   Sulu   Mindanao   Mariana Trench   Yap   FEDERATED STATES   Atoll
                Gulf of   Sea   4101   10,497   Mindanao Trench   OF MICRONESIA   Chuuk (Truk)
G   Kuala Lumpur   Thailand   SABAH   Celebes   PALAU   Caroline Islands   Pohnpei   Jaluit
PEN.   BRUNEI   Sea   Melanesia   Gilbert Is.
MALAYSIA   MALAYSIA   SARAWAK   Moluccas   Butaritari   O
Singapore   Borneo   Halmahera   Admiralty Is.   NAURU   Banaba   Abarir
                Sumatra   Celebes   Ceram   Buru   Bismarck   New Ireland
H   Palembang   Java Sea   Ujung   Irian   Arch.   Rabaul   K
        Jakarta   Pandang   Banda   Jaya 5029   New   New Britain   SOLOMON IS.   TUVALU
Sunda   Flores   Sea   7440   Guinea   Lae   9103   (Ellice Is.)   Tok
Strait   Surabaya   Sea   NEW   Honiara   Sta. Cruz I.   Wallis &
        Bali   Flores   Timor   GUINEA   Port Moresby   Guadalcanal   9165   Futuna (Fr.)   Rotuma
Christmas I.   Java   7450   Sumbawa   Sumba   Arafura Sea   Torres Strait   Louisiade Arch.   VANUATU   Vanua Levu   FIJI
(Austral.)   Trench   Sunda Islands   Timor   C. Arnhem   C. York   (Austral.)   Coral Sea   Chesterfield Is.   Viti Levu   Suva   Ton
Cocos (Keeling) Is.   Darwin   G. of   Sea   7670   New   Tre
(Austral.)   INDIAN   Carpentaria   Cairns   Caledonia   TON
J   NORTHERN   Townsville   (Fr.)   Loyalty Is.   Frien
OCEAN   TERRITORY   Mt. Isa   Great   Rockhampton   Nouméa
K   N.W.   AUSTRALIA   Alice Springs   Divide   Brisbane   Norfolk I. (Aust.)   Kermadec
Cape   WESTERN AUSTRALIA   QUEENSLAND   (N.Z.)
                                L. Eyre   SOUTH AUSTRALIA   Lord Howe I. (Aust.)   Kern
                                        Darling   NEW SOUTH WALES   Tren
L   Amsterdam I.   St. Paul I. (Fr.)   Perth   Sydney   10,047
(Fr.)   Adelaide   Murray   Canberra   Tasman
Midian Indian Ridge   Great   VICTORIA   Mt. Kosciuszko 2237   Auckland
                Australian Bight   Melbourne   Ridge   Cook Strait   NEW ZEALA
M   Crozet Is.   Bass Strait   Mt. Cook   Wellington
(Fr.)   Kerguelen   TASMANIA   Hobart   3753   Christchurch   Chath
(Fr.)   Invercargill   Dunedin   Bounty Is.
N   Heard Is. (Aust.)   Auckland Is. (N.Z.)   Antipode
                                        Macquarie I.   Campbell I.
                                        (Aust.)   (N.Z.)

ft   m
18,000 6000
12,000 4000
6000   2000
3000   1000
600   200
0   0
200   600
2000   6000
4000   12,000
6000   18,000
8000   24,000
m   ft

12 13 14 15 16 17 18 19 20

A

Gulf of Alaska
Prince of Wales I.
Prince Rupert
Queen Charlotte Is.
Kitimat
Juneau

ALASKA
5959

CANADA
Hudson Bay
GREENLAND
C. Farewell

NORTH AMERICA
Labrador
Newfoundland

Edmonton
L. Winnipeg

B

Vancouver
Vancouver I.
Victoria
Seattle
Calgary
Regina
Winnipeg
Montréal
Quebec
Pr. Edward I.
Saint John

Portland
L. Superior
Ottawa
Toronto
L. Huron
Michigan
Detroit
L. Ontario
Boston
C. Sable

C

Minneapolis
CHICAGO
Pittsburgh
Buffalo
Erie
NEW YORK
Philadelphia
Baltimore
Washington

C. Mendocino
Salt Lake City
Denver
Kansas
St. Louis
Cincinnati

ATLANTIC

D

San Francisco
4418
UNITED STATES
Oklahoma
Memphis
Atlanta
C. Hatteras

6741
Los Angeles
San Diego
Dallas
Mississippi
Appalachian Mts.
Jacksonville

Bermuda (U.K.)

OCEAN

E

Ciudad Juárez
6225
San Antonio
Houston
New Orleans
Miami
Florida Strait
BAHAMAS

Hawaiian Is.
(U.S.)
Tropic of Cancer
Sierra Madre
Gulf of California
MEXICO
Monterrey
Gulf of Mexico
Havana
CUBA
Yucatan Channel
West Indies
Hispaniola
DOM. REP.
9200

Honolulu
Oahu
Hawaii
(U.S.)
Revilla Gigedo Is.
(Mexico)
Guadalajara
México
Puebla
6700
Mérida
7680
JAMAICA
HAITI
Kingston
PUERTO RICO
Leeward Is.

F

PACIFIC
Acapulco
BELIZE
GUATEMALA
Guatemala
HONDURAS
Caribbean Sea
BARBADOS
Windward Is.
TRINIDAD & TOBAGO

El SALVADOR
NICARAGUA
Managua
CENTRAL AMERICA
San José
COSTA RICA
Barranquilla
Maracaibo
Caracas
VENEZUELA

Clipperton I. (Fr.)
Cocos I.
Colón
PANAMA
Panamá
Canal
Orinoco

G

Palmyra Is. (U.S.)
Teraina
Tabuaeran
Kiritimati
Jarvis I. (U.S.)
Medellín
Bogotá
Cali
COLOMBIA

OCEAN
Malden I.
Starbuck I.
Equator
Galápagos
(Ecuador)
Guayaquil
Quito
ECUADOR
Manaus
Amazon

H

Tongareva
Penrhyn Is.
Manihiki
Suwarrow Is.
Caroline I.
Vostok I.
Flint I.
Marquesas Is.
C. Pariñas
Iquitos
BRAZIL
SOUTH

Trujillo

J

Cook Islands
(N.Z.)
Society Is.
Windward Is.
Tahiti
Leeward Is.
Tuamotu Archipelago
6369
PERU
Lima
Cuzco
AMERICA

Manuae
Rarotonga
FRENCH POLYNESIA
Mururoa
Arequipa
L. Titicaca
Illampu & Ancohuma
6550
La Paz
BOLIVIA
Peru
6866

K

Tubuai Is.
(Austral Is.)
Rapa Iti
Pitcairn I. (U.K.)
Ducie I. (U.K.)
Tropic of Capricorn
Sala-y-Gomez
(Chile)
Easter Is.
(Chile)
San Félix (Chile)
San Ambrosio (Chile)
Iquique
Chile
8050
Antofagasta Trench
PARAGUAY
Asunción
Tucumán
Pto. Alegre

L

East Pacific Ridge
Arch. de Juan Fernández
(Chile)
Valparaíso
Santiago
6960
Córdoba
Rosario
Buenos Aires
URUGUAY
Montevideo
Río de la Plata

Concepción
ARGENTINA

M

Pacific - Antarctic Ridge
Chile Rise
SOUTH
ATLANTIC

Chonos Arch.
OCEAN

N

G. of Penas
6212
Falkland Is. (U.K.)

Punta Arenas
Str. of Magellan
C. Horn
Tierra del Fuego
South Georgia

12 13 14 15 16 17 18 19 20

West from Greenwich

1:54 000 000

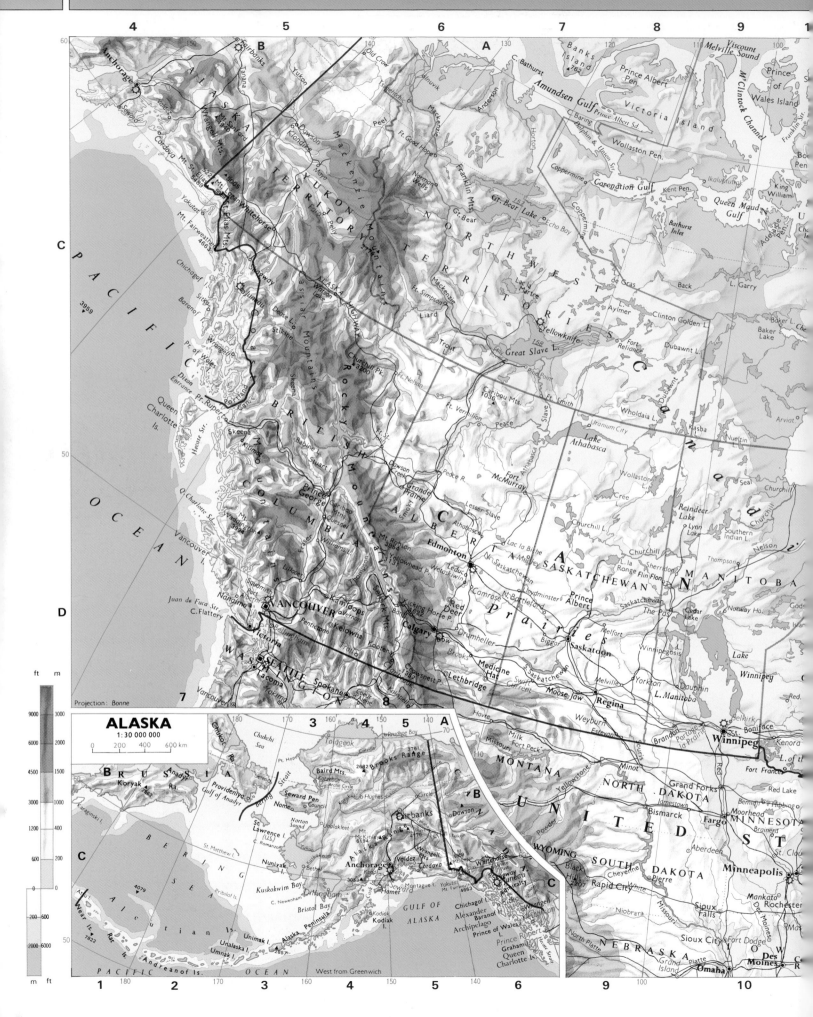

Projection: Bonne

ALASKA

1:30 000 000

0   200   400   600 km

1:15 000 000

West from Greenwich

COPYRIGHT. GEORGE PHILIP & SON. LTD

100   0   100   200   300   400 miles

100   0   100   200   300   400   500   600 km

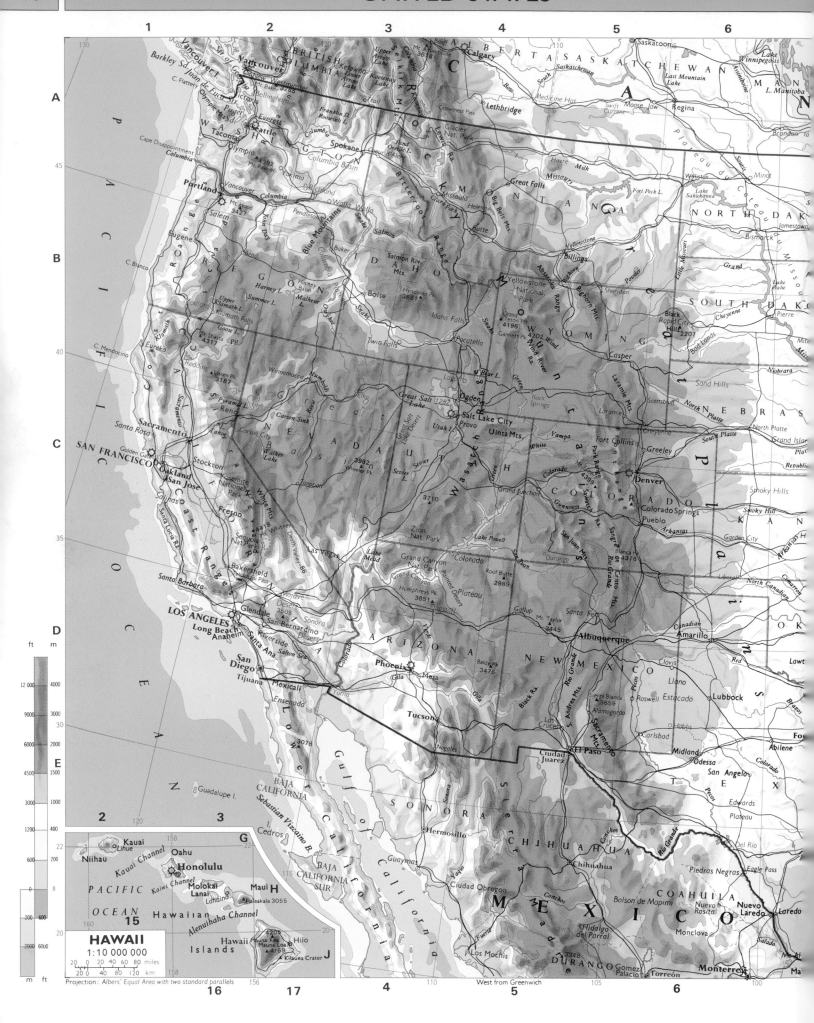

HAWAII
1:10 000 000
20 0 20 40 60 80 miles
20 0 40 80 120 km
Projection: Albers' Equal Area with two standard parallels

Empty

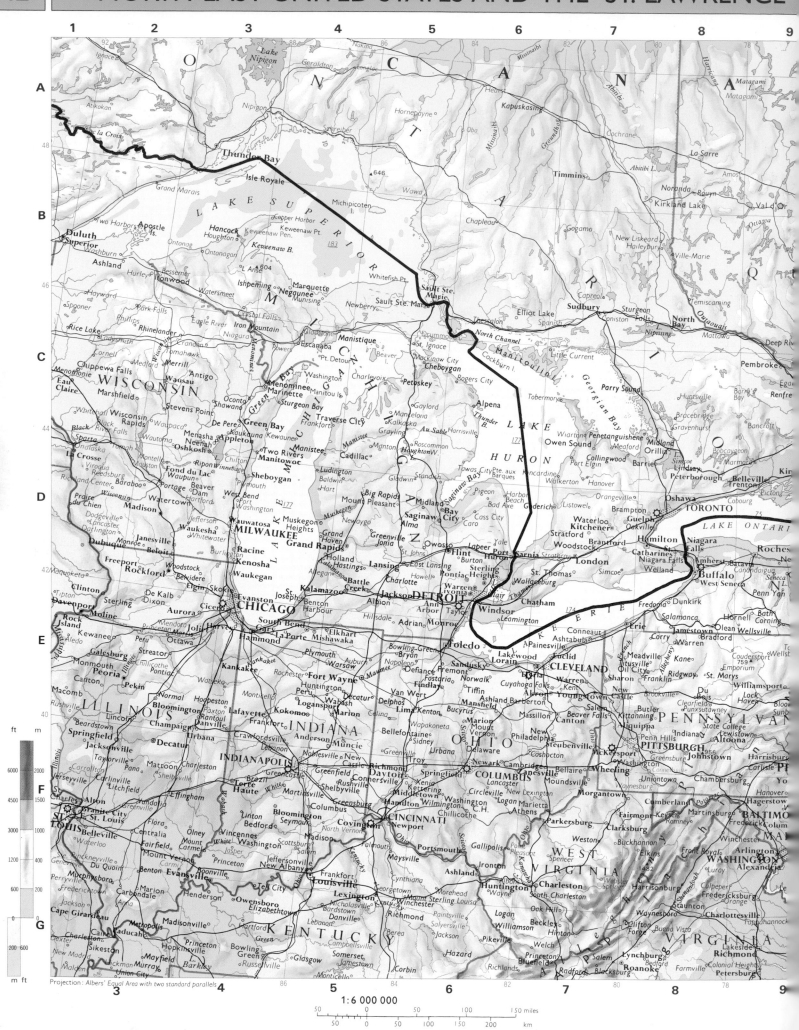

Projection: Albers' Equal Area with two standard parallels

1 : 6 000 000

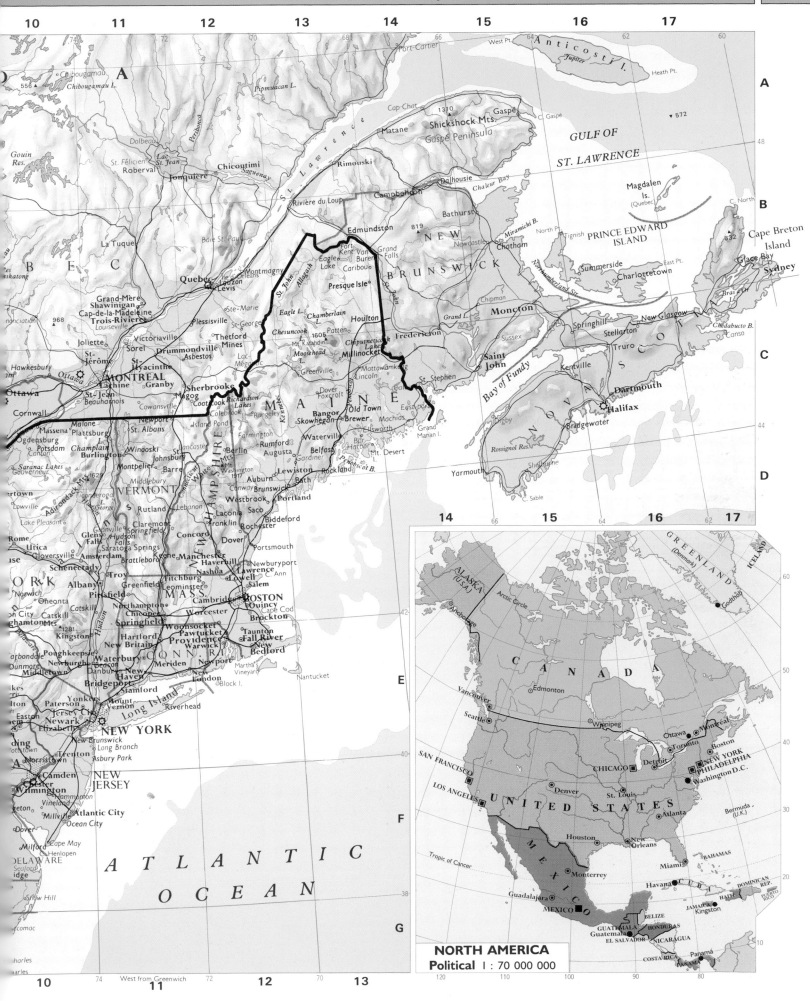

NORTH AMERICA
Political 1 : 70 000 000

A map of the Caribbean region, showing:

ATLANTIC OCEAN

Bermuda (U.K.) • Hamilton

Columbus • C. Fear • Augusta • Charleston • avannah

Jacksonville • Daytona Beach • C. Canaveral • Orlando • West Palm Beach • Grand Bahama I. • Freeport • Gt. Abaco I. • New Providence I. • Eleuthera I.

Miami • Fort Lauderdale • C. Sable • ey West • Nassau • BAHAMAS • Andros I. • Cat I. • S. Salvador • Long I.

Tropic of Cancer

avana • Matanzas • Cárdenas • Sagua la Grande • Sta. Clara • Morón • Mayaguana • Acklins • Turks & Caicos Is. (U.K.)

uventud • Cienfuegos • Sancti Spiritus • Ciego de Ávila • Camagüey • Holguín • Gt. Inagua I.

C • U • B • A • Manzanillo • Bayamo • Guantánamo • Cap Hoitien • San Francisco de Macoris • Santiago

rand Cayman (U.K.) • Santiago de Cuba • Gonaives • DOMINICAN REP. • La Romana • PUERTO RICO (U.S.A.) • San Juan • St. Thomas (U.S.A.) • Charlotte Amalie • Virgin Is. (U.K.) • Anguilla • St. Martin (Fr. & Neth.)

Montego Bay • Kingston • JAMAICA • Les Coyes • Port au Prince • Santo Domingo • 2280 • 1754 • Barahona • Jacmel • Ponce • Mayagüez • Caguas • St. Croix (U.S.A.) • ST. KITTS–NEVIS • ANTIGUA & BARBUDA • St. John's • Montserrat (U.K.) • Guadeloupe (Fr.) • Pointe à Pitre

GREATER • **ANTILLES** • **Hispaniola** • Windward Passage • Mona Passage • 1338 • Leeward Islands • DOMINICA • **LESSER**

atasca Lagoon • C. Gracias á Dios

CARIBBEAN SEA • **ANTILLES** • Windward • ST. LUCIA • BARBADOS • Fort de France • Martinique (Fr.) • Bridgetown • ST. VINCENT • THE GRENADINES • Islands • GRENADA

Providencia (Col.) • San Andrés (Col.) • Pta. Gallinas • Gulf of Venezuela • Aruba (Neth.) • Curaçao • Willemstad • Bonaire • La Blanquilla (Ven.) • Margarita • Tobago • Port of Spain • TRINIDAD & TOBAGO

uefields • Pen. de la Guajira • Pen. de Paraguaná • NETH. ANTILLES • La Tortuga (Ven.) • Carúpano • San Fernando

Barranquilla • Santa Marta • Punto Fijo • Coro • Cumana • G. of Paria • Delta of the Orinoco

Limón • Colón • Cartagena • 5800 • Sierra Nevada de Santa Marta • **Maracaibo** • Cabimas • **Caracas** • **Maracay** • Barcelona • Maturin

Vol. Barú • 3374 • **Panama** • G. of Darién • Sincelejo • L. de Maracaibo • **Barquisimeto** • **Valencia** • El Tigre • Ciudad Guayana

David • Azuero Pen. • Coiba • G. of Panama • Valera • **Mérida** • Cord. de Mérida • Barinas • Apure • San Fernando de Apure • Ciudad Bolívar • Orinoco • Georgetown • New Amsterdam

Cúcuta • 4104 • **San Cristóbal** • Arauca • Arauca • **GUYANA**

Barrancabermeja • 3960 • **Bucaramanga** • **VENEZUELA** • Meta • Angel Falls • 2560 • Caroní • Cuyuni • Essequibo

Quibdó • **Medellín** • Tunja • Pto. Ayacucho • 2285 • Roraima • 2810 • **SURINAM**

Manizales • Pereira • 5215 • **Bogotá** • **COLOMBIA** • Sierra Pacaraima • 280

Armenia • Girardot • Sa. Parú

Buenaventura • Guaviare • Casiquiare

Cali • 5750 • Magdalena • Popayán • 4646 • **BRAZIL**

COPYRIGHT. GEORGE PHILIP & SON. LTD.

1:15 000 000

100 0 100 200 300 400 miles

100 0 100 200 300 400 500 600 km

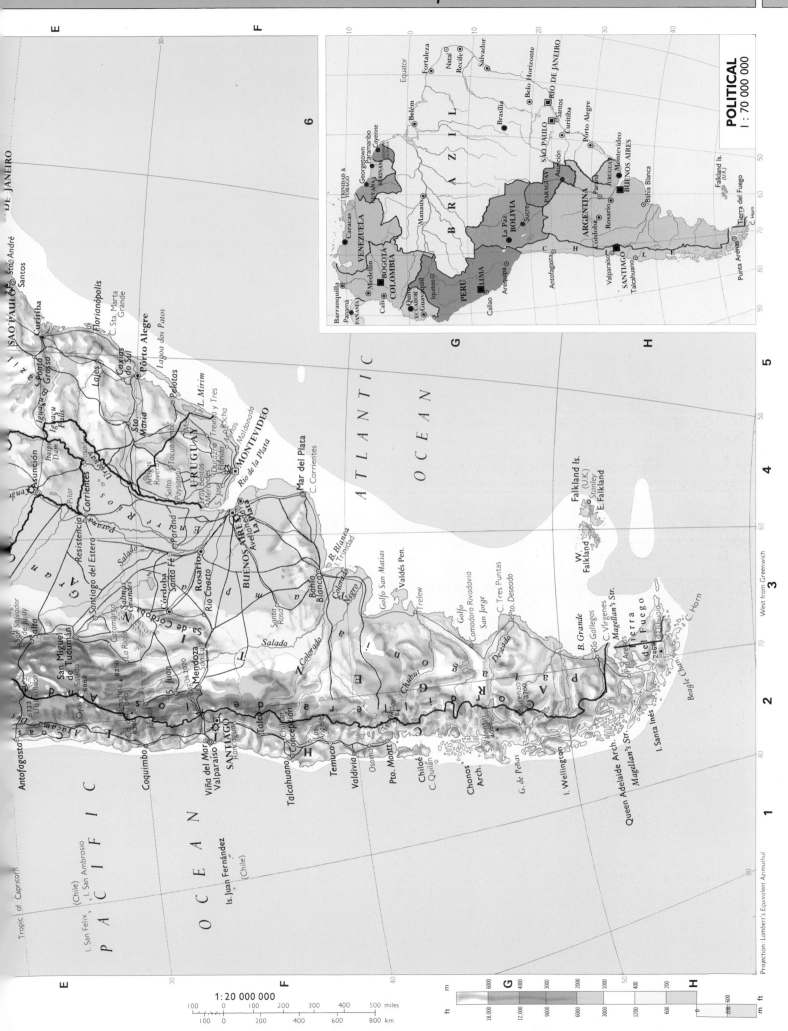

Projection: Lambert's Equivalent Azimuthal

POLITICAL
1 : 70 000 000

1:20 000 000

100   0   100   200   300   400   500 miles
100   0   200   400   600   800 km

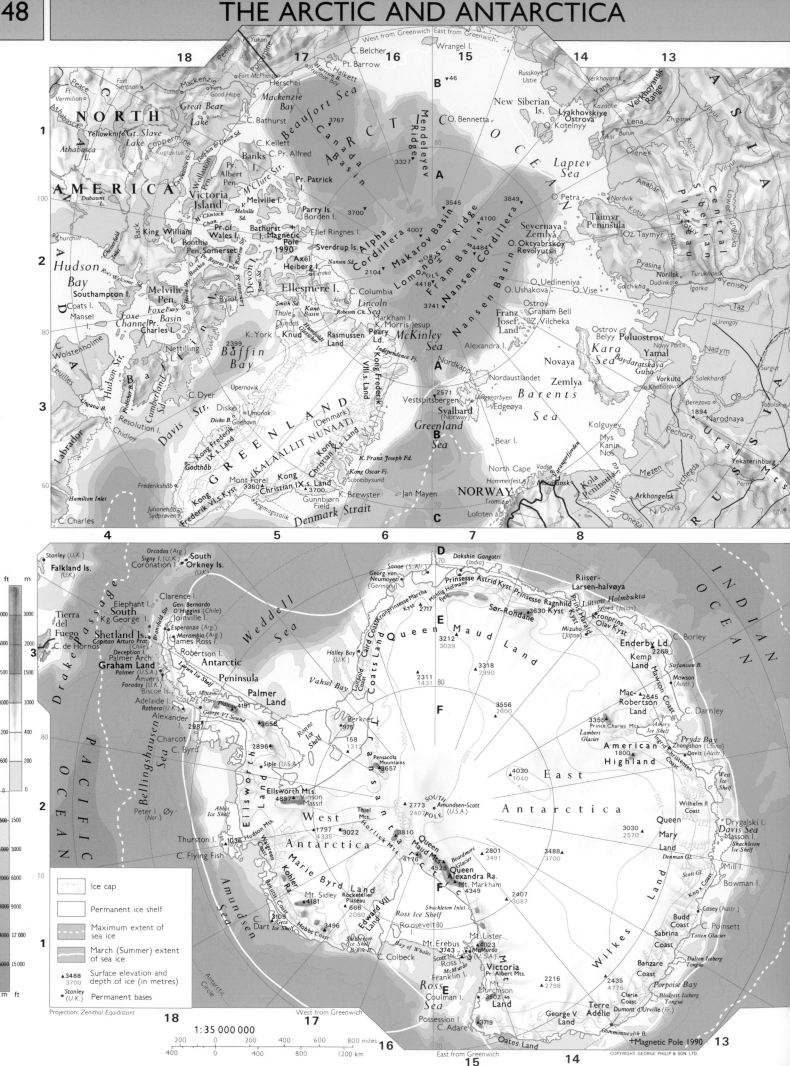

WORLD THEMATIC MAPS

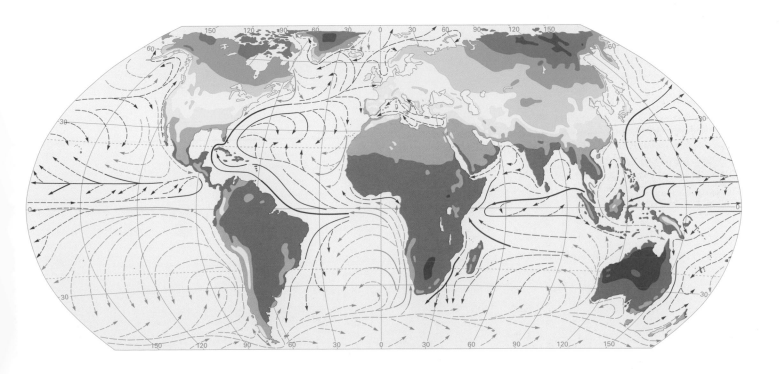

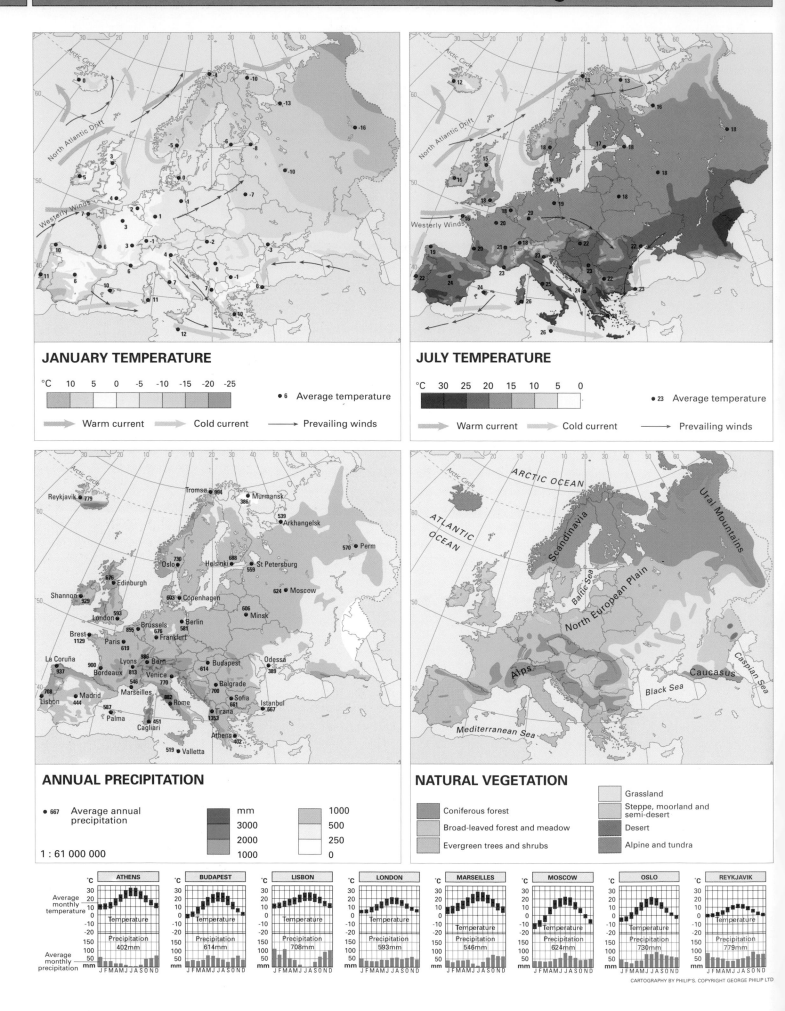

JANUARY TEMPERATURE

°C   10   5   0   -5   -10   -15   -20   -25

● 6   Average temperature

→ Warm current   ⇒ Cold current   → Prevailing winds

JULY TEMPERATURE

°C   30   25   20   15   10   5   0

● 23   Average temperature

→ Warm current   ⇒ Cold current   → Prevailing winds

ANNUAL PRECIPITATION

● 667   Average annual precipitation

mm		1000
3000		500
2000		250
1000		0

1 : 61 000 000

NATURAL VEGETATION

- Coniferous forest
- Broad-leaved forest and meadow
- Evergreen trees and shrubs
- Grassland
- Steppe, moorland and semi-desert
- Desert
- Alpine and tundra

ATHENS — Temperature — Precipitation 402mm

BUDAPEST — Temperature — Precipitation 614mm

LISBON — Temperature — Precipitation 708mm

LONDON — Temperature — Precipitation 593mm

MARSEILLES — Temperature — Precipitation 546mm

MOSCOW — Temperature — Precipitation 624mm

OSLO — Temperature — Precipitation 730mm

REYKJAVIK — Temperature — Precipitation 779mm

Average monthly temperature

Average monthly precipitation

CARTOGRAPHY BY PHILIP'S. COPYRIGHT GEORGE PHILIP LTD

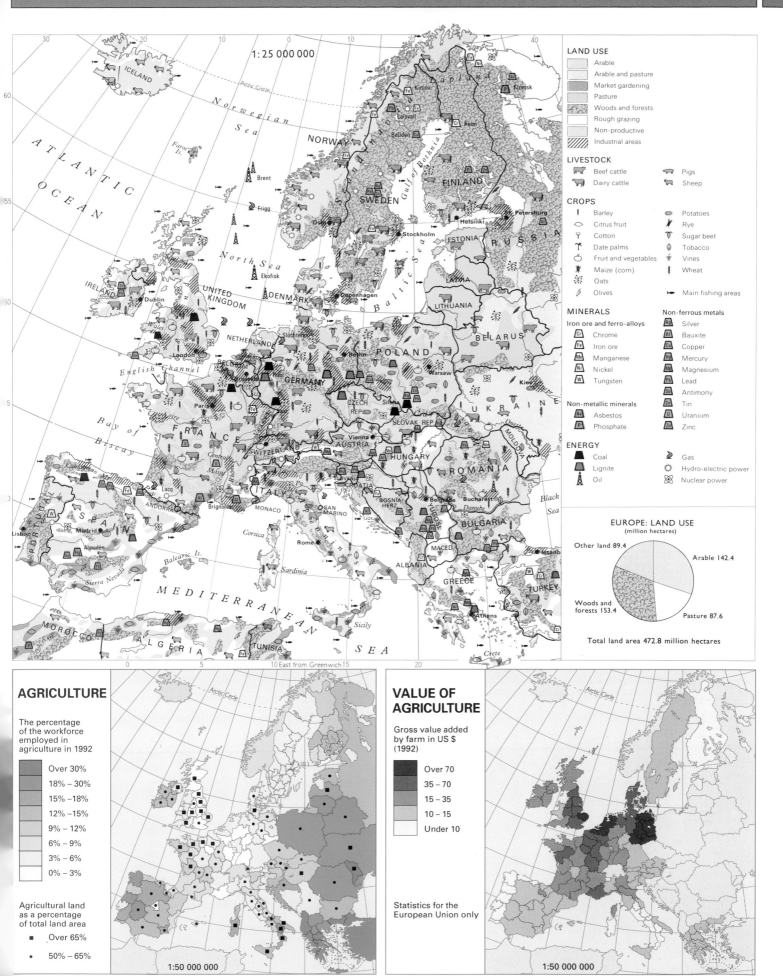

LAND USE
- Arable
- Arable and pasture
- Market gardening
- Pasture
- Woods and forests
- Rough grazing
- Non-productive
- Industrial areas

LIVESTOCK
- Beef cattle
- Dairy cattle
- Pigs
- Sheep

CROPS
- Barley
- Citrus fruit
- Cotton
- Date palms
- Fruit and vegetables
- Maize (corn)
- Oats
- Olives
- Potatoes
- Rye
- Sugar beet
- Tobacco
- Vines
- Wheat
- Main fishing areas

MINERALS
Iron ore and ferro-alloys
- Cr Chrome
- Fe Iron ore
- Mn Manganese
- Ni Nickel
- W Tungsten

Non-metallic minerals
- As Asbestos
- P Phosphate

Non-ferrous metals
- Ag Silver
- Al Bauxite
- Cu Copper
- Hg Mercury
- Mg Magnesium
- Pb Lead
- Sb Antimony
- Sn Tin
- U Uranium
- Zn Zinc

ENERGY
- Coal
- Lignite
- Oil
- Gas
- Hydro-electric power
- Nuclear power

EUROPE: LAND USE
(million hectares)

Other land 89.4
Arable 142.4
Woods and forests 153.4
Pasture 87.6

Total land area 472.8 million hectares

AGRICULTURE

The percentage of the workforce employed in agriculture in 1992
- Over 30%
- 18% – 30%
- 15% –18%
- 12% –15%
- 9% – 12%
- 6% – 9%
- 3% – 6%
- 0% – 3%

Agricultural land as a percentage of total land area
- ■ Over 65%
- • 50% – 65%

1:50 000 000

VALUE OF AGRICULTURE

Gross value added by farm in US $ (1992)
- Over 70
- 35 – 70
- 15 – 35
- 10 – 15
- Under 10

Statistics for the European Union only

1:50 000 000

Projection: Bonne

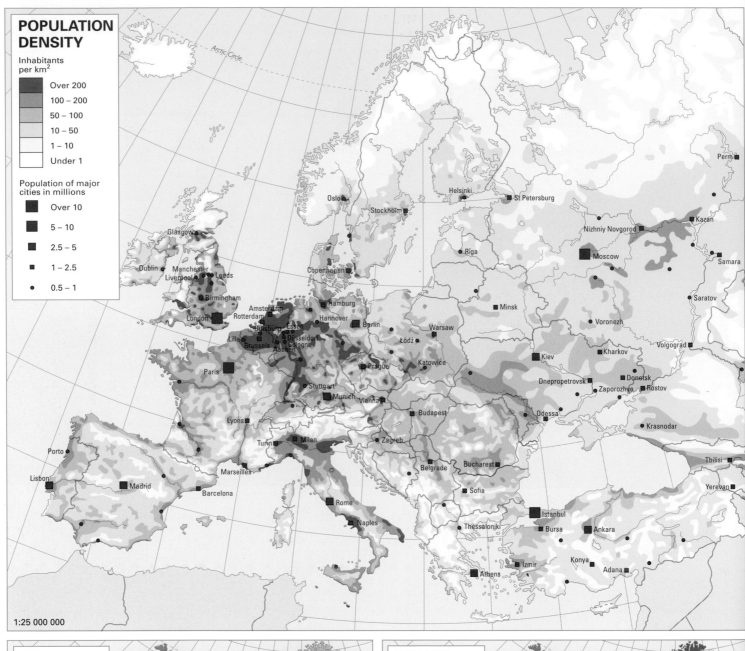

POPULATION DENSITY

Inhabitants per km²

- Over 200
- 100 – 200
- 50 – 100
- 10 – 50
- 1 – 10
- Under 1

Population of major cities in millions

- Over 10
- 5 – 10
- 2.5 – 5
- 1 – 2.5
- 0.5 – 1

1:25 000 000

Glasgow
Dublin Manchester Leeds
Liverpool
Birmingham
London
Amsterdam Hamburg
Rotterdam Hannover Berlin
Duisburg Essen Warsaw
Lille Düsseldorf Łódź
Brussels Cologne
Aachen Katowice
Paris Prague
Stuttgart
Munich Vienna
Lyons Budapest
Turin Milan Zagreb
Porto Marseilles Belgrade Bucharest
Lisbon Rome Sofia
Madrid
Barcelona Naples Istanbul
Thessaloniki Bursa Ankara
Athens Izmir Konya Adana

Oslo
Stockholm
Copenhagen
Helsinki
St Petersburg
Riga
Minsk
Moscow Kazan
Nizhniy Novgorod
Samara
Saratov
Voronezh
Kiev Kharkov Volgograd
Dnepropetrovsk Donetsk
Zaporozhye Rostov
Odessa Krasnodar
Tbilisi
Yerevan
Perm

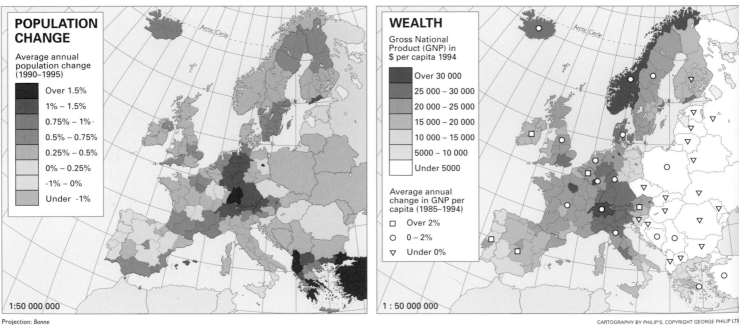

POPULATION CHANGE

Average annual population change (1990–1995)

- Over 1.5%
- 1% – 1.5%
- 0.75% – 1%
- 0.5% – 0.75%
- 0.25% – 0.5%
- 0% – 0.25%
- -1% – 0%
- Under -1%

1:50 000 000

WEALTH

Gross National Product (GNP) in $ per capita 1994

- Over 30 000
- 25 000 – 30 000
- 20 000 – 25 000
- 15 000 – 20 000
- 10 000 – 15 000
- 5000 – 10 000
- Under 5000

Average annual change in GNP per capita (1985–1994)

- ☐ Over 2%
- ○ 0 – 2%
- ▽ Under 0%

1 : 50 000 000

Projection: *Bonne*

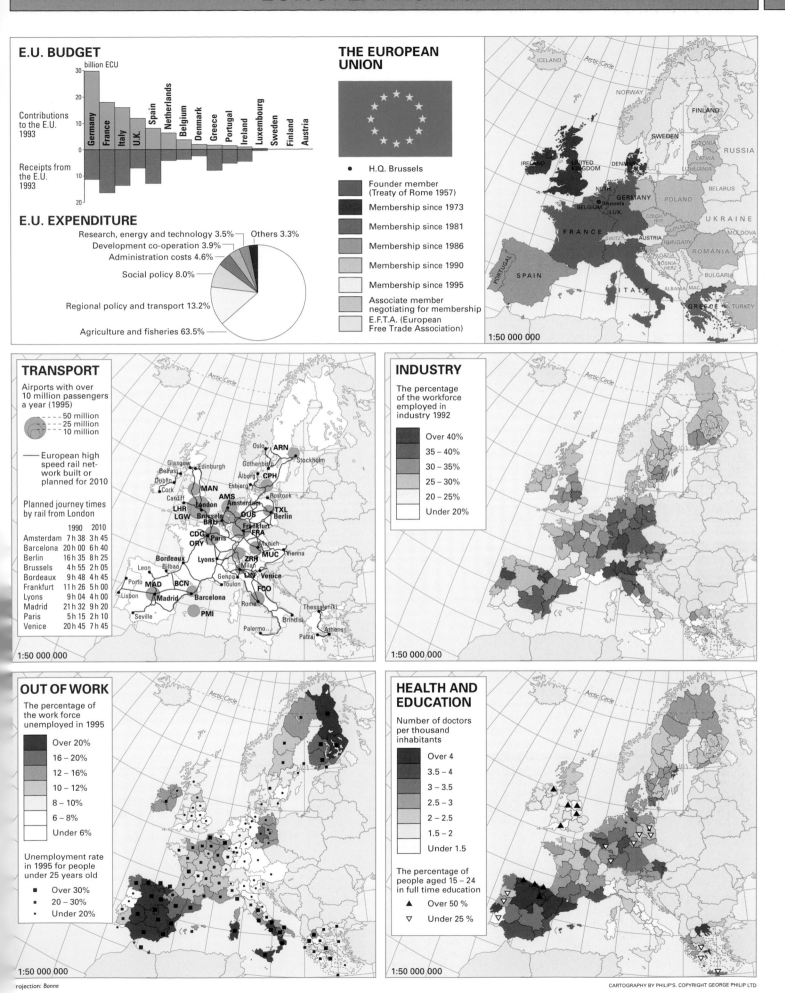

E.U. BUDGET

billion ECU

Contributions to the E.U. 1993

Receipts from the E.U. 1993

Germany, France, Italy, U.K., Spain, Netherlands, Belgium, Denmark, Greece, Portugal, Ireland, Luxembourg, Sweden, Finland, Austria

E.U. EXPENDITURE

- Research, energy and technology 3.5%
- Others 3.3%
- Development co-operation 3.9%
- Administration costs 4.6%
- Social policy 8.0%
- Regional policy and transport 13.2%
- Agriculture and fisheries 63.5%

THE EUROPEAN UNION

- ● H.Q. Brussels
- Founder member (Treaty of Rome 1957)
- Membership since 1973
- Membership since 1981
- Membership since 1986
- Membership since 1990
- Membership since 1995
- Associate member negotiating for membership
- E.F.T.A. (European Free Trade Association)

1:50 000 000

TRANSPORT

Airports with over 10 million passengers a year (1995)
- 50 million
- 25 million
- 10 million

— European high speed rail network built or planned for 2010

Planned journey times by rail from London

	1990	2010
Amsterdam	7 h 38	3 h 45
Barcelona	20 h 00	6 h 40
Berlin	16 h 35	8 h 25
Brussels	4 h 55	2 h 05
Bordeaux	9 h 48	4 h 45
Frankfurt	11 h 26	5 h 00
Lyons	9 h 04	4 h 00
Madrid	21 h 32	9 h 20
Paris	5 h 15	2 h 10
Venice	20 h 45	7 h 45

1:50 000 000

INDUSTRY

The percentage of the workforce employed in industry 1992
- Over 40%
- 35 – 40%
- 30 – 35%
- 25 – 30%
- 20 – 25%
- Under 20%

1:50 000 000

OUT OF WORK

The percentage of the work force unemployed in 1995
- Over 20%
- 16 – 20%
- 12 – 16%
- 10 – 12%
- 8 – 10%
- 6 – 8%
- Under 6%

Unemployment rate in 1995 for people under 25 years old
- ■ Over 30%
- ▪ 20 – 30%
- • Under 20%

1:50 000 000

HEALTH AND EDUCATION

Number of doctors per thousand inhabitants
- Over 4
- 3.5 – 4
- 3 – 3.5
- 2.5 – 3
- 2 – 2.5
- 1.5 – 2
- Under 1.5

The percentage of people aged 15 – 24 in full time education
- ▲ Over 50 %
- ▽ Under 25 %

1:50 000 000

Projection: Bonne

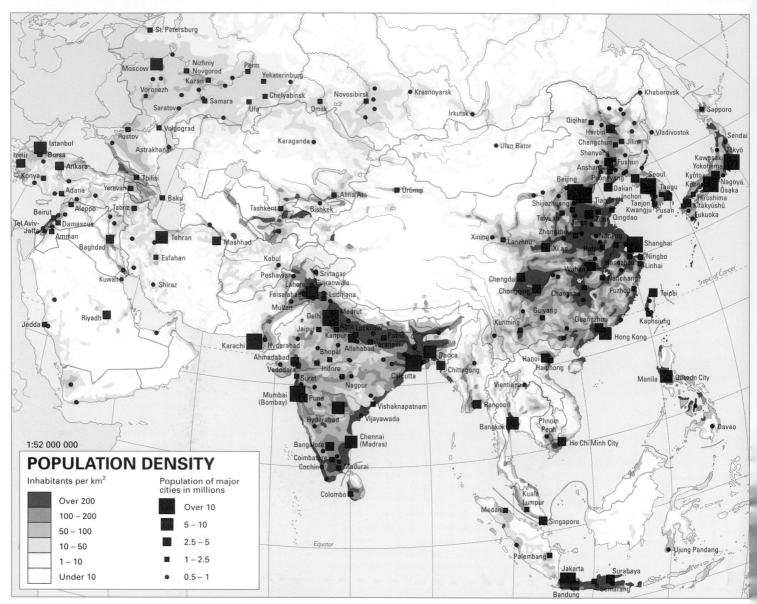

POPULATION DENSITY

1:52 000 000

Inhabitants per km²

- Over 200
- 100 – 200
- 50 – 100
- 10 – 50
- 1 – 10
- Under 10

Population of major cities in millions

- Over 10
- 5 – 10
- 2.5 – 5
- 1 – 2.5
- 0.5 – 1

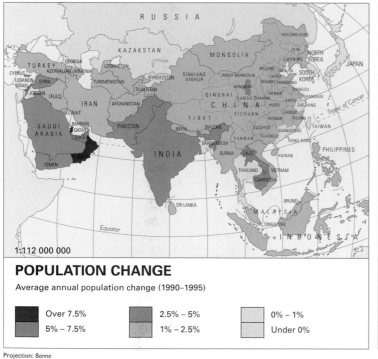

POPULATION CHANGE

Average annual population change (1990–1995)

1:112 000 000

- Over 7.5%
- 5% – 7.5%
- 2.5% – 5%
- 1% – 2.5%
- 0% – 1%
- Under 0%

Projection: Bonne

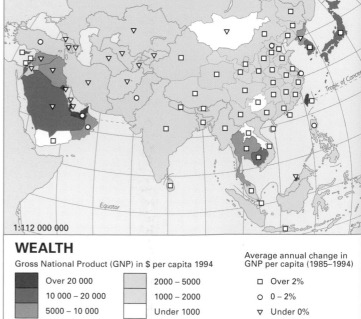

WEALTH

Gross National Product (GNP) in $ per capita 1994

1:112 000 000

- Over 20 000
- 10 000 – 20 000
- 5000 – 10 000
- 2000 – 5000
- 1000 – 2000
- Under 1000

Average annual change in GNP per capita (1985–1994)

- □ Over 2%
- ○ 0 – 2%
- ▽ Under 0%

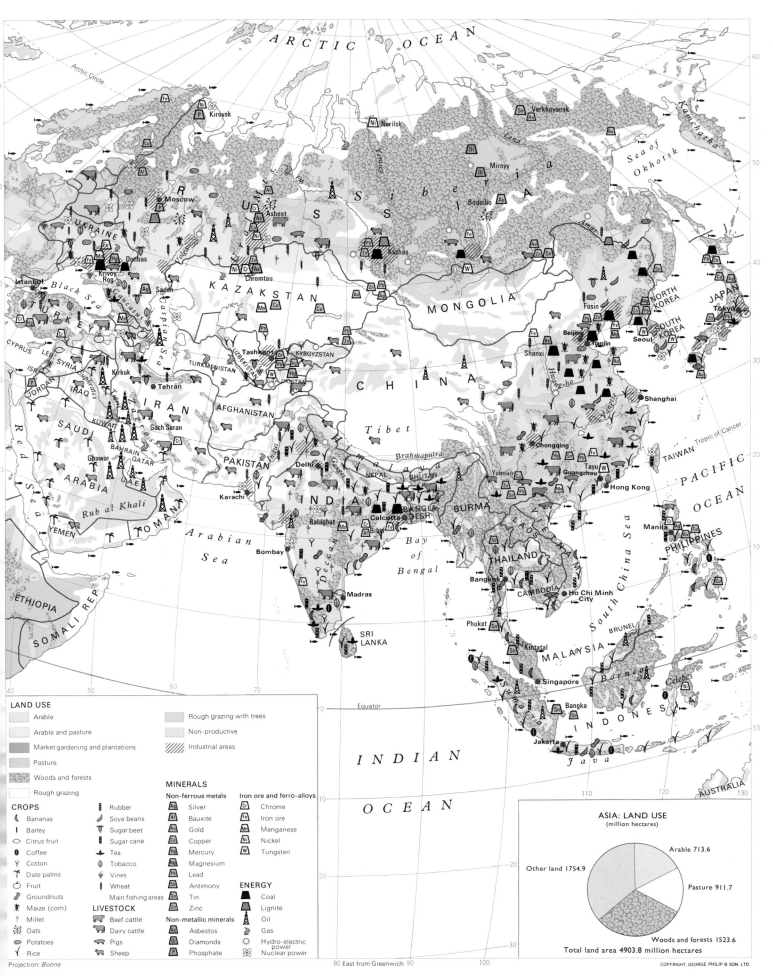

LAND USE

- Arable
- Arable and pasture
- Market gardening and plantations
- Pasture
- Woods and forests
- Rough grazing
- Rough grazing with trees
- Non-productive
- Industrial areas

CROPS

- Bananas
- Barley
- Citrus fruit
- Coffee
- Cotton
- Date palms
- Fruit
- Groundnuts
- Maize (corn)
- Millet
- Oats
- Potatoes
- Rice
- Rubber
- Soya beans
- Sugar beet
- Sugar cane
- Tea
- Tobacco
- Vines
- Wheat
- Main fishing areas

LIVESTOCK

- Beef cattle
- Dairy cattle
- Pigs
- Sheep

MINERALS

Non-ferrous metals

- Ag Silver
- Al Bauxite
- Au Gold
- Cu Copper
- Hg Mercury
- Mg Magnesium
- Pb Lead
- Sb Antimony
- Sn Tin
- Zn Zinc

Non-metallic minerals

- As Asbestos
- Di Diamonds
- P Phosphate

Iron ore and ferro-alloys

- Cr Chrome
- Fe Iron ore
- Mn Manganese
- Ni Nickel
- W Tungsten

ENERGY

- Coal
- Lignite
- Oil
- Gas
- Hydro-electric power
- Nuclear power

ASIA: LAND USE
(million hectares)

Other land 1754.9

Arable 713.6

Pasture 911.7

Woods and forests 1523.6

Total land area 4903.8 million hectares

Projection: *Bonne*

80 East from Greenwich 90 100

COPYRIGHT. GEORGE PHILIP & SON. LTD.

1 : 50 000 000

200 0 200 400 600 800 1000 miles

200 0 400 800 1200 1600 km

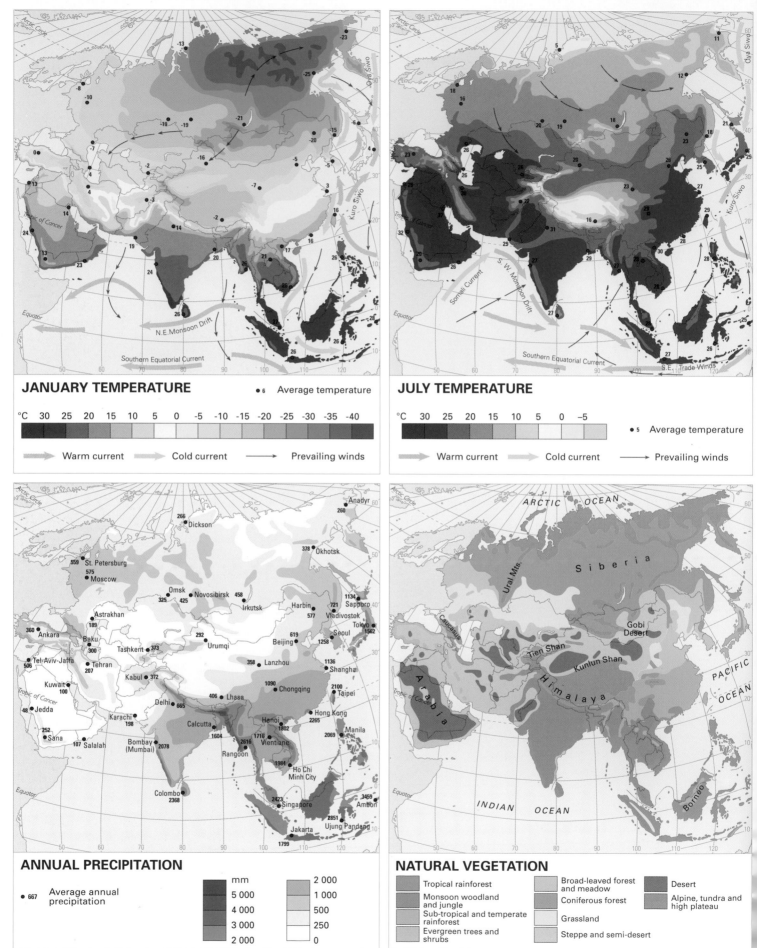

JANUARY TEMPERATURE

●₆ Average temperature

°C 30 25 20 15 10 5 0 -5 -10 -15 -20 -25 -30 -35 -40

→ Warm current   → Cold current   → Prevailing winds

JULY TEMPERATURE

°C 30 25 20 15 10 5 0 -5

●₅ Average temperature

→ Warm current   → Cold current   → Prevailing winds

ANNUAL PRECIPITATION

●₆₆₇ Average annual precipitation

mm	
5 000	2 000
4 000	1 000
3 000	500
2 000	250
	0

NATURAL VEGETATION

- Tropical rainforest
- Monsoon woodland and jungle
- Sub-tropical and temperate rainforest
- Evergreen trees and shrubs
- Broad-leaved forest and meadow
- Coniferous forest
- Grassland
- Steppe and semi-desert
- Desert
- Alpine, tundra and high plateau

Projection: *Modified Hammer Equal Area*   1 : 105 000 000

CARTOGRAPHY BY PHILIP'S. COPYRIGHT GEORGE PHILIP LTD

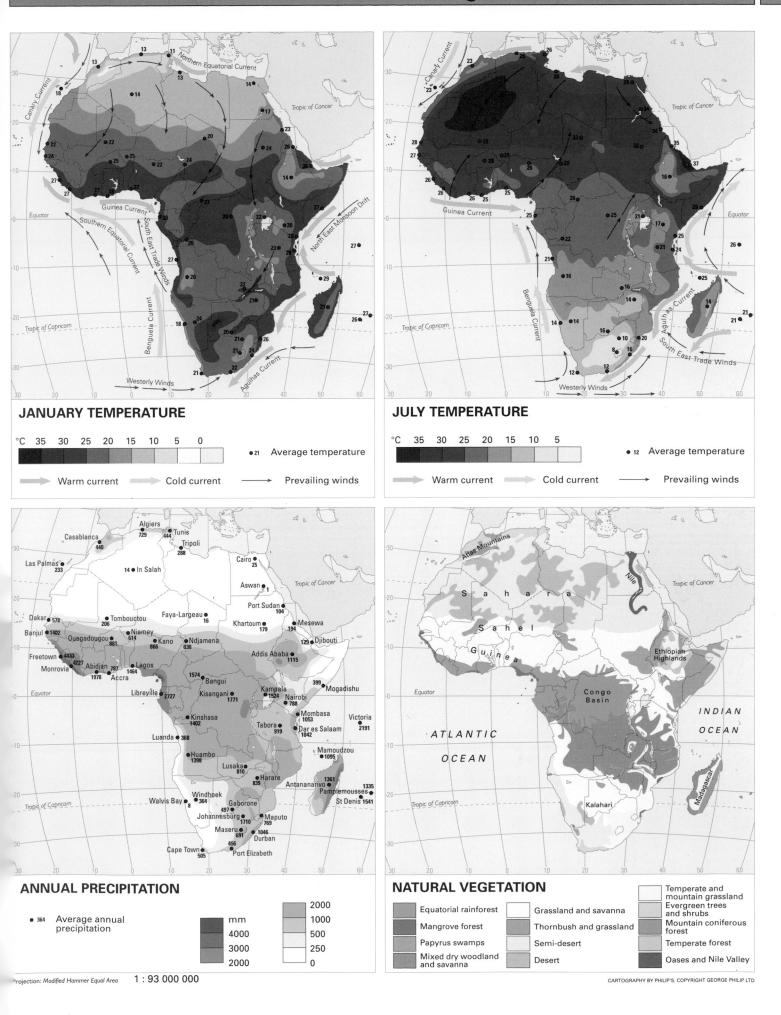

JANUARY TEMPERATURE

°C 35 30 25 20 15 10 5 0

• 21 Average temperature

⟶ Warm current   ⟹ Cold current   → Prevailing winds

JULY TEMPERATURE

°C 35 30 25 20 15 10 5

• 12 Average temperature

⟶ Warm current   ⟹ Cold current   → Prevailing winds

ANNUAL PRECIPITATION

Algiers 729
Casablanca 440
Tunis 444
Tripoli 288
Las Palmas 233
In Salah 14
Cairo 25
Aswan 1
Port Sudan 104
Dakar 578
Tombouctou 206
Faya-Largeau 16
Khartoum 179
Mesewa 194
Banjul 1402
Ouagadougou 881
Niamey 614
Kano 866
Ndjamena 636
Djibouti 129
Freetown 4433
Abidjan 787
Lagos 1464
Addis Ababa 1115
Monrovia 4227
Accra 1978
Bangui 1574
Libreville 2727
Kisangani 1771
Kampala 1524
Nairobi 788
Mogadishu 399
Kinshasa 1402
Mombasa 1053
Victoria 2191
Luanda 368
Tabora 919
Dar es Salaam 1042
Huambo 1398
Lusaka 810
Harare 839
Mamoudzou 1095
Antananarivo 1361
Pamplemousses 1335
Walvis Bay 8
Windhoek 364
Gaborone 497
St Denis 1541
Johannesburg 1710
Maputo 769
Maseru 691
Durban 1046
Cape Town 505
Port Elizabeth 456

• 364 Average annual precipitation

mm
2000
1000
4000
3000
500
2000
250
0

NATURAL VEGETATION

Atlas Mountains
Sahara
Sahel
Guinea
Nile
Ethiopian Highlands
Congo Basin
ATLANTIC OCEAN
INDIAN OCEAN
Kalahari
Madagascar

Equatorial rainforest
Mangrove forest
Papyrus swamps
Mixed dry woodland and savanna
Grassland and savanna
Thornbush and grassland
Semi-desert
Desert
Temperate and mountain grassland
Evergreen trees and shrubs
Mountain coniferous forest
Temperate forest
Oases and Nile Valley

Projection: *Modified Hammer Equal Area*   1 : 93 000 000

CARTOGRAPHY BY PHILIP'S. COPYRIGHT GEORGE PHILIP LTD

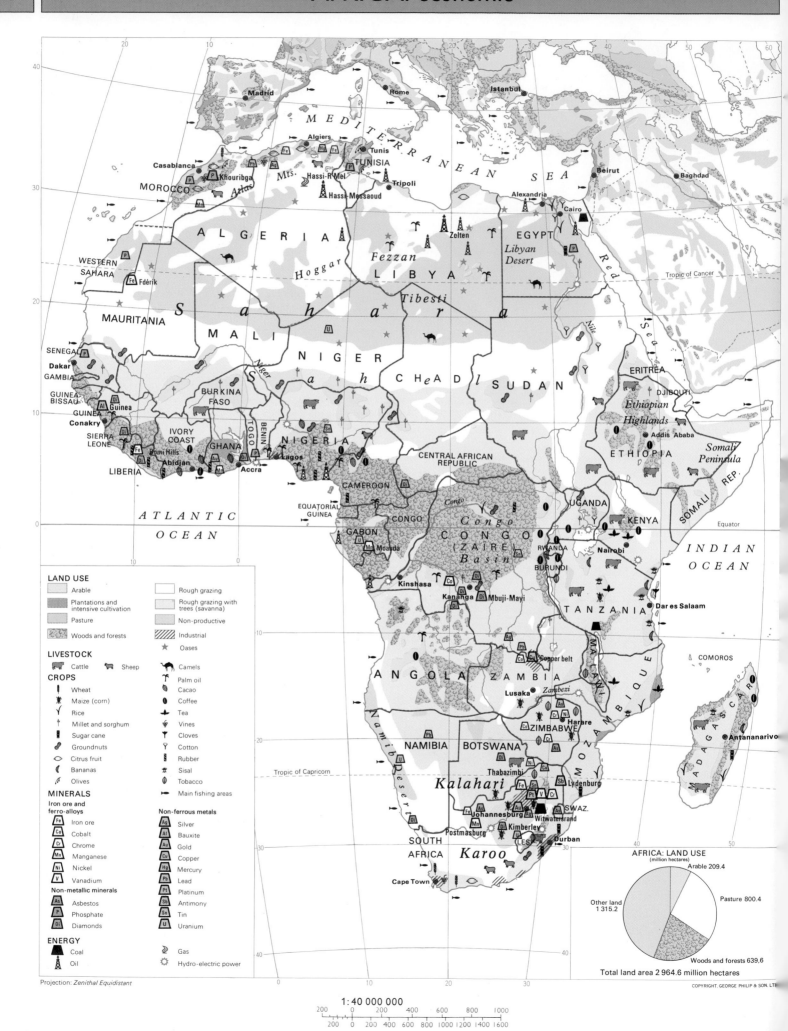

LAND USE
- Arable
- Plantations and intensive cultivation
- Pasture
- Woods and forests
- Rough grazing
- Rough grazing with trees (savanna)
- Non-productive
- Industrial
- Oases ★

LIVESTOCK
- Cattle
- Sheep
- Camels

CROPS
- Wheat
- Maize (corn)
- Rice
- Millet and sorghum
- Sugar cane
- Groundnuts
- Citrus fruit
- Bananas
- Olives
- Palm oil
- Cacao
- Coffee
- Tea
- Vines
- Cloves
- Cotton
- Rubber
- Sisal
- Tobacco
- Main fishing areas

MINERALS
Iron ore and ferro-alloys
- Fe Iron ore
- Co Cobalt
- Cr Chrome
- Mn Manganese
- Ni Nickel
- V Vanadium

Non-metallic minerals
- As Asbestos
- P Phosphate
- D Diamonds

Non-ferrous metals
- Ag Silver
- Al Bauxite
- Au Gold
- Cu Copper
- Hg Mercury
- Pb Lead
- Pt Platinum
- Sb Antimony
- Sn Tin
- U Uranium

ENERGY
- Coal
- Oil
- Gas
- Hydro-electric power

AFRICA: LAND USE
(million hectares)
Arable 209.4
Pasture 800.4
Other land 1 315.2
Woods and forests 639.6
Total land area 2 964.6 million hectares

Projection: Zenithal Equidistant

1:40 000 000

200 0 200 400 600 800 1000
200 0 200 400 600 800 1000 1200 1400 1600

COPYRIGHT. GEORGE PHILIP & SON. LTD

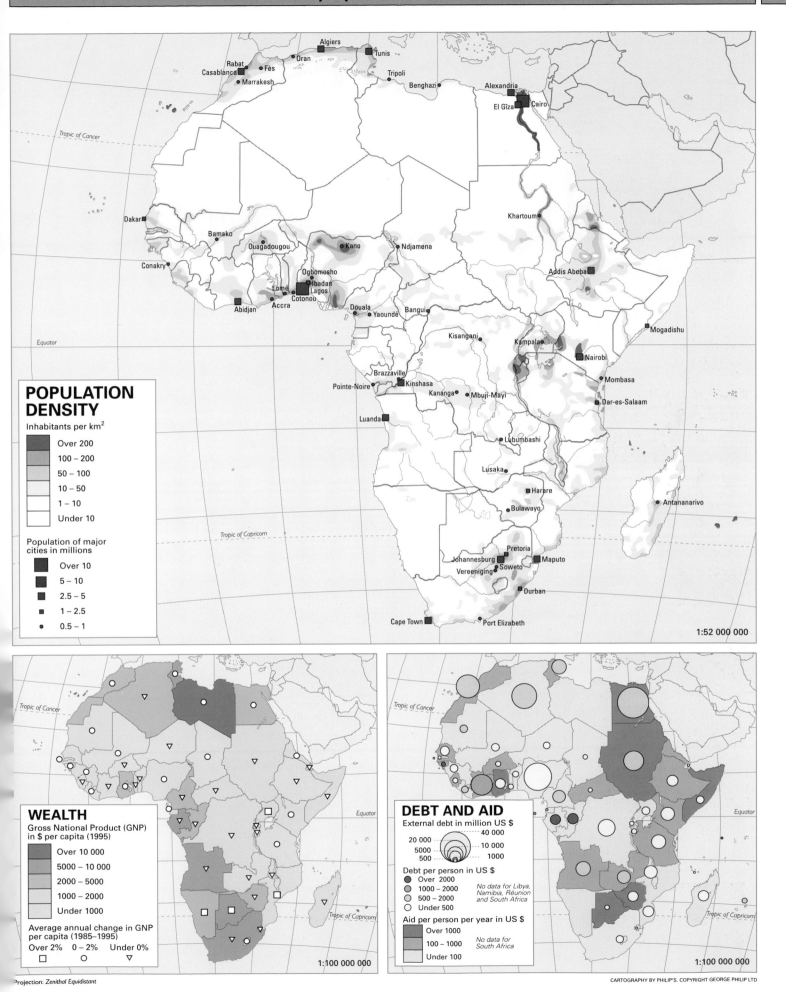

POPULATION DENSITY

Inhabitants per km²

- Over 200
- 100 – 200
- 50 – 100
- 10 – 50
- 1 – 10
- Under 10

Population of major cities in millions

- Over 10
- 5 – 10
- 2.5 – 5
- 1 – 2.5
- 0.5 – 1

1:52 000 000

Cities labelled (top map): Algiers, Tunis, Rabat, Oran, Fès, Casablanca, Marrakesh, Tripoli, Benghazi, Alexandria, El Gîza, Cairo, Dakar, Bamako, Ouagadougou, Kano, Ndjamena, Khartoum, Conakry, Ogbomosho, Ibadan, Lagos, Addis Abeba, Lomé, Cotonou, Abidjan, Accra, Douala, Yaoundé, Banguí, Mogadishu, Kisangani, Kampala, Nairobi, Brazzaville, Kinshasa, Pointe-Noire, Kananga, Mbuji-Mayi, Mombasa, Dar-es-Salaam, Luanda, Lubumbashi, Lusaka, Harare, Bulawayo, Antananarivo, Pretoria, Maputo, Johannesburg, Soweto, Vereeniging, Durban, Cape Town, Port Elizabeth

WEALTH
Gross National Product (GNP) in $ per capita (1995)

- Over 10 000
- 5000 – 10 000
- 2000 – 5000
- 1000 – 2000
- Under 1000

Average annual change in GNP per capita (1985–1995)

- Over 2% □
- 0 – 2% ○
- Under 0% ▽

1:100 000 000

DEBT AND AID
External debt in million US $

- 40 000
- 20 000
- 10 000
- 5000
- 5000
- 1000
- 500

Debt per person in US $

- Over 2000
- 1000 – 2000
- 500 – 2000
- Under 500

No data for Libya, Namibia, Réunion and South Africa

Aid per person per year in US $

- Over 1000
- 100 – 1000
- Under 100

No data for South Africa

1:100 000 000

Projection: *Zenithal Equidistant*

CARTOGRAPHY BY PHILIP'S. COPYRIGHT GEORGE PHILIP LTD

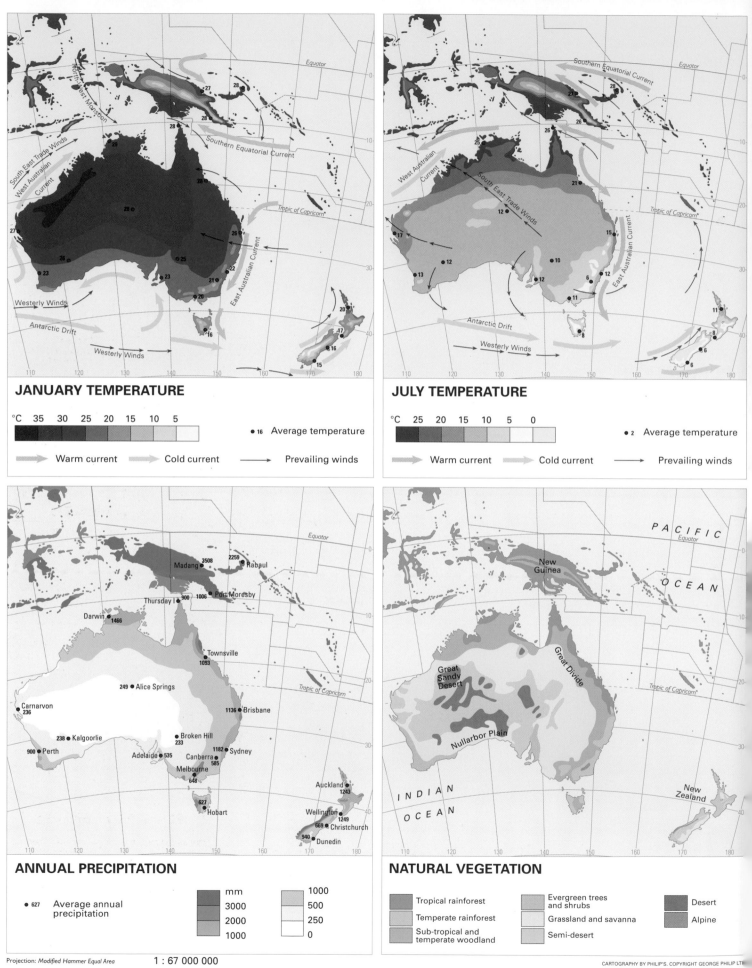

JANUARY TEMPERATURE

°C   35   30   25   20   15   10   5

• 16   Average temperature

Warm current   Cold current   Prevailing winds

JULY TEMPERATURE

°C   25   20   15   10   5   0

• 2   Average temperature

Warm current   Cold current   Prevailing winds

ANNUAL PRECIPITATION

• 627   Average annual precipitation

mm	
3000	1000
2000	500
1000	250
	0

NATURAL VEGETATION

- Tropical rainforest
- Temperate rainforest
- Sub-tropical and temperate woodland
- Evergreen trees and shrubs
- Grassland and savanna
- Semi-desert
- Desert
- Alpine

Projection: *Modified Hammer Equal Area*   1 : 67 000 000

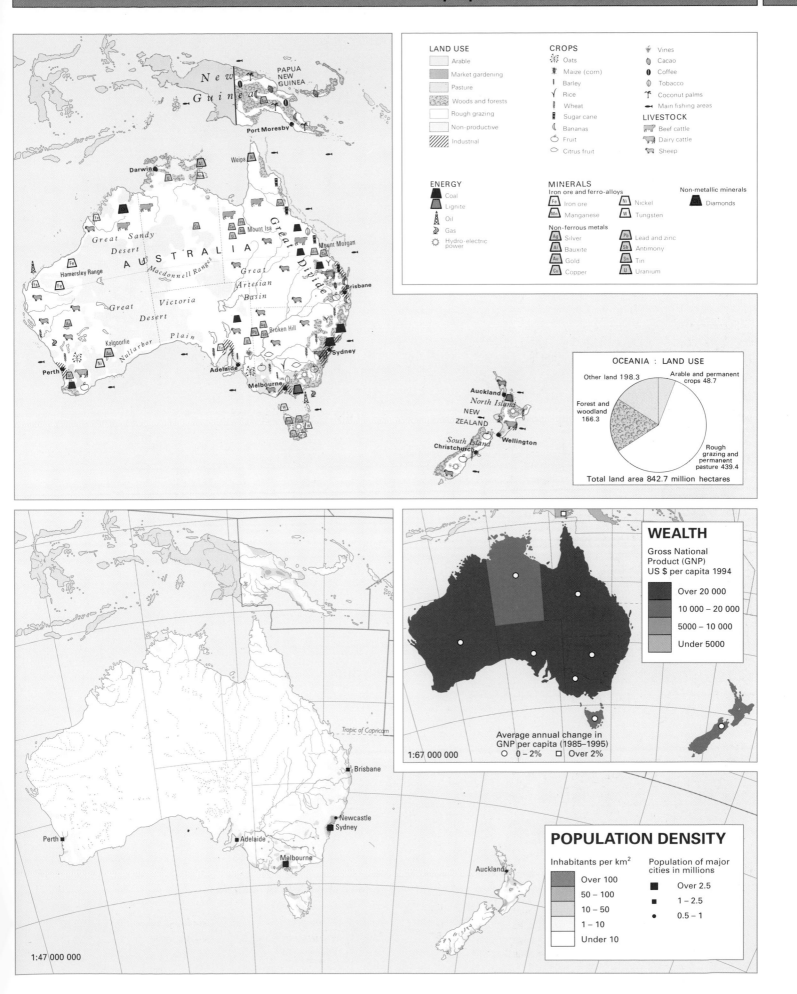

LAND USE
- Arable
- Market gardening
- Pasture
- Woods and forests
- Rough grazing
- Non-productive
- Industrial

CROPS
- Oats
- Maize (corn)
- Barley
- Rice
- Wheat
- Sugar cane
- Bananas
- Fruit
- Citrus fruit
- Vines
- Cacao
- Coffee
- Tobacco
- Coconut palms
- Main fishing areas

LIVESTOCK
- Beef cattle
- Dairy cattle
- Sheep

ENERGY
- Coal
- Lignite
- Oil
- Gas
- Hydro-electric power

MINERALS
Iron ore and ferro-alloys
- Fe Iron ore
- Mn Manganese
- Ni Nickel
- W Tungsten

Non-ferrous metals
- Ag Silver
- Al Bauxite
- Au Gold
- Cu Copper
- Pb Lead and zinc
- Sb Antimony
- Sn Tin
- U Uranium

Non-metallic minerals
- Diamonds

OCEANIA : LAND USE
- Other land 198.3
- Arable and permanent crops 48.7
- Forest and woodland 166.3
- Rough grazing and permanent pasture 439.4

Total land area 842.7 million hectares

WEALTH
Gross National Product (GNP) US $ per capita 1994
- Over 20 000
- 10 000 – 20 000
- 5000 – 10 000
- Under 5000

Average annual change in GNP per capita (1985–1995)
- ○ 0 – 2%
- □ Over 2%

1:67 000 000

POPULATION DENSITY
Inhabitants per km²
- Over 100
- 50 – 100
- 10 – 50
- 1 – 10
- Under 10

Population of major cities in millions
- ■ Over 2.5
- ■ 1 – 2.5
- ● 0.5 – 1

1:47 000 000

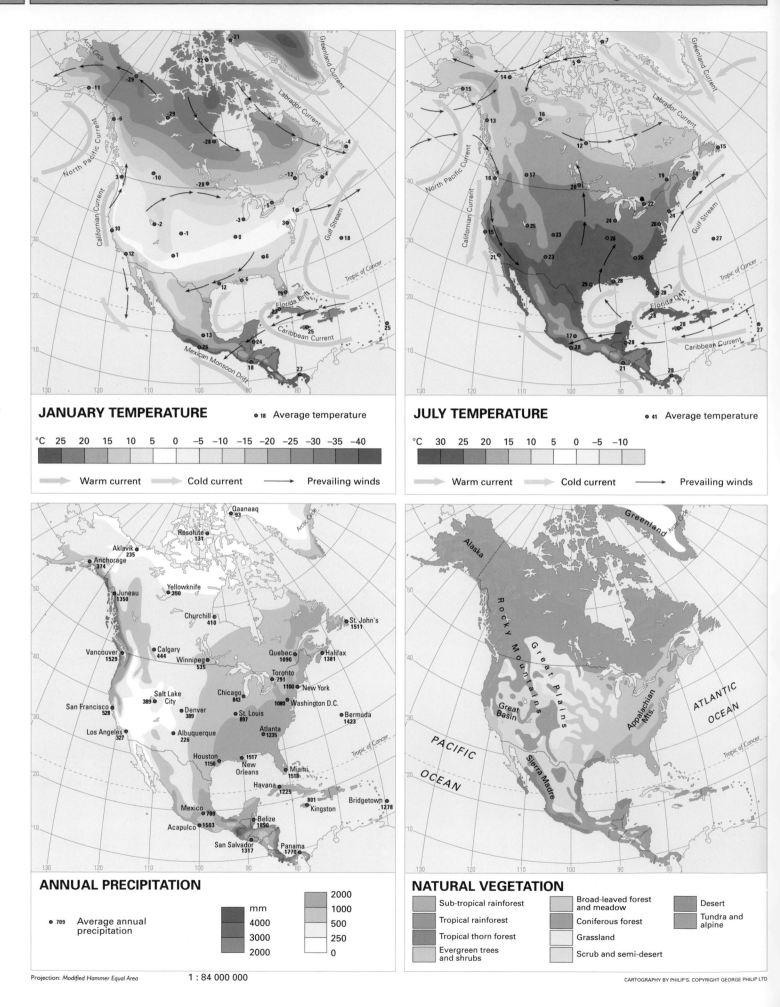

JANUARY TEMPERATURE   • 18   Average temperature

°C 25 20 15 10 5 0 −5 −10 −15 −20 −25 −30 −35 −40

Warm current   Cold current   → Prevailing winds

JULY TEMPERATURE   • 41   Average temperature

°C 30 25 20 15 10 5 0 −5 −10

Warm current   Cold current   → Prevailing winds

ANNUAL PRECIPITATION

• 709   Average annual precipitation

mm
2000
1000
500
250
0

4000
3000
2000

NATURAL VEGETATION

Sub-tropical rainforest
Tropical rainforest
Tropical thorn forest
Evergreen trees and shrubs
Broad-leaved forest and meadow
Coniferous forest
Grassland
Scrub and semi-desert
Desert
Tundra and alpine

Projection: *Modified Hammer Equal Area*   1 : 84 000 000

CARTOGRAPHY BY PHILIP'S. COPYRIGHT GEORGE PHILIP LTD

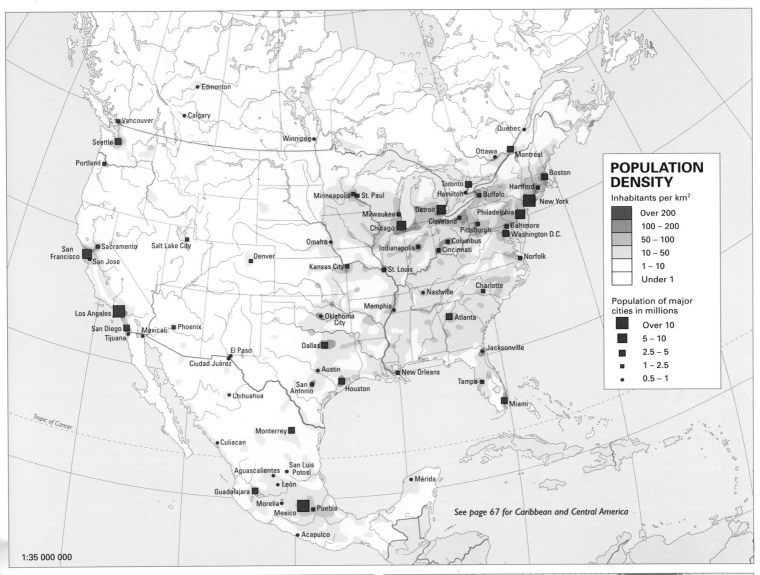

POPULATION DENSITY

Inhabitants per km²

- Over 200
- 100 – 200
- 50 – 100
- 10 – 50
- 1 – 10
- Under 1

Population of major cities in millions

- Over 10
- 5 – 10
- 2.5 – 5
- 1 – 2.5
- 0.5 – 1

See page 67 for Caribbean and Central America

1:35 000 000

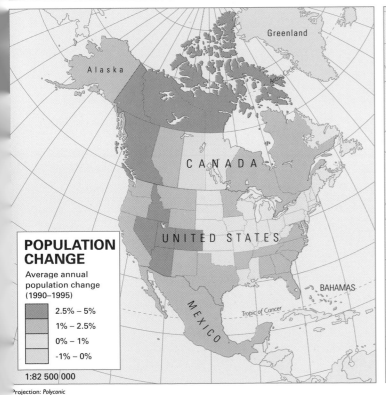

POPULATION CHANGE

Average annual population change (1990–1995)

- 2.5% – 5%
- 1% – 2.5%
- 0% – 1%
- -1% – 0%

1:82 500 000

Projection: *Polyconic*

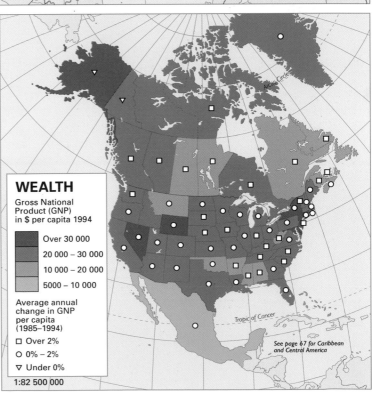

WEALTH

Gross National Product (GNP) in $ per capita 1994

- Over 30 000
- 20 000 – 30 000
- 10 000 – 20 000
- 5000 – 10 000

Average annual change in GNP per capita (1985–1994)

- □ Over 2%
- ○ 0% – 2%
- ▽ Under 0%

See page 67 for Caribbean and Central America

1:82 500 000

CARTOGRAPHY BY PHILIP'S. COPYRIGHT GEORGE PHILIP LTD

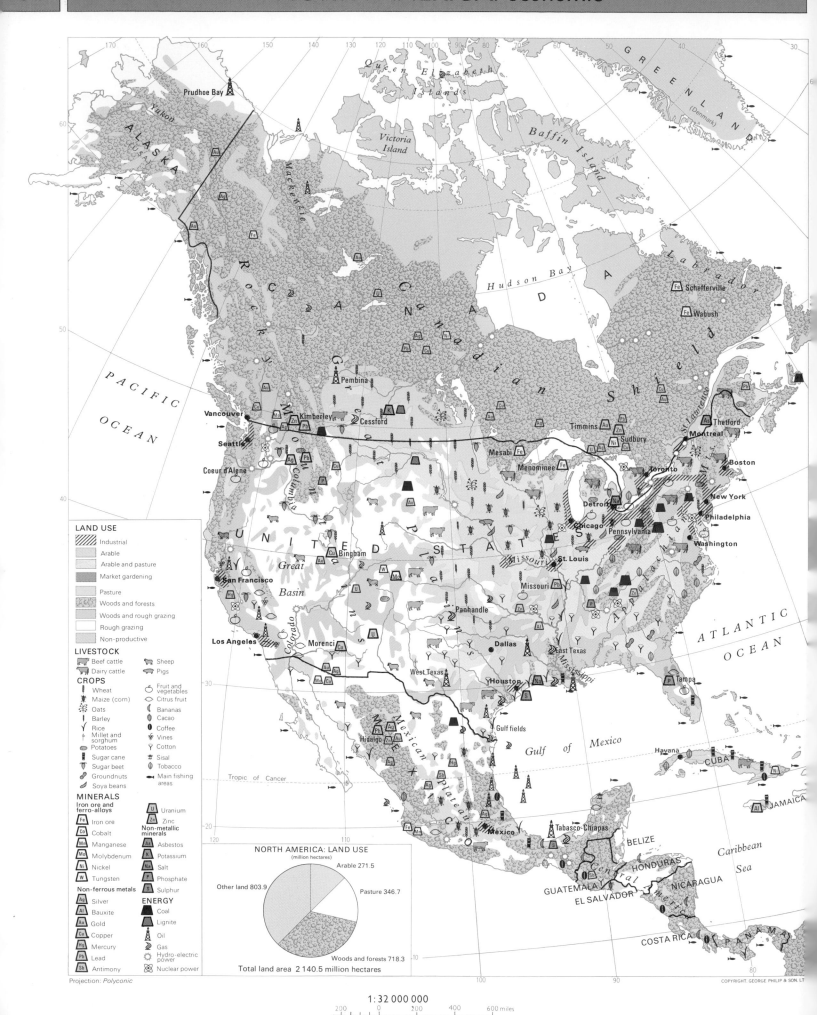

LAND USE

- Industrial
- Arable
- Arable and pasture
- Market gardening
- Pasture
- Woods and forests
- Woods and rough grazing
- Rough grazing
- Non-productive

LIVESTOCK

- Beef cattle
- Dairy cattle
- Sheep
- Pigs

CROPS

- Wheat
- Maize (corn)
- Oats
- Barley
- Rice
- Millet and sorghum
- Potatoes
- Sugar cane
- Sugar beet
- Groundnuts
- Soya beans
- Fruit and vegetables
- Citrus fruit
- Bananas
- Cacao
- Coffee
- Vines
- Cotton
- Sisal
- Tobacco
- Main fishing areas

MINERALS

Iron ore and ferro-alloys

- Fe Iron ore
- Co Cobalt
- Mn Manganese
- Mo Molybdenum
- Ni Nickel
- W Tungsten

- U Uranium
- Zn Zinc

Non-metallic minerals

- As Asbestos
- K Potassium
- Na Salt
- P Phosphate
- S Sulphur

Non-ferrous metals

- Ag Silver
- Al Bauxite
- Au Gold
- Cu Copper
- Hg Mercury
- Pb Lead
- Sb Antimony

ENERGY

- Coal
- Lignite
- Oil
- Gas
- Hydro-electric power
- Nuclear power

NORTH AMERICA: LAND USE
(million hectares)

- Arable 271.5
- Other land 803.9
- Pasture 346.7
- Woods and forests 718.3

Total land area 2 140.5 million hectares

Projection: *Polyconic*

COPYRIGHT. GEORGE PHILIP & SON. LT

1:32 000 000

200   0   200   400   600 miles
400   0   400   800 km

SOUTH AMERICA: LAND USE
(million hectares)

Arable 104.1

Other land 283.5

Pasture 441.8

Woods and
forests 924.3

Total land area 1 753.7 million hectares

LAND USE

Industrial

Arable

Market gardening
and plantations

Pasture

Woods and forests

Rough grazing

Non-productive

LIVESTOCK

Beef cattle   Sheep

Dairy cattle   Pigs

CROPS

Wheat   Coconut
                     palms
Maize (corn)   Cacao
Rice   Coffee
Millet and   Tea
sorghum
Potatoes   Vines
Sugar cane   Cotton
Groundnuts   Rubber
Fruit   and   Tobacco
vegetables
Citrus fruit   Main fishing
                     areas
Bananas

MINERALS   Non-ferrous
Iron ore and   metals
ferro-alloys
Fe Iron ore   Ag Silver
Cr Chrome   Al Bauxite
Mn Manganese   Au Gold
Mo Molybdenum   Cu Copper
W Tungsten   Pb Lead
Non-metallic minerals   Sb Antimony
N Saltpetre   Sn Tin
ENERGY   Zn Zinc
Coal   Nuclear power
Oil   Gas
                     Hydro-electric
                     power

Projection: Lambert's Equivalent Azimuthal

COPYRIGHT GEORGE PHILIP & SON LTD

1:30 000 000

200   0   200   400   600 miles

200   0   200   400   600   800 km

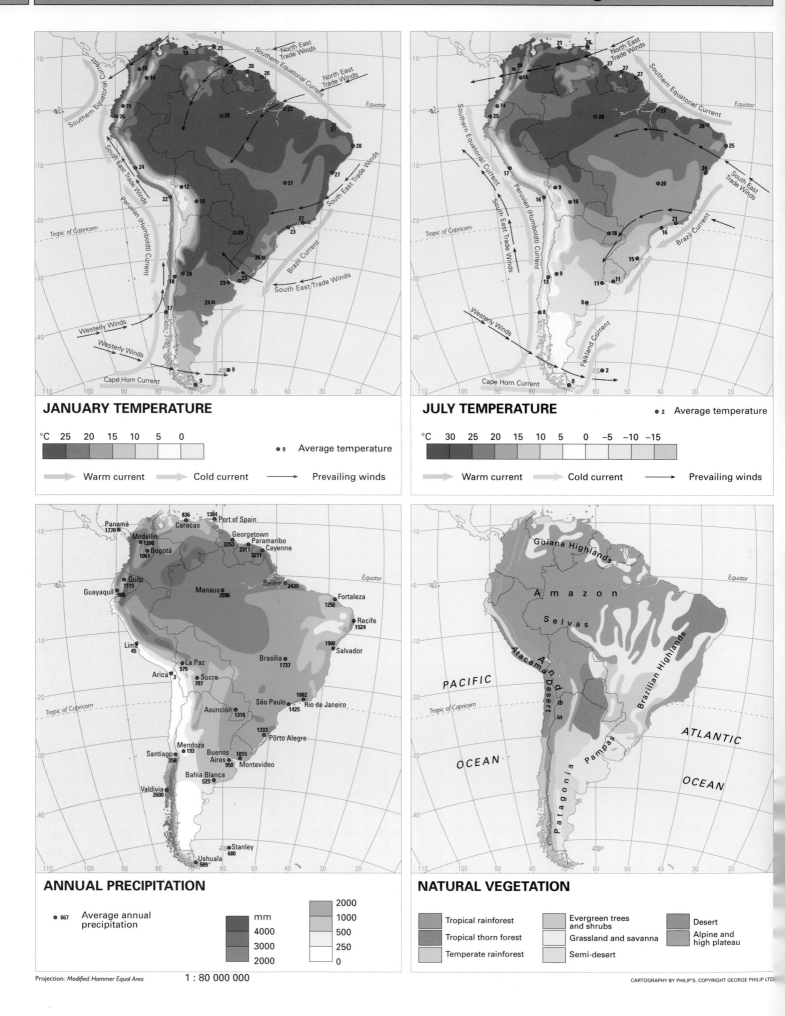

JANUARY TEMPERATURE

°C 25 20 15 10 5 0

● 9 Average temperature

Warm current   Cold current   Prevailing winds

JULY TEMPERATURE

● 2 Average temperature

°C 30 25 20 15 10 5 0 −5 −10 −15

Warm current   Cold current   Prevailing winds

ANNUAL PRECIPITATION

● 667 Average annual precipitation

mm	
4000	2000
3000	1000
2000	500
	250
	0

NATURAL VEGETATION

Tropical rainforest	Evergreen trees and shrubs	Desert
Tropical thorn forest	Grassland and savanna	Alpine and high plateau
Temperate rainforest	Semi-desert	

Projection: *Modified Hammer Equal Area*   1 : 80 000 000

CARTOGRAPHY BY PHILIP'S. COPYRIGHT GEORGE PHILIP LTD

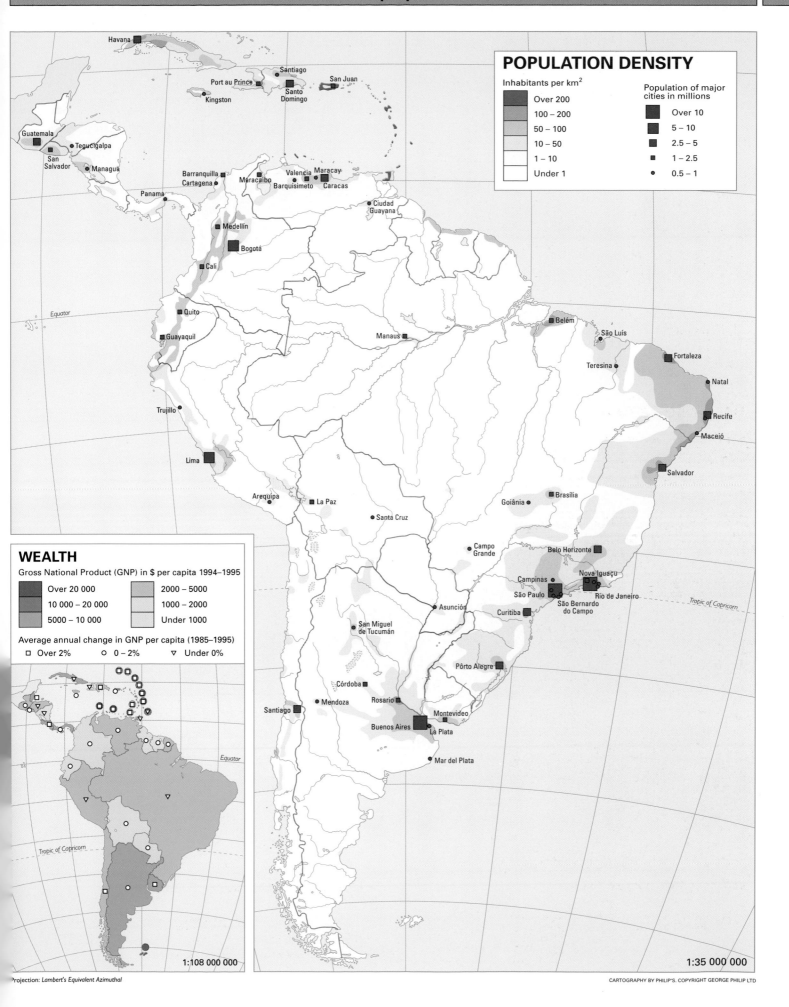

POPULATION DENSITY

Inhabitants per km²

- Over 200
- 100 – 200
- 50 – 100
- 10 – 50
- 1 – 10
- Under 1

Population of major cities in millions

- Over 10
- 5 – 10
- 2.5 – 5
- 1 – 2.5
- 0.5 – 1

WEALTH

Gross National Product (GNP) in $ per capita 1994–1995

- Over 20 000
- 10 000 – 20 000
- 5000 – 10 000
- 2000 – 5000
- 1000 – 2000
- Under 1000

Average annual change in GNP per capita (1985–1995)

- ☐ Over 2%
- ○ 0 – 2%
- ▽ Under 0%

Equator

Tropic of Capricorn

1:108 000 000

1:35 000 000

Projection: Lambert's Equivalent Azimuthal

CARTOGRAPHY BY PHILIP'S. COPYRIGHT GEORGE PHILIP LTD

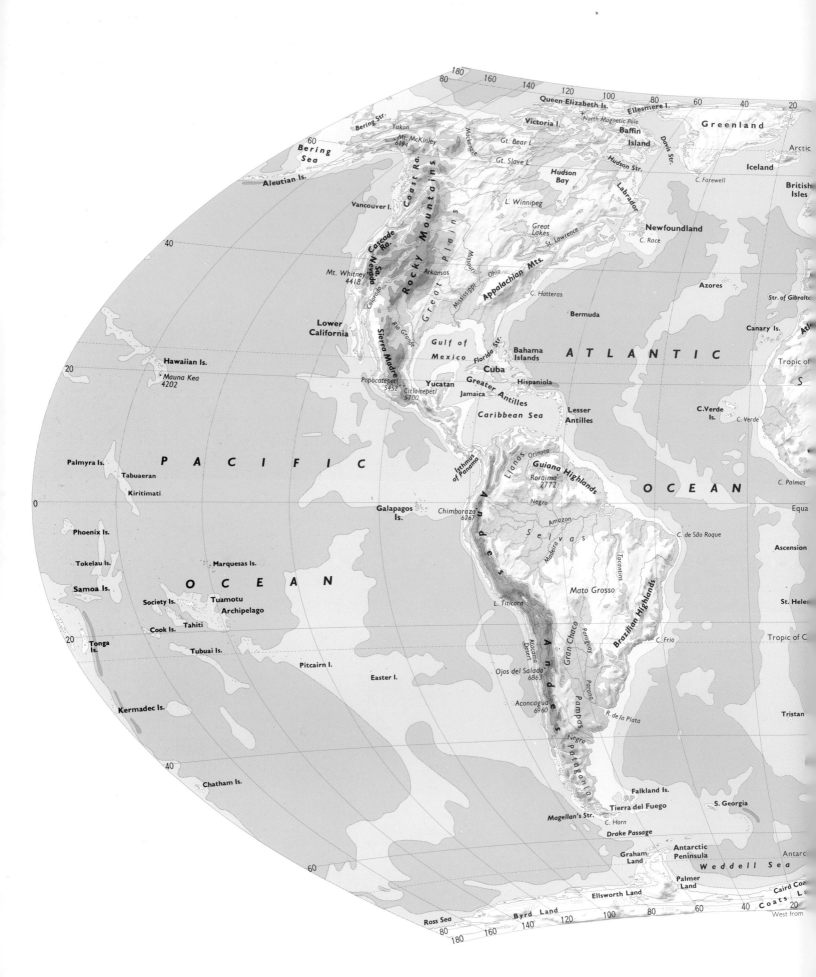

Projection: Hammer Equal Area

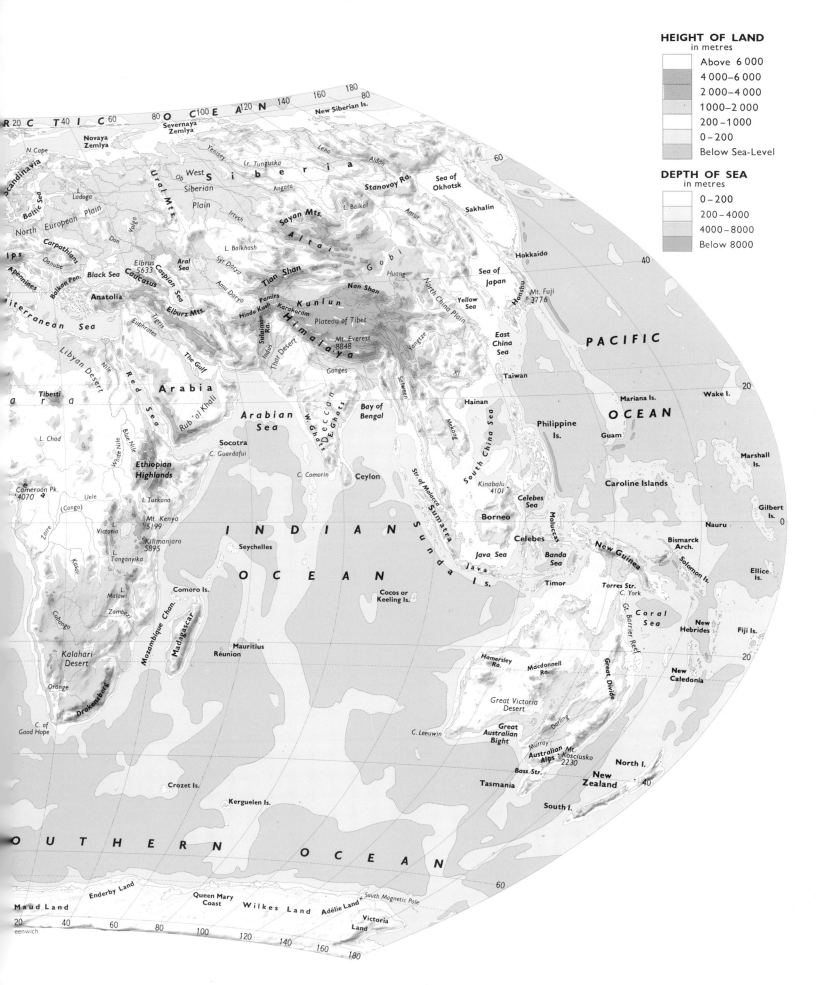

HEIGHT OF LAND
in metres

Above 6 000
4 000–6 000
2 000–4 000
1000–2 000
200–1000
0–200
Below Sea-Level

DEPTH OF SEA
in metres

0–200
200–4000
4000–8000
Below 8000

ARCTIC OCEAN

N. Cape
Scandinavia
Novaya Zemlya
Severnaya Zemlya
New Siberian Is.
Baltic Sea
L. Ladoga
North European Plain
West Siberian Plain
Siberia
Lr. Tunguska
Lena
Aldan
Alps
Carpathians
Danube
Ural Mts.
Ob
Yenisey
Irtysh
Angara
Stanovoy Ra.
Sea of Okhotsk
Apennines
Balkan Pen.
Black Sea
Caucasus
Elbrus 5633
Caspian Sea
Aral Sea
Volga
Don
L. Balkhash
Soyan Mts.
L. Baikal
Amur
Sakhalin
Hokkaido
Mediterranean Sea
Anatolia
Elburz Mts.
Syr Darya
Amu Darya
Tian Shan
Altai
Gobi
Huang
North China Plain
Sea of Japan
Honshu
Mt. Fuji 3776
Sahara
Libyan Desert
Tibesti
Nile
Red Sea
Tigris
Euphrates
The Gulf
Hindu Kush
Sulaiman Ra.
Pamirs
Karakoram
Kunlun
Nan Shan
Yellow Sea
East China Sea
PACIFIC
Arabia
Rub 'al Khali
Indus
Thar Desert
Himalaya
Mt. Everest 8848
Plateau of Tibet
Ganges
Yangtze
Xi
Taiwan
Wake I.
L. Chad
Blue Nile
White Nile
Socotra
C. Guardafui
Arabian Sea
W. Ghats
Deccan
E. Ghats
Bay of Bengal
Salween
Mekong
Hainan
Philippine Is.
Mariana Is.
OCEAN
Guam
Cameroon Pk. 4070
Uele
(Congo)
Ethiopian Highlands
L. Turkana
C. Comorin
Ceylon
South China Sea
Kinabalu 4101
Caroline Islands
Marshall Is.
Zaire
L. Victoria
Mt. Kenya 5199
Kilimanjaro 5895
INDIAN
Seychelles
Borneo
Celebes Sea
Moluccas
Celebes
Nauru
Gilbert Is.
Kasai
L. Tanganyika
Sumatra
Java Sea
Banda Sea
New Guinea
Bismarck Arch.
Solomon Is.
Ellice Is.
Cubango
Comoro Is.
Mozambique Chan.
OCEAN
Java
Sunda Is.
Timor
New Hebrides
Fiji Is.
L. Malawi
Zambezi
Madagascar
Cocos or Keeling Is.
Torres Str.
C. York
Gt. Barrier Reef
Coral Sea
Kalahari Desert
Mauritius
Réunion
Hamersley Ra.
Macdonnell Ra.
Great Divide
New Caledonia
Orange
Drakensberg
Great Victoria Desert
C. of Good Hope
C. Leeuwin
Great Australian Bight
Murray
Darling
Australian Alps
Mt. Kosciusko 2230
North I.
Crozet Is.
Bass Str.
Tasmania
New Zealand
Kerguelen Is.
South I.
SOUTHERN OCEAN
Maud Land
Enderby Land
Queen Mary Coast
Wilkes Land
Adélie Land
South Magnetic Pole
Victoria Land
Greenwich

1:80 000 000

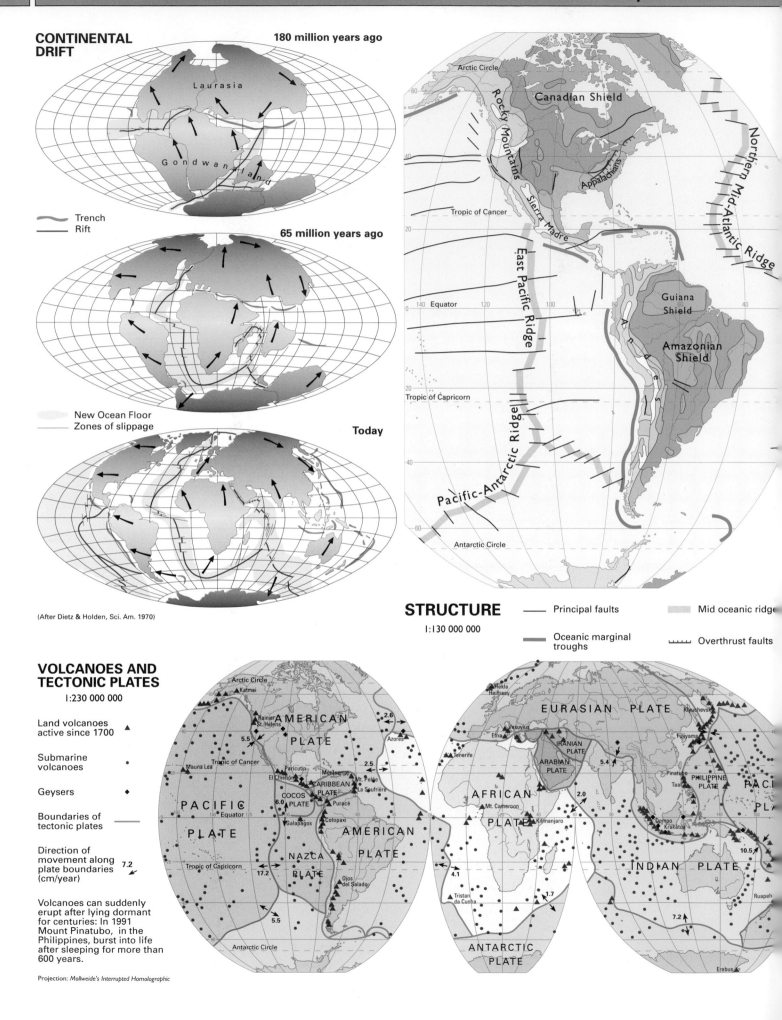

CONTINENTAL DRIFT

180 million years ago

Laurasia

Gondwanaland

〜〜 Trench
── Rift

65 million years ago

New Ocean Floor
Zones of slippage

Today

(After Dietz & Holden, Sci. Am. 1970)

Arctic Circle

Canadian Shield

Rocky Mountains

Appalachians

Tropic of Cancer

Sierra Madre

East Pacific Ridge

Northern Mid-Atlantic Ridge

140 Equator 120 100 40

Guiana Shield

Andes

Amazonian Shield

Tropic of Capricorn

Pacific-Antarctic Ridge

Antarctic Circle

STRUCTURE

1:130 000 000

── Principal faults

━━ Oceanic marginal troughs

▨ Mid oceanic ridge

⊥⊥⊥ Overthrust faults

VOLCANOES AND TECTONIC PLATES

1:230 000 000

▲ Land volcanoes active since 1700

· Submarine volcanoes

✦ Geysers

── Boundaries of tectonic plates

Direction of movement along plate boundaries (cm/year) 7.2

Volcanoes can suddenly erupt after lying dormant for centuries: In 1991 Mount Pinatubo, in the Philippines, burst into life after sleeping for more than 600 years.

Projection: Mollweide's Interrupted Homolographic

Arctic Circle

Katmai

AMERICAN PLATE

Rainier
St. Helens

2.6

5.5

Azores

Tropic of Cancer

Mauna Loa

Paricutín

El Chichón

2.5

PACIFIC

CARIBBEAN PLATE

Montserrat

Mt. Pelée

La Soufrière

COCOS PLATE 6.0

Puracé

Equator 120

Galapagos

Cotopaxi

AMERICAN PLATE

PLATE

NAZCA PLATE

Tropic of Capricorn

7.2

17.2

Ojos del Salado

5.5

Antarctic Circle

Hekla
Heimaey

EURASIAN PLATE

Klyuchevsk

Vesuvius

Etna

Fujiyama

IRANIAN PLATE

ARABIAN PLATE

5.4

Tenerife

Pinatubo

PHILIPPINE PLATE

Taal

PACI PLA

AFRICAN PLATE

2.0

Mt. Cameroon

Kilimanjaro

Dempo

Krakatoa

10.5

4.1

INDIAN PLATE

Tristan da Cunha

1.7

Ruapeh

7.2

ANTARCTIC PLATE

Erebus

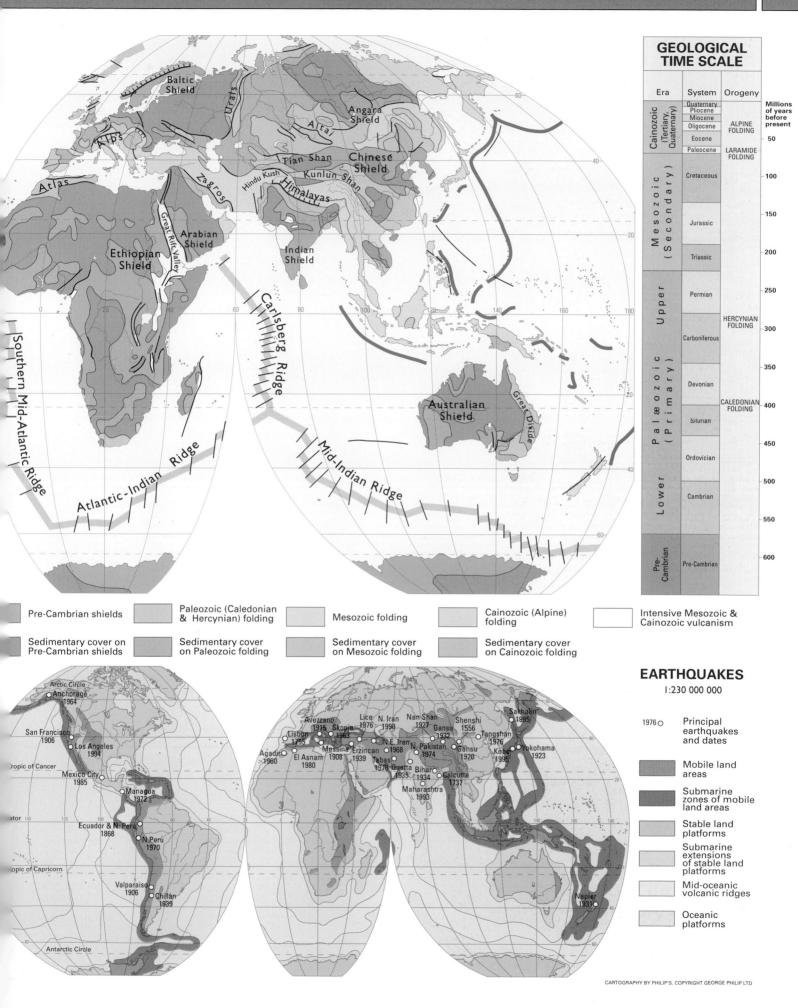

GEOLOGICAL TIME SCALE

Era	System	Orogeny	Millions of years before present
Cainozoic (Tertiary, Quaternary)	Quaternary / Pliocene / Miocene / Oligocene / Eocene	ALPINE FOLDING	50
	Paleocene	LARAMIDE FOLDING	
Mesozoic (Secondary)	Cretaceous		100
	Jurassic		150
	Triassic		200
Upper Palaeozoic (Primary)	Permian		250
	Carboniferous	HERCYNIAN FOLDING	300
	Devonian		350
Lower Palaeozoic (Primary)	Silurian	CALEDONIAN FOLDING	400
	Ordovician		450
	Cambrian		500 / 550
Pre-Cambrian	Pre-Cambrian		600

Pre-Cambrian shields
Paleozoic (Caledonian & Hercynian) folding
Mesozoic folding
Cainozoic (Alpine) folding
Intensive Mesozoic & Cainozoic vulcanism
Sedimentary cover on Pre-Cambrian shields
Sedimentary cover on Paleozoic folding
Sedimentary cover on Mesozoic folding
Sedimentary cover on Cainozoic folding

EARTHQUAKES
1:230 000 000

1976 ○ Principal earthquakes and dates

Mobile land areas
Submarine zones of mobile land areas
Stable land platforms
Submarine extensions of stable land platforms
Mid-oceanic volcanic ridges
Oceanic platforms

CARTOGRAPHY BY PHILIP'S. COPYRIGHT GEORGE PHILIP LTD

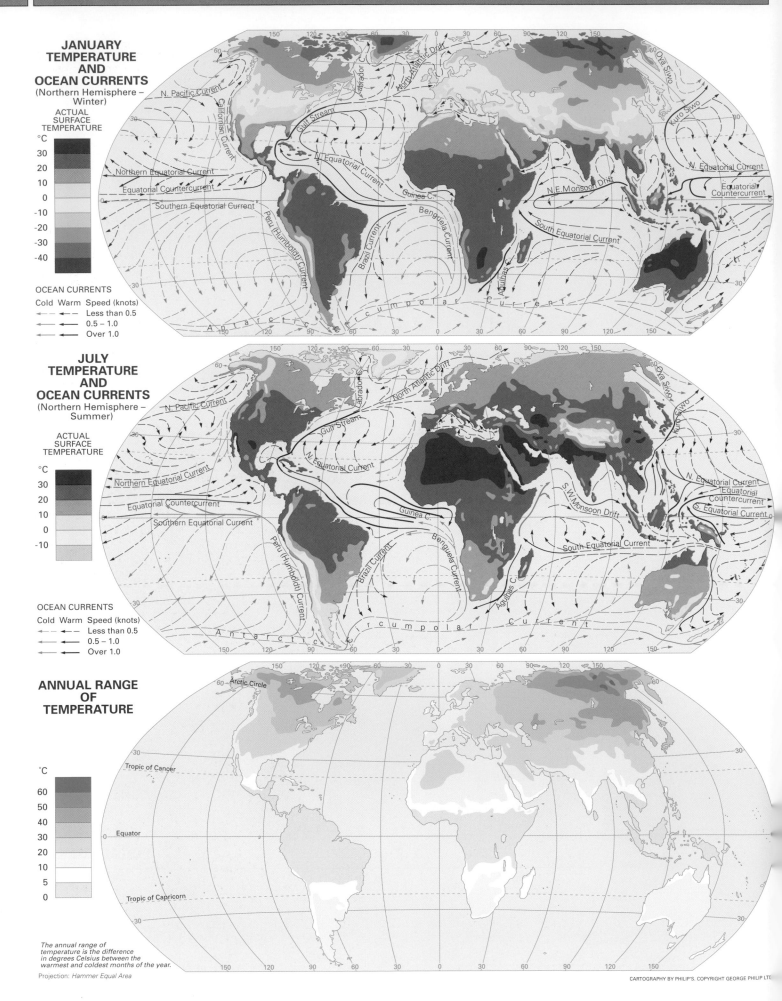

JANUARY TEMPERATURE AND OCEAN CURRENTS
(Northern Hemisphere – Winter)

ACTUAL SURFACE TEMPERATURE

°C
30
20
10
0
-10
-20
-30
-40

OCEAN CURRENTS

Cold	Warm	Speed (knots)
		Less than 0.5
		0.5 – 1.0
		Over 1.0

JULY TEMPERATURE AND OCEAN CURRENTS
(Northern Hemisphere – Summer)

ACTUAL SURFACE TEMPERATURE

°C
30
20
10
0
-10

OCEAN CURRENTS

Cold	Warm	Speed (knots)
		Less than 0.5
		0.5 – 1.0
		Over 1.0

ANNUAL RANGE OF TEMPERATURE

°C
60
50
40
30
20
10
5
0

The annual range of temperature is the difference in degrees Celsius between the warmest and coldest months of the year.

Projection: *Hammer Equal Area*

CARTOGRAPHY BY PHILIP'S. COPYRIGHT GEORGE PHILIP LTD

1 : 190 000 000

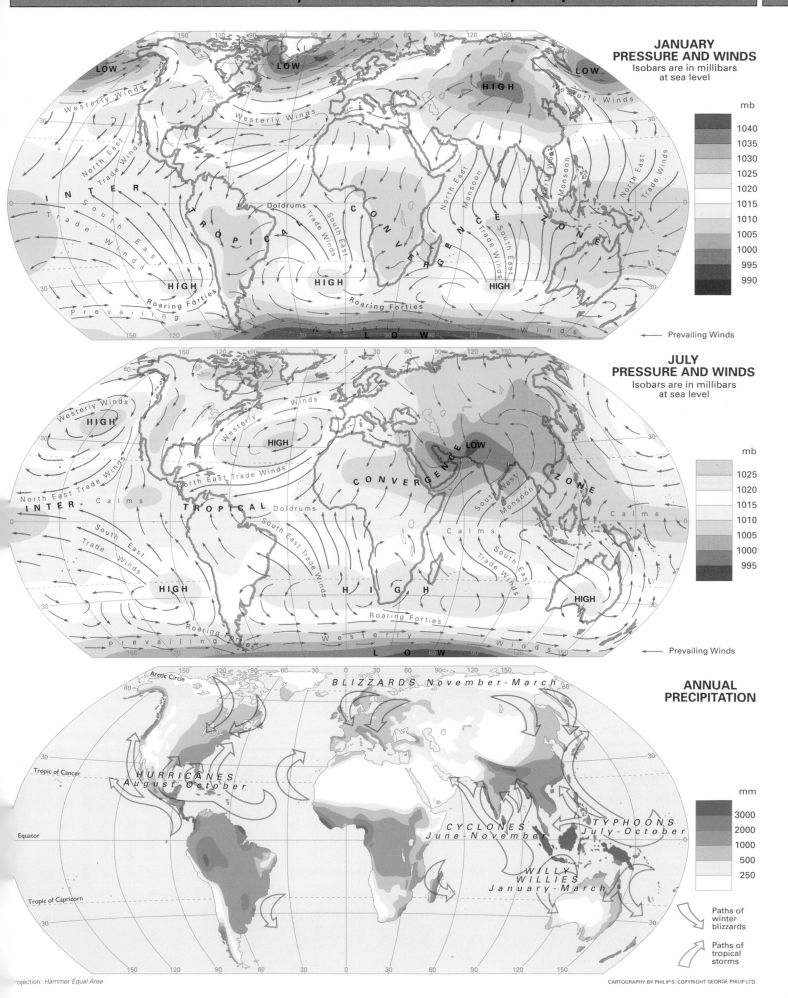

**JANUARY
PRESSURE AND WINDS**
Isobars are in millibars
at sea level

mb
1040
1035
1030
1025
1020
1015
1010
1005
1000
995
990

⟵ Prevailing Winds

**JULY
PRESSURE AND WINDS**
Isobars are in millibars
at sea level

mb
1025
1020
1015
1010
1005
1000
995

⟵ Prevailing Winds

**ANNUAL
PRECIPITATION**

mm
3000
2000
1000
500
250

Paths of
winter
blizzards

Paths of
tropical
storms

Projection: *Hammer Equal Area*

CARTOGRAPHY BY PHILIP'S. COPYRIGHT GEORGE PHILIP LTD

1 : 190 000 000

CLIMATIC REGIONS   after Köppen

Köppen's classification recognises five major climatic regions corresponding broadly to the five principal vegetation types and these are designated by the letters A, B, C, D and E. Each one of these are subdivided on the basis of temperature and rainfall. This map shows a climate graph for a selected place within each of the 12 sub-regions.

TROPICAL RAINY CLIMATES A

Af	Rain Forest Climate	All mean monthly temperatures above 18°C and an annual variation in temperature of less than 6°C.
Am	Monsoon Climate	
Aw	Savanna Climate	All monthly temperatures above 18°C but with an annual variation in temperature of less than 12°C.

DRY CLIMATES B

BS	Steppe Climate	The principal difference between this grouping and groups A, C, D and E is the combination of a wide range of temperatures with low rainfall.
BW	Desert Climate	

WARM TEMPERATE RAINY CLIMATES C

The climatic group is separated from group A by having the mean temperature of the coolest month below 18°C but above -3°C. The mean temperature of the warmest month is over 10°C.

Cw	Dry Winter Climate	The wettest month of summer has at least ten times as much rain as the driest winter month
Cs	Dry Summer Climate (Mediterranean)	The wettest month of winter has at least three times as much rain as the driest month of summer. The driest summer month itself has less than 30mm rainfall.
Cf	Climate with no Dry Season	Even rainfall throughout the year.

COLD TEMPERATE RAINY CLIMATES D

Dw	Dry Winter Climate	The mean temperature of the coldest month is below -3°C but the mean temperature of the warmest month is still over 10°C.
Df	Climate with no Dry Season	

POLAR CLIMATES E

ET	Tundra Climate	The mean temperature of the warmest month is below 10°C giving permanently frozen subsoil.
EF	Polar Climate	The mean temperature of the warmest month is below 0°C giving permanently ice and snow.

The classification is in some cases subdivided by the addition of the following letters after the major types :-

Used with groups C and D	**a**	Hot summer – mean temperature of the hottest month above 22°C and with more than four months of over 10°C.
	b	Warm summer – mean temperature of the hottest month below 22°C but still with more than four months of over 10°C.
	c	Cool short summer – mean temperature of the hottest month below 22°C but with less than four months of over 10°C.
Used with group D	**d**	Cool short summer and cold winter – mean temperature of the hottest month below 22°C and of the coolest month below -38°C.
Used with group B	**h**	Hot dry climate – mean annual temperature above 18°C.
	k	Cool dry climate – mean annual temperature below 18°C.
Used with group E	**H**	Polar climate due to elevation being over 1500m.

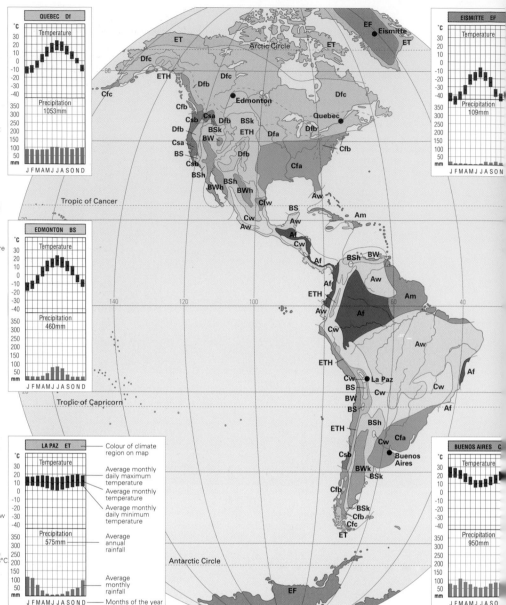

SOIL REGIONS

1:220 000 000

after Glinka, Stremme, Marbut, and others

	Tundra soil
	Podzols
	Brown forest soil
	Lightly leached dry forest soil
	Red and yellow sub-tropical forest soil
	Reddish savanna soil and tropical red earths
	Laterites
	Chernozem
	Degraded chernozem
	Black savanna soil
	Chestnut steppe soil
	Grey and brown desert steppe soils
	Alluvium
	Mountain and high plateau soils
	Oases soil
	Tropical and mangrove swamp

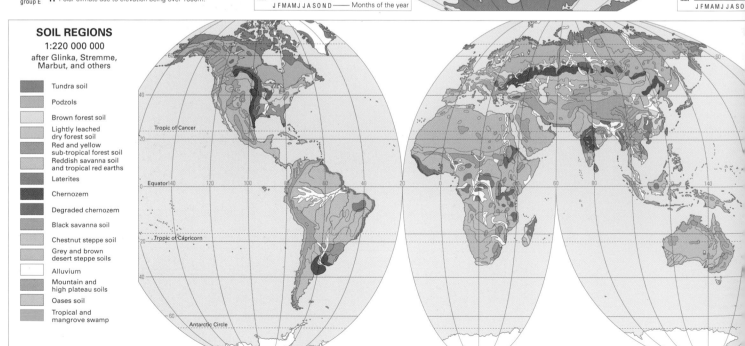

Projection: *Interrupted Mollweide's Homolographic*

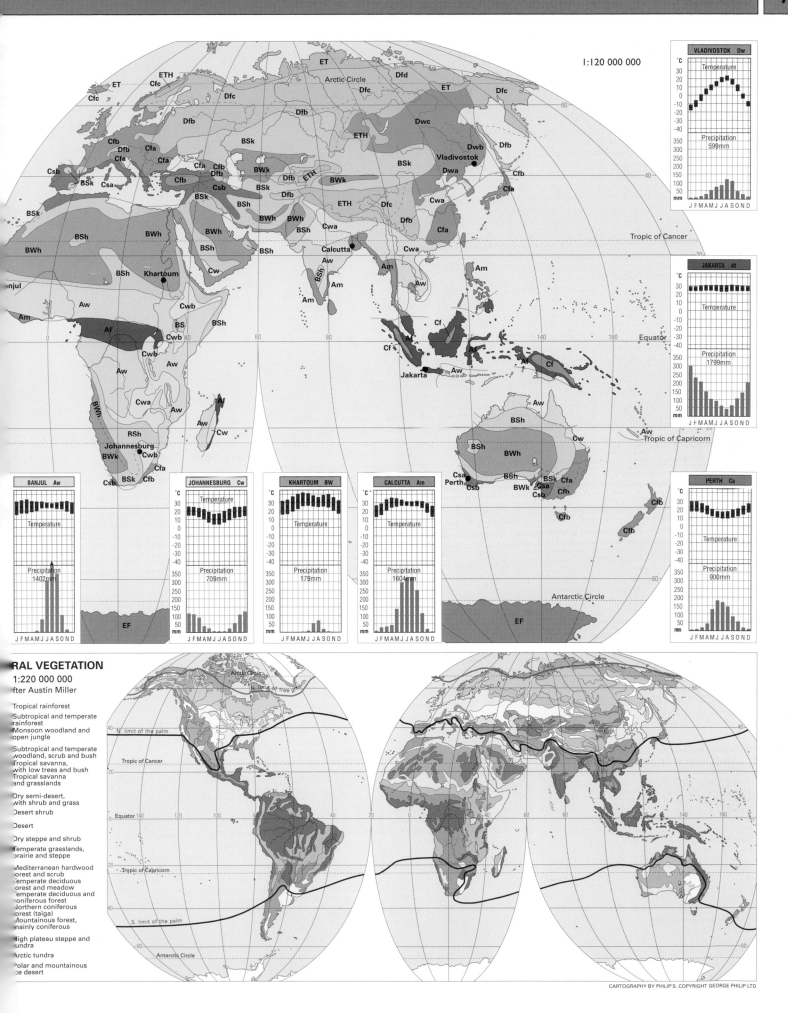

	Jan	Feb
Addis Ababa Ethiopia 2410m		
Temperature Daily Max.°C	23	24
Daily Min.°C	6	7
Average Monthly °C	14	15
Rainfall Monthly Total mm	13	35
Sunshine Hours per Day	8.7	8.2

- Height of meteorological station above sea level in metres
- Average monthly maximum temperature in degrees Celsius
- Average monthly minimum temperature in degrees Celsius
- Average monthly temperature in degrees Celsius
- Average monthly precipitation in millimetres
- Average daily duration of bright sunshine per month in hours

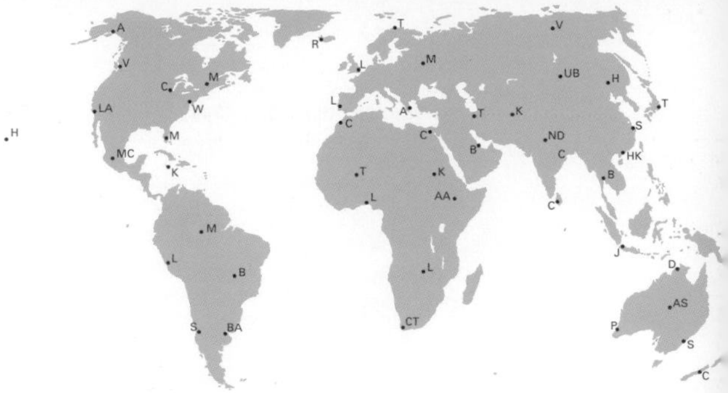

	Jan	Feb	Mar	Apr	May	June	July	Aug	Sep	Oct	Nov	Dec	Year
Addis Ababa Ethiopia 2410m													
Temperature Daily Max.°C	23	24	25	24	25	23	20	20	21	22	23	22	23
Daily Min.°C	6	7	9	10	9	10	11	11	10	7	5	5	8
Average Monthly °C	14	15	17	17	17	16	16	15	15	15	14	14	15
Rainfall Monthly Total mm	13	35	67	91	81	117	247	255	167	29	8	5	1115
Sunshine Hours per Day	8.7	8.2	7.6	8.1	6.5	4.8	2.8	3.2	5.2	7.6	6.7	7	6.4
Alice Springs Australia 580m													
Temperature Daily Max.°C	35	35	32	27	23	19	19	23	27	31	33	35	28
Daily Min.°C	21	20	17	12	8	5	4	6	10	15	18	20	13
Average Monthly °C	28	27	25	20	15	12	12	14	18	23	25	27	21
Rainfall Monthly Total mm	44	33	27	10	15	13	7	8	7	18	29	38	249
Sunshine Hours per Day	10.3	10.4	9.3	9.2	8	8	8.9	9.8	10	9.7	10.1	10	9.5
Anchorage USA 183m													
Temperature Daily Max.°C	-7	-3	0	7	13	18	19	17	13	6	-2	-6	-6
Daily Min.°C	-15	-12	-9	-2	4	8	10	9	5	-2	-9	-14	-2
Average Monthly °C	-11	-7	-4	3	9	13	15	13	9	2	-5	-10	-4
Rainfall Monthly Total mm	20	18	13	11	13	25	47	64	64	47	28	24	374
Sunshine Hours per Day	2.4	4.1	6.6	8.3	8.3	9.2	8.5	6	4.4	3.1	2.6	1.6	5.4
Athens Greece 107m													
Temperature Daily Max.°C	13	14	16	20	25	30	33	33	29	24	19	15	23
Daily Min.°C	6	7	8	11	16	20	23	23	19	15	12	8	14
Average Monthly °C	10	10	12	16	20	25	28	28	24	20	15	11	18
Rainfall Monthly Total mm	62	37	37	23	23	14	6	7	15	51	56	71	402
Sunshine Hours per Day	3.9	5.2	5.8	7.7	8.9	10.7	11.9	11.5	9.4	6.8	4.8	3.8	7.3
Bahrain City Bahrain 2m													
Temperature Daily Max.°C	20	21	25	29	33	36	37	38	36	32	27	22	30
Daily Min.°C	14	15	18	22	25	29	31	32	29	25	22	16	23
Average Monthly °C	17	18	21	25	29	32	34	35	32	29	25	19	26
Rainfall Monthly Total mm	18	12	10	9	2	0	0	0	0	0.4	3	16	70
Sunshine Hours per Day	5.9	6.9	7.9	8.8	10.6	13.2	12.1	12	12	10.3	7.7	6.4	9.5
Bangkok Thailand 10m													
Temperature Daily Max.°C	32	33	34	35	34	33	32	32	32	31	31	31	33
Daily Min.°C	20	23	24	26	25	25	25	24	24	24	23	20	24
Average Monthly °C	26	28	29	30	30	29	28	28	28	28	27	26	28
Rainfall Monthly Total mm	9	30	36	82	165	153	168	183	310	239	55	8	1438
Sunshine Hours per Day	8.2	8	8	10	7.5	6.1	4.7	5.2	5.2	6.1	7.3	7.8	7
Brasilia Brazil 910m													
Temperature Daily Max.°C	28	28	28	28	27	27	27	29	30	29	28	27	28
Daily Min.°C	18	18	18	17	15	13	13	14	16	18	18	18	16
Average Monthly °C	23	23	23	22	21	20	20	21	23	24	23	22	22
Rainfall Monthly Total mm	252	204	227	93	17	3	6	3	30	127	255	343	1560
Sunshine Av. Monthly Dur.	5.8	5.7	6	7.4	8.7	9.3	9.6	9.8	7.9	6.5	4.8	4.4	7.2
Buenos Aires Argentina 25m													
Temperature Daily Max.°C	30	29	26	22	18	14	14	16	18	21	25	28	22
Daily Min.°C	17	17	16	12	9	5	6	6	8	10	14	16	11
Average Monthly °C	23	23	21	17	13	10	10	11	13	15	19	22	16
Rainfall Monthly Total mm	79	71	109	89	76	61	56	61	79	86	84	99	950
Sunshine Hours per Day	9.2	8.5	7.5	6.8	4.9	3.5	3.8	5.2	6	6.8	8.1	8.5	6.6
Cairo Egypt 75m													
Temperature Daily Max.°C	19	21	24	28	32	35	35	35	33	30	26	21	28
Daily Min.°C	9	9	12	14	18	20	22	22	20	18	14	10	16
Average Monthly °C	14	15	18	21	25	28	29	28	26	24	20	16	22
Rainfall Monthly Total mm	4	4	3	1	2	1	0	0	1	1	3	7	27
Sunshine Hours per Day	6.9	8.4	8.7	9.7	10.5	11.9	11.7	11.3	10.4	9.4	8.3	6.4	9.5
Calcutta India 5m													
Temperature Daily Max.°C	27	29	34	36	35	34	32	32	32	32	29	26	31
Daily Min.°C	13	15	21	24	25	26	26	26	26	23	18	13	21
Average Monthly °C	20	22	27	30	30	30	29	29	29	28	23	20	26
Rainfall Monthly Total mm	10	30	34	44	140	297	325	332	253	114	20	5	1604
Sunshine Hours per Day	8.6	8.7	8.9	9	8.7	5.4	4.1	4.1	5.1	6.5	8.3	8.4	7.1
Cape Town South Africa 44m													
Temperature Daily Max.°C	26	26	25	23	20	18	17	18	19	21	24	25	22
Daily Min.°C	15	15	14	11	9	7	7	7	8	10	13	15	11
Average Monthly °C	21	20	20	17	14	13	12	12	14	16	18	20	16
Rainfall Monthly Total mm	12	19	17	42	67	98	68	76	36	45	12	13	505
Sunshine Hours per Day	11.4	10.2	9.4	7.7	6.1	5.7	6.4	6.6	7.6	8.6	10.2	10.9	8.4

	Jan	Feb	Mar	Apr	May	June	July	Aug	Sep	Oct	Nov	Dec
Casablanca Morocco 59m												
Temperature Daily Max.°C	17	18	20	21	22	24	26	26	26	24	21	18
Daily Min.°C	8	9	11	12	15	18	19	20	18	15	12	10
Average Monthly °C	13	13	15	16	18	21	23	23	22	20	17	14
Rainfall Monthly Total mm	78	61	54	37	20	3	0	1	6	28	58	94
Sunshine Hours per Day	5.2	6.3	7.3	9	9.4	9.7	10.2	9.7	9.1	7.4	5.9	5.3
Chicago USA 186m												
Temperature Daily Max.°C	0.6	1.5	6.4	14.1	20.6	26.4	28.9	28	23.8	17.4	8.4	2.1
Daily Min.°C	-7	-6	-2	5	11	16	20	19	14	8	0	-5
Average Monthly °C	-3	-2	2	9	16	21	24	23	19	13	4	-2
Rainfall Monthly Total mm	47	41	70	77	96	103	86	80	69	71	56	48
Sunshine Hours per Day	4	5	6.6	6.9	8.9	10.2	10	9.2	8.2	6.9	4.5	3.7
Christchurch New Zealand 5m												
Temperature Daily Max.°C	21	21	19	17	13	11	10	11	14	17	19	21
Daily Min.°C	12	12	10	7	4	2	1	3	5	7	8	11
Average Monthly °C	16	16	15	12	9	6	6	7	9	12	13	16
Rainfall Monthly Total mm	56	46	43	46	76	69	61	58	51	51	51	61
Sunshine Hours per Day	7	6.5	5.6	4.7	4.3	3.9	4.1	4.7	5.6	6.1	6.9	6.3
Colombo Sri Lanka 10m												
Temperature Daily Max.°C	30	31	31	31	30	30	29	29	30	29	29	30
Daily Min.°C	22	22	23	24	25	25	25	25	25	24	23	22
Average Monthly °C	26	26	27	28	28	27	27	27	27	27	26	26
Rainfall Monthly Total mm	101	66	118	230	394	220	140	102	174	348	333	142
Sunshine Hours per Day	7.9	9	8.1	7.2	6.4	5.4	6.1	6.3	6.2	6.5	6.4	7.8
Darwin Australia 30m												
Temperature Daily Max.°C	32	32	33	33	33	31	31	32	33	34	34	33
Daily Min.°C	25	25	25	24	23	21	19	21	23	25	26	26
Average Monthly °C	29	29	29	29	28	26	25	26	28	29	30	29
Rainfall Monthly Total mm	405	309	279	77	8	2	0	1	15	48	108	214
Sunshine Hours per Day	5.8	5.8	6.6	9.8	9.3	10	9.9	10.4	10.1	9.4	9.6	6.8
Harbin China 175m												
Temperature Daily Max.°C	-14	-9	0	12	21	26	29	27	20	12	-1	-11
Daily Min.°C	-26	-23	-12	-1	7	14	18	16	8	0	-12	-22
Average Monthly °C	-20	-16	-6	6	14	20	23	22	14	6	-7	-17
Rainfall Monthly Total mm	4	6	17	23	44	92	167	119	52	36	12	5
Sunshine Hours per Day	6.4	7.8	8	7.8	8.3	8.6	8.6	8.2	7.2	6.9	6.1	5.7
Hong Kong China 35m												
Temperature Daily Max.°C	18	18	20	24	28	30	31	31	30	27	24	20
Daily Min.°C	13	13	16	19	23	26	26	26	25	23	19	15
Average Monthly °C	16	15	18	22	25	28	28	28	27	25	21	17
Rainfall Monthly Total mm	30	60	70	133	332	479	286	415	364	33	46	17
Sunshine Hours per Day	4.7	3.5	3.1	3.8	5	5.4	6.8	6.5	6.6	7	6.2	5.5
Honolulu Hawaii 5m												
Temperature Daily Max.°C	26	26	26	27	28	29	29	29	30	29	28	26
Daily Min.°C	19	19	19	20	21	22	23	23	23	22	21	20
Average Monthly °C	23	22	23	23	24	26	26	26	26	26	24	23
Rainfall Monthly Total mm	96	84	73	33	25	8	11	23	25	47	55	76
Sunshine Hours per Day	7.3	7.7	8.3	8.6	8.8	9.1	9.4	9.3	9.2	8.3	7.5	6.2
Jakarta Indonesia 10m												
Temperature Daily Max.°C	29	29	30	31	31	31	31	31	31	31	30	29
Daily Min.°C	23	23	23	24	24	23	23	23	23	23	23	23
Average Monthly °C	26	26	27	27	27	27	27	27	27	27	27	26
Rainfall Monthly Total mm	300	300	211	147	114	97	64	43	66	112	142	203
Sunshine Av. Monthly Dur.	6.1	6.5	7.7	8.5	8.4	8.5	9.1	9.5	9.6	9	7.7	7.1
Kabul Afghanistan 1791 m												
Temperature Daily Max.°C	2	4	12	19	26	31	33	33	30	22	17	8
Daily Min.°C	-8	-6	1	6	11	13	16	15	11	6	1	-3
Average Monthly °C	-3	-1	6	13	18	22	25	24	20	14	9	3
Rainfall Monthly Total mm	28	61	72	117	33	1	7	1	0	1	37	14
Sunshine Av. Monthly Dur.	5.9	6	5.7	6.8	10.1	11.5	11.4	11.2	9.8	9.4	7.8	6.1
Khartoum Sudan 380m												
Temperature Daily Max.°C	32	33	37	40	42	41	38	36	38	39	35	32
Daily Min.°C	16	17	20	23	26	27	26	25	25	25	21	17
Average Monthly °C	24	25	28	32	34	34	32	30	32	32	28	25
Rainfall Monthly Total mm	0	0	0	1	7	5	56	80	28	2	0	[illegible]
Sunshine Av. Monthly Dur.	10.6	11.2	10.4	10.8	10.4	10.1	8.6	8.6	9.6	10.3	10.8	10.[illegible]

	Jan	Feb	Mar	Apr	May	June	July	Aug	Sep	Oct	Nov	Dec	Year
n Jamaica 35m													
ture Daily Max.°C	30	30	30	31	31	32	32	32	32	31	31	31	31
Daily Min.°C	20	20	20	21	22	24	23	23	23	23	22	21	22
verage Monthly °C	25	25	25	26	26	28	28	28	27	27	26	26	26
Monthly Total mm	23	15	23	31	102	89	38	91	99	180	74	36	801
Av. Monthly Dur.	8.3	8.8	8.7	8.7	8.3	7.8	8.5	8.5	7.6	7.3	8.3	7.7	8.2
Nigeria 40m													
ture Daily Max.°C	32	33	33	32	31	29	28	28	29	30	31	32	31
Daily Min.°C	22	23	23	23	23	22	22	21	22	22	23	22	22
verage Monthly °C	27	28	28	28	27	26	25	24	25	26	27	27	26
Monthly Total mm	28	41	99	99	203	300	180	56	180	190	63	25	1464
Av. Monthly Dur.	5.9	6.8	6.3	6.1	5.6	3.8	2.8	3.3	3	5.1	6.6	6.5	5.2
eru 120m													
ure Daily Max.°C	28	29	29	27	24	20	20	19	20	22	24	26	24
Daily Min.°C	19	20	19	17	16	15	14	14	14	15	16	17	16
verage Monthly °C	24	24	24	22	20	17	17	16	17	18	20	21	20
Monthly Total mm	1	1	1	1	5	5	8	8	8	3	3	1	45
Av. Monthly Dur.	6.3	6.8	6.9	6.7	4	1.4	1.1	1	1.1	2.5	4.1	5	3.9
Portugal 77m													
ure Daily Max.°C	14	15	17	20	21	25	27	28	26	22	17	15	21
Daily Min.°C	8	8	10	12	13	15	17	17	17	14	11	9	13
verage Monthly °C	11	12	14	16	17	20	22	23	21	18	14	12	17
Monthly Total mm	111	76	109	54	44	16	3	4	33	62	93	103	708
Av. Monthly Dur.	4.7	5.9	6	8.3	9.1	10.6	11.4	10.7	8.4	6.7	5.2	4.6	7.7
(Kew) United Kingdom 5m													
ure Daily Max.°C	6	7	10	13	17	20	22	21	19	14	10	7	14
Daily Min.°C	2	2	3	6	8	12	14	13	11	8	5	4	7
erage Monthly °C	4	5	7	9	12	16	18	17	15	11	8	5	11
Monthly Total mm	54	40	37	37	46	45	57	59	49	57	64	48	593
Av. Monthly Dur.	1.7	2.3	3.5	5.7	6.7	7	6.6	6	5	3.3	1.9	1.4	4.3
eles USA 30m													
ure Daily Max.°C	18	18	18	19	20	22	24	24	24	23	22	19	21
Daily Min.°C	7	8	9	11	13	15	17	17	16	14	11	9	12
erage Monthly °C	12	13	14	15	17	18	21	21	20	18	16	14	17
Monthly Total mm	69	74	46	28	3	3	0	0	5	10	28	61	327
Av. Monthly Dur.	6.9	8.2	8.9	8.8	9.5	10.3	11.7	11	10.1	8.6	8.2	7.6	9.2
Zambia 1154m													
re Daily Max.°C	26	26	26	27	25	23	23	26	29	31	29	27	27
Daily Min.°C	17	17	16	15	12	10	9	11	15	18	18	17	15
erage Monthly °C	22	22	21	21	18	17	16	19	22	25	23	22	21
Monthly Total mm	224	173	90	19	3	1	0	1	1	17	85	196	810
Av. Monthly Dur.	5.1	5.4	6.9	8.9	9	9	9.1	9.6	9.5	9	7	5.5	7.8
Brazil 45m													
re Daily Max.°C	31	31	31	31	31	31	32	33	34	34	33	32	32
Daily Min.°C	24	24	24	24	24	24	24	24	24	25	25	24	24
rage Monthly °C	28	28	28	27	28	28	28	29	29	29	29	28	28
lonthly Total mm	278	278	300	287	193	99	61	41	62	112	165	220	2096
Av. Monthly Dur.	3.9	4	3.6	3.9	5.4	6.9	7.9	8.2	7.5	6.6	5.9	4.9	5.7
ity Mexico 2309m													
re Daily Max.°C	21	23	26	27	26	25	23	24	23	22	21	21	24
Daily Min.°C	5	6	7	9	10	11	11	11	11	9	6	5	8
rage Monthly °C	13	15	16	18	18	18	17	17	17	16	14	13	16
lonthly Total mm	8	4	9	23	57	111	160	149	119	46	16	7	709
Av. Monthly Dur.	7.3	8.1	8.5	8.1	7.8	7	6.2	6.4	5.6	6.3	7	7.3	7.1
SA 2m													
e Daily Max.°C	24	25	27	28	30	31	32	32	31	29	27	25	28
Daily Min.°C	14	15	16	19	21	23	24	24	24	22	18	15	20
rage Monthly °C	19	20	21	23	25	27	28	28	27	25	22	20	24
onthly Total mm	51	48	58	99	163	188	170	178	241	208	71	43	1518
v. Monthly Dur.	7.7	8.3	8.7	9.4	8.9	8.5	8.7	8.4	7.1	6.5	7.5	7.1	8.1
Canada 57m													
e Daily Max.°C	-6	-4	2	11	18	23	26	25	20	14	5	-3	11
Daily Min.°C	-13	-11	-5	2	9	14	17	16	11	6	0	-9	3
age Monthly °C	-9	-8	-2	6	13	19	22	20	16	10	3	-6	7
onthly Total mm	87	76	86	83	81	91	98	87	96	84	89	89	1047
v. Monthly Dur.	2.8	3.4	4.5	5.2	6.7	7.7	8.2	7.7	5.6	4.3	2.4	2.2	5.1
Russia 156m													
e Daily Max.°C	-6	-4	1	9	18	22	24	22	17	10	1	-5	9
Daily Min.°C	-14	-16	-11	-1	5	9	12	9	4	-2	-6	-12	-2
age Monthly °C	-10	-10	-5	4	12	15	18	16	10	4	-2	-8	4
onthly Total mm	31	28	33	35	52	67	74	74	58	51	36	36	575
v. Monthly Dur.	1	1.9	3.7	5.2	7.8	8.3	8.4	7.1	4.4	2.4	1	0.6	4.4
India 220m													
e Daily Max.°C	21	24	29	36	41	39	35	34	34	34	28	23	32
Daily Min.°C	6	10	14	20	26	28	27	26	24	17	11	7	18
age Monthly °C	14	17	22	28	33	34	31	30	29	26	20	15	25
onthly Total mm	25	21	13	8	13	77	178	184	123	10	2	11	665
v. Monthly Dur.	7.7	8.2	8.2	8.7	9.2	7.9	6	6.3	6.9	9.4	8.7	8.3	8

	Jan	Feb	Mar	Apr	May	June	July	Aug	Sep	Oct	Nov	Dec	Year
Perth Australia 60m													
Temperature Daily Max.°C	29	30	27	25	21	18	17	18	19	21	25	27	23
Daily Min.°C	17	18	16	14	12	10	9	9	10	11	14	16	13
Average Monthly °C	23	24	22	19	16	14	13	13	15	16	19	22	18
Rainfall Monthly Total mm	8	13	22	44	128	189	177	145	84	58	19	13	900
Sunshine Av. Monthly Dur.	10.4	9.8	8.8	7.5	5.7	4.8	5.4	6	7.2	8.1	9.6	10.4	7.8
Reykjavik Iceland 18m													
Temperature Daily Max.°C	2	3	5	6	10	13	15	14	12	8	5	4	8
Daily Min.°C	-3	-3	-1	1	4	7	9	8	6	3	0	-2	3
Average Monthly °C	0	0	2	4	7	10	12	11	9	5	3	1	5
Rainfall Monthly Total mm	89	64	62	56	42	42	50	56	67	94	78	79	779
Sunshine Av. Monthly Dur.	0.8	2	3.6	4.5	5.9	6.1	5.8	5.4	3.5	2.3	1.1	0.3	3.7
Santiago Chile 520m													
Temperature Daily Max.°C	30	29	27	24	19	15	15	17	19	22	26	29	23
Daily Min.°C	12	11	10	7	5	3	3	4	6	7	9	11	7
Average Monthly °C	21	20	18	15	12	9	9	10	12	15	17	20	15
Rainfall Monthly Total mm	3	3	5	13	64	84	76	56	31	15	8	5	363
Sunshine Av. Monthly Dur.	10.8	8.9	8.5	5.5	3.6	3.3	3.3	3.6	4.8	6.1	8.7	10.1	6.4
Shanghai China 5m													
Temperature Daily Max.°C	8	8	13	19	24	28	32	32	27	23	17	10	20
Daily Min.°C	-1	0	4	9	14	19	23	23	19	13	7	2	11
Average Monthly °C	3	4	8	14	19	23	27	27	23	18	12	6	15
Rainfall Monthly Total mm	48	59	84	94	94	180	147	142	130	71	51	36	1136
Sunshine Av. Monthly Dur.	4	3.7	4.4	4.8	5.4	4.7	6.9	7.5	5.3	5.6	4.7	4.5	5.1
Sydney Australia 40m													
Temperature Daily Max.°C	26	26	25	22	19	17	17	18	20	22	24	25	22
Daily Min.°C	18	19	17	14	11	9	8	9	11	13	16	17	14
Average Monthly °C	22	22	21	18	15	13	12	13	16	18	20	21	18
Rainfall Monthly Total mm	89	101	127	135	127	117	117	76	74	71	74	74	1182
Sunshine Av. Monthly Dur.	7.5	7	6.4	6.1	5.7	5.3	6.1	7	7.3	7.5	7.5	7.5	6.8
Tehran Iran 1191m													
Temperature Daily Max.°C	9	11	16	21	29	30	37	36	29	24	16	11	22
Daily Min.°C	-1	1	4	10	16	20	23	23	18	12	6	1	11
Average Monthly °C	4	6	10	15	22	25	30	29	23	18	11	6	17
Rainfall Monthly Total mm	37	23	36	31	14	2	1	1	1	5	29	27	207
Sunshine Av. Monthly Dur.	5.9	6.7	7.5	7.4	8.6	11.6	11.2	11	10.1	7.6	6.9	6.3	8.4
Timbuktu Mali 269m													
Temperature Daily Max.°C	31	35	38	41	43	42	38	35	38	40	37	31	37
Daily Min.°C	13	16	18	22	26	27	25	24	24	23	18	14	21
Average Monthly °C	22	25	28	31	34	34	32	30	31	31	28	23	29
Rainfall Monthly Total mm	0	0	0	1	4	20	54	93	31	3	0	0	206
Sunshine Av. Monthly Dur.	9.1	9.6	9.6	9.7	9.8	9.4	9.6	9	9.3	9.5	9.5	8.9	9.4
Tokyo Japan 5m													
Temperature Daily Max.°C	9	9	12	18	22	25	29	30	27	20	16	11	19
Daily Min.°C	-1	-1	3	4	13	17	22	23	19	13	7	1	10
Average Monthly °C	4	4	8	11	18	21	25	26	23	17	11	6	14
Rainfall Monthly Total mm	48	73	101	135	131	182	146	147	217	220	101	61	1562
Sunshine Av. Monthly Dur.	6	5.9	5.7	6	6.2	5	5.8	6.6	4.5	4.4	4.8	5.4	5.5
Tromsø Norway 100m													
Temperature Daily Max.°C	-2	-2	0	3	7	12	16	14	10	5	2	0	5
Daily Min.°C	-6	-6	-5	-2	1	6	9	8	5	1	-2	-4	0
Average Monthly °C	-4	-4	-3	0	4	9	13	11	7	3	0	-2	3
Rainfall Monthly Total mm	96	79	91	65	61	59	56	80	109	115	88	95	994
Sunshine Av. Monthly Dur.	0.1	1.6	2.9	6.1	5.7	6.9	7.9	4.8	3.5	1.7	0.3	0	3.52
Ulan Bator Mongolia 1305m													
Temperature Daily Max.°C	-19	-13	-4	7	13	21	22	21	14	6	-6	-16	4
Daily Min.°C	-32	-29	-22	-8	-2	7	11	8	2	-8	-20	-28	-11
Average Monthly °C	-26	-21	-13	-1	6	14	16	14	8	-1	-13	-22	-4
Rainfall Monthly Total mm	1	1	2	5	10	28	76	51	23	5	5	2	209
Sunshine Av. Monthly Dur.	6.4	7.8	8	7.8	8.3	8.6	8.6	8.2	7.2	6.9	6.1	5.7	7.5
Vancouver Canada 5m													
Temperature Daily Max.°C	6	7	10	14	17	20	23	22	19	14	9	7	14
Daily Min.°C	0	1	3	5	8	11	13	12	10	7	3	2	6
Average Monthly °C	3	4	6	9	13	16	18	17	14	10	6	4	10
Rainfall Monthly Total mm	214	161	151	90	69	65	39	44	83	172	198	243	1529
Sunshine Av. Monthly Dur.	1.6	3	3.8	5.9	7.5	7.4	9.5	8.2	6	3.7	2	1.4	5
Verkhoyansk Russia 137m													
Temperature Daily Max.°C	-47	-40	-20	-1	11	21	24	21	12	-8	-33	-42	-8
Daily Min.°C	-51	-48	-40	-25	-7	4	6	1	-6	-20	-39	-50	-23
Average Monthly °C	-49	-44	-30	-13	2	12	15	11	3	-14	-36	-46	-16
Rainfall Monthly Total mm	7	5	5	4	5	25	33	30	13	11	10	7	155
Sunshine Av. Monthly Dur.	0	2.6	6.9	9.6	9.7	10	9.7	7.5	4.1	2.4	0.6	0	5.4
Washington USA 22m													
Temperature Daily Max.°C	7	8	12	19	25	29	31	30	26	20	14	8	19
Daily Min.°C	-1	-1	2	8	13	18	21	20	16	10	4	-1	9
Average Monthly °C	3	3	7	13	19	24	26	25	21	15	9	4	14
Rainfall Monthly Total mm	84	68	96	85	103	88	108	120	100	78	75	75	1080
Sunshine Av. Monthly Dur.	4.4	5.7	6.7	7.4	8.2	8.8	8.6	8.2	7.5	6.5	5.3	4.5	6.8

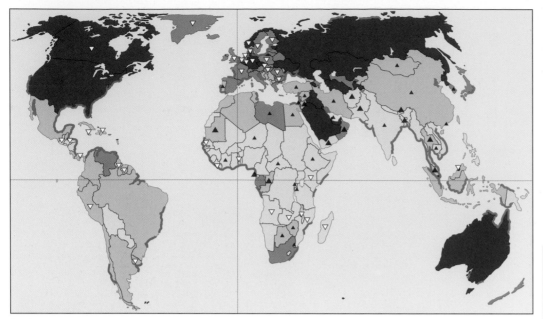

GLOBAL WARMING

Carbon dioxide emissions in tonnes per person per year (1992)

- Over 10 tonnes of CO_2
- 5 – 10 tonnes of CO_2
- 1 – 5 tonnes of CO_2
- Under 1 tonne of CO_2

Changes in CO_2 emissions 1980 – 1990

- ▲ Over 100% increase in emissions
- ▲ 50 – 100% increase in emissions
- ▽ Reduction in emissions
- ▬▬ Coasts in danger of flooding from rising sea levels caused by global warming

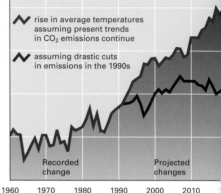

- rise in average temperatures assuming present trends in CO_2 emissions continue
- assuming drastic cuts in emissions in the 1990s

Recorded change   Projected changes

1960   1970   1980   1990   2000   2010

5%   10%   15%   20%

U.S.A.
Former U.S.S.R.
China
Japan
Brazil
Germany
India
U.K.

Largest percentage share of total world greenhouse gas emissions 1992

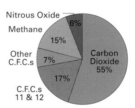

Contribution to the greenhouse effect by the major heat-absorbing gases in the atmosphere

- Nitrous Oxide 6%
- Methane 15%
- Other C.F.C.s 7%
- C.F.C.s 11 & 12 17%
- Carbon Dioxide 55%

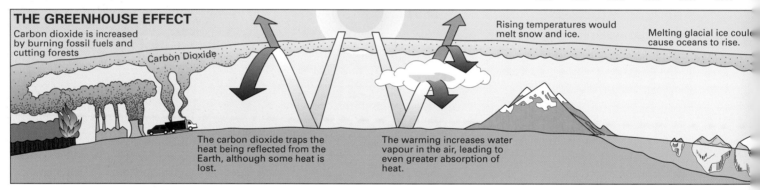

THE GREENHOUSE EFFECT

Carbon dioxide is increased by burning fossil fuels and cutting forests

Carbon Dioxide

Rising temperatures would melt snow and ice.

Melting glacial ice could cause oceans to rise.

The carbon dioxide traps the heat being reflected from the Earth, although some heat is lost.

The warming increases water vapour in the air, leading to even greater absorption of heat.

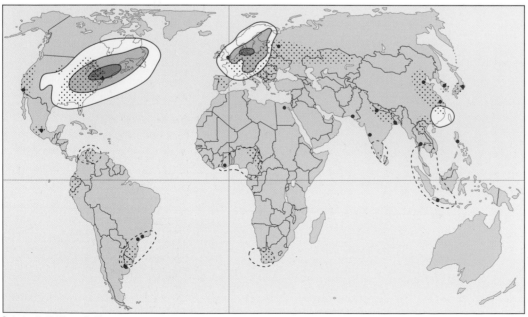

ACID RAIN

Acid rain is caused by high levels of sulphu
nitrogen in the atmosphere. They combine
water vapour and oxygen to form acids (H_2
and HNO_3) which fall as precipitation.

- Main areas of sulphur and nitrogen emissions (from the burning of fossil fuels)
- Major cities with levels of air pollution exceeding World Health Organisation guidelines

Areas of acid deposition

(pH numbers measure acidity: normal rain is

- pH less than 4.0 (most acidic)
- pH 4.0 – 4.5
- pH 4.5 – 5.0
- Potential problem areas

Projection: *Modified Hammer Equal Area*

WATER POLLUTION

	Severely polluted sea areas and lakes
	Less polluted sea areas and lakes
	Areas of frequent oil pollution by shipping

◤ Major oil tanker spills

▲ Major oil rig blow-outs

▼ Offshore dumpsites for industrial and municipal waste

─── Severely polluted rivers and estuaries

Sources of marine oil pollution		Sources of river pollution	
Tanker operations	22%	Agriculture	64%
Municipal waste	22%	Mining	9%
Tanker accidents	13%	Land disposal	9%
River runoff	12%	Forestry	6%
Others	31%	Others	11%

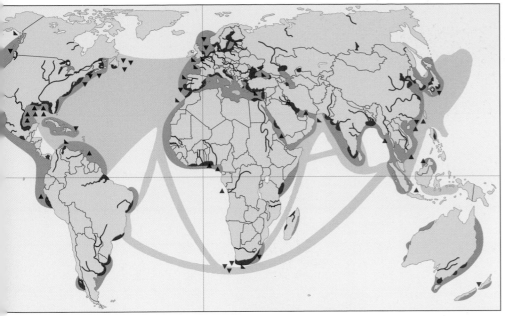

DESERTIFICATION

	Existing deserts
	Areas with a high risk of desertification
	Areas with a moderate risk of desertification

DEFORESTATION IN THE TROPICS

	Former areas of rainforest
	Existing rainforest

Deforestation 1990-1995

	Extent of forest cleared annually (thousand ha)	Annual deforestation rate (%)
Brazil	2554	0.5
Indonesia	1084	1.0
Congo (Zaire)	740	0.7
Bolivia	581	1.2
Mexico	508	0.9
Venezuela	503	1.1
Malaysia	400	2.4

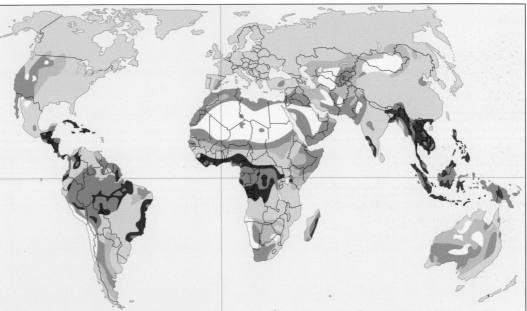

NATURAL DISASTERS

	Earthquake zones
●	Major earthquakes since 1900 (with dates)
▲	Major volcanoes (notable eruptions since 1900 with dates)
	Areas liable to flood
⇒	Paths of tropical storms
⇒	Paths of winter blizzards
	Areas liable to invasion by locusts
■	Major famines since 1900 (with dates)
⑨	Major storms and floods

1 Texas 1900
2 Central America 1966, 1974
3 West Indies 1928, 1963, 1979, 1988
4 Bangladesh 1960, 1963, 1965, 1970, 1985, 1988, 1989, 1991
5 Huang He 1887, 1931
6 Yangtze 1911, 1989, 1995
7 Hunan 1991
8 Haiphong 1881
9 Philippines 1970, 1991
10 Mississippi 1993

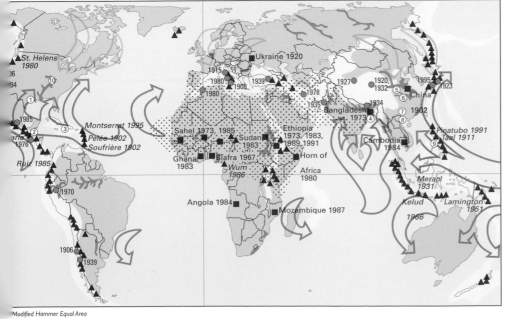

Modified Hammer Equal Area

CARTOGRAPHY BY PHILIP'S. COPYRIGHT GEORGE PHILIP LTD

	Population									Land and Agriculture					Energy	Trade	
	Population Total 1997	Population Density 1997	Average Annual Change 1970-80	Average Annual Change 1990-97	Birth Rate 1997	Death Rate 1997	Fertility Rate 1995	Life Expectancy Average 1997	Urban Population 1995	Land Area	Arable and Permanent Crops	Permanent grassland	Forest	Agriculture Population 1995	Consumption per capita 1994	Imports per capita 1995	Exports per capita 1995
	millions	persons per km²	%	%	births per thousand population	deaths per thousand population	children	years	%	thousand km²	% of land area	% of land area	% of land area	% of economically active pop.	tonnes of coal	US $	US $
Afghanistan	23	35	1.7	4.8	43	18	6.9	46	20	652	12	46	3	69	0.04	19	6
Albania	3.6	131	2.3	1.5	22	8	2.6	68	37	27.4	26	15	38	54	0.3	178	42
Algeria	29.3	12	3.1	2.3	28	6	3.5	69	56	2382	3	13	2	24	1.58	375	375
Angola	11.2	9	3.3	1.6	44	17	6.9	47	32	1247	3	43	18	74	0.08	198	309
Argentina	35.4	13	1.7	1.3	20	8	2.7	74	88	2737	10	52	19	11	2.15	579	603
Armenia	3.8	134	2	1.9	17	8	1.8	69	69	28.4	20	54	15	15	0.61	105	603
Australia	18.4	2	1.6	1.2	14	7	1.9	80	86	7644	6	54	19	5	7.61	3342	2942
Austria	8.2	99	0.1	1.1	11	10	1.5	77	65	82.7	18	24	39	7	4.16	8253	7166
Azerbaijan	7.7	89	1.8	1	22	9	2.3	65	56	86.1	23	52	11	30	2.6	105	86
Bahamas	0.3	28	2.1	1.5	18	6	2	73	85	10	1	0	32	5	2.97	4439	5418
Bangladesh	124	953	2.8	1	30	11	3.5	56	18	130	74	5	15	62	0.09	55	27
Barbados	0.3	616	0.4	0.6	15	8	1.8	75	46	0.43	37	5	12	6	1.58	2946	915
Belarus	10.5	51	0.7	0.3	11	13	1.4	69	69	208	31	14	34	18	3.38	297	243
Belgium	10.2	335	0.2	0.5	12	10	1.6	77	97	30.5	24	21	21	3	6.86	14702	16078
Benin	5.8	52	2.5	2.9	46	13	6	53	36	111	17	4	31	60	0.05	125	34
Bolivia	7.7	7	2.6	2.4	32	10	4.5	60	62	1084	2	24	53	45	0.49	192	149
Bosnia-Herzegovina	3.6	70	1	-2.7	6	7	1	60	41	51.2	16	24	39	10	0.36	204	12
Botswana	1.5	3	3.8	2.2	33	7	4.4	62	31	567	1	45	47	39	...	1153	1302
Brazil	159.5	19	2.4	1.4	20	9	2.4	62	78	8457	6	22	58	19	0.85	345	298
Bulgaria	8.6	77	0.4	-0.7	8	14	1.2	71	71	111	38	16	35	11	3.26	598	606
Burkina Faso	10.9	40	2.3	2.8	46	20	6.7	42	27	274	13	22	50	92	0.05	54	53
Burma	47.5	72	2.4	1.9	30	11	3.4	57	27	658	15	1	49	72	0.08	30	19
Burundi	6.3	243	1.6	0.5	42	15	6.5	49	7	25.7	46	39	13	91	0.02	39	18
Cambodia	10.5	59	-0.8	3.5	43	15	4.7	50	21	177	22	8	69	73	0.02	43	24
Cameroon	13.8	30	2.7	2.6	42	14	5.7	52	45	465	15	4	77	68	0.14	94	154
Canada	30.2	3	1.2	1.9	13	7	1.7	79	77	9221	5	3	54	3	11.21	5676	649
Central African Rep.	3.4	5	2.3	1.8	40	18	5.1	45	39	623	3	5	75	79	0.04	54	53
Chad	6.8	5	2.1	2.5	44	17	5.9	48	22	1259	3	36	26	81	0.01	67	7
Chile	14.7	20	1.6	1.6	18	6	2.3	75	85	749	6	18	22	17	1.45	1121	1130
China	1210	130	1.8	1.2	17	7	1.9	70	29	9326	10	43	14	71	0.92	106	12
Colombia	35.9	35	2.3	1.2	21	5	2.8	73	73	1039	5	39	48	24	1	395	288
Congo	2.7	8	2.8	2.9	39	17	6	46	59	342	0	29	58	45	0.34	259	329
Congo (Zaïre)	47.2	21	2.9	4.1	48	17	6	47	29	2267	3	7	77	66	0.06	8	
Costa Rica	3.5	69	2.8	2.2	23	4	2.8	76	50	51.1	10	46	31	22	0.87	977	81
Croatia	4.9	86	0.4	0.2	10	11	1.5	73	55	56.4	22	20	38	15	1.59	1586	96
Cuba	11.3	102	1.3	0.8	13	7	1.7	75	75	110	31	27	24	16	1.14	258	14
Cyprus	0.8	83	0.2	1.4	15	8	2.2	77	68	9.24	15	0	13	10	3.03	4986	166
Czech Rep.	10.5	136	0.5	0.3	11	11	1.3	74	65	77	44	12	34	11	4.97	2450	209
Denmark	5.4	126	0.4	0.3	12	10	1.8	78	86	42.4	56	7	10	4	5.15	8266	937
Dominican Rep.	8.2	168	2.6	1.8	23	6	2.9	69	62	48.4	31	43	12	21	0.65	376	9
Ecuador	11.8	43	3	1.6	25	5	3.2	72	59	277	11	18	56	29	0.77	366	37
Egypt	63	63	2.1	2.6	28	9	3.4	62	45	995	4	0	0	33	0.66	199	5
El Salvador	6	287	2.3	1.8	27	6	3.7	69	52	20.7	35	29	5	32	0.5	504	17
Estonia	1.5	34	0.8	-1.1	12	14	1.3	68	73	43.2	27	7	48	14	4.9	1714	124
Ethiopia	58.5	53	2.4	3.5	46	18	7	47	13	1101	11	20	13	86	0.03	19	
Finland	5.2	17	0.4	0.6	11	11	1.8	76	63	305	9	0	76	7	7.4	5502	7747
France	58.8	107	0.6	0.7	13	9	1.7	79	74	550	35	19	27	4	5.15	4763	4947
Gabon	1.2	5	4.8	1.5	28	13	5.2	56	73	258	2	18	77	45	0.87	667	2057
Gambia, The	1.2	120	3.3	4.9	44	19	5.3	53	26	10	17	19	10	80	0.1	192	3
Georgia	5.5	78	0.8	0	14	9	1.9	68	58	69.7	16	24	33	25	0.85	39	2
Germany	82.3	236	0.1	0.5	9	11	1.2	76	87	349	34	15	31	3	5.48	5445	622
Ghana	18.1	80	2.2	2.7	34	11	5.1	57	36	228	19	37	42	56	0.14	129	7
Greece	10.6	82	0.9	0.8	10	10	1.4	78	65	129	27	41	20	20	3.22	2056	89
Guatemala	11.3	104	2.8	2.9	33	7	4.7	66	42	108	18	24	54	51	0.29	310	20
Guinea	7.5	30	1.4	3.8	42	18	6.5	46	30	246	3	44	27	85	0.08	116	9
Guinea-Bissau	1.2	41	4.2	2.6	39	16	6	49	22	28.1	12	38	38	84	0.1	66	2
Guyana	0.8	4	0.7	-0.8	19	10	2.4	59	35	197	3	6	84	20	0.6	594	55
Haiti	7.4	269	1.7	1.8	33	15	4.4	50	32	27.6	33	18	5	66	0.04	91	17
Honduras	6.3	56	3.4	3	33	6	4.6	69	48	112	18	14	54	33	0.31	205	17
Hungary	10.2	110	0.4	-0.6	11	15	1.6	69	64	92.3	54	12	19	14	3.27	1472	121
Iceland	0.3	3	1.1	1.2	17	6	2.1	81	92	100	0	23	1	10	6.7	6500	667
India	980	330	2.2	2.5	25	9	3.2	60	27	2973	57	4	23	62	0.37	37	3
Indonesia	203.5	112	2.3	1.8	23	8	2.7	62	33	1812	17	7	62	53	0.47	211	23
Iran	69.5	42	3.2	3.5	33	6	4.5	68	58	1636	11	27	7	36	1.88	537	34
Iraq	22.5	51	3.6	2.5	43	6	5.4	67	73	437	12	9	4	12	1.76	278	35

GNP 1995 (million US$)	GNP per capita 1995 US $	Real GDP per capita 1995 US $	Average Annual growth of Real GNP per capita 1985-95 %	GDP share Agriculture 1995 %	GDP share Industry 1995 %	GDP share services 1995 %	HDI Human Development Index 1994	Food Intake calories per day	Population per doctor 1993 persons	% of GNP spent on health 1990-95 %	% of GNP spent on education 1993-94 %	%o GNP spent on military 1995 %	Adult Illiteracy Female %	Adult Illiteracy Male %	Aid given (*) and received per capita 1994 US $	
000	300	800	-6	52	32	16	...	1523	7000	...	...	9.1	85	53	10	Afghanistan
199	670	2750	-7	56	21	23	0.655	2605	735	2.7	3	2.8	0	0	21	Albania
509	1600	5300	-2.6	13	47	40	0.737	2897	1062	4.6	5.6	2.5	51	26	11	Algeria
422	410	1310	-6.1	12	59	29	0.335	1839	23725	4	...	4.8	71	44	40	Angola
431	8030	8310	1.9	6	31	63	0.884	2880	330	10.6	3.8	1.7	4	4	7	Argentina
752	730	2260	-15.1	44	35	21	0.651	...	261	7.8	7.3	4.4	2	1	27	Armenia
009	18720	18940	1.4	3	28	69	0.931	3179	500	8.4	6	2.5	...	...	*62	Australia
547	26890	21250	1.9	2	34	64	0.932	3497	231	9.7	5.5	1	0	0	*82	Austria
501	480	1460	-16.3	27	32	41	0.636	...	257	7.5	5.5	5	4	1	3	Azerbaijan
297	11940	14710	-1	3	9	88	0.894	2624	700	...	3.9	0.6	2	1	15	Bahamas
599	240	1380	2.1	31	18	51	0.368	2019	12884	2.4	2.3	1.8	74	51	11	Bangladesh
745	6560	10620	-0.2	5	17	78	0.907	3207	1000	5	7.5	0.7	3	2	...	Barbados
456	2070	4220	-5.2	13	35	52	0.806	...	236	6.4	6.1	3.3	3	1	11	Belarus
710	24710	21660	2.2	2	31	67	0.932	3681	274	8.2	5.6	1.7	0	0	*81	Belgium
34	370	1760	-0.4	34	12	54	0.368	2532	14216	1.7	...	1.3	74	51	53	Benin
05	800	2540	1.7	17	30	53	0.589	2094	2348	5	5.4	2.6	24	10	96	Bolivia
50	2600	...	1.8	...	...	...	...	...	600	...	...	...	23	3	...	Bosnia-Herzegovina
81	3020	5580	6	5	46	49	0.673	2266	5151	1.9	8.5	7.1	40	20	64	Botswana
87	3640	5400	-0.7	14	37	49	0.783	2824	844	7.4	1.6	1.5	17	17	2	Brazil
25	1330	4480	-2.2	13	34	53	0.78	2831	306	4	4.5	3.3	3	1	6	Bulgaria
17	230	780	-0.1	34	27	39	0.221	2387	34804	5.5	3.6	2.4	91	71	48	Burkina Faso
00	1000	1050	0.4	63	9	28	0.475	2598	12528	0.9	2.4	6.2	22	11	3	Burma
84	160	630	-1.3	56	18	26	0.247	1941	17153	0.9	3.8	5.3	78	51	46	Burundi
18	270	1084	2	51	14	35	0.348	2021	9374	7.2	...	4.7	47	20	57	Cambodia
15	650	2110	-7	39	23	38	0.468	1981	11996	1.4	3.1	1.8	48	25	35	Cameroon
95	19380	21130	0.4	3	30	67	0.96	3094	464	9.8	7.6	1.6	2	2	*73	Canada
23	340	1070	-2	44	13	43	0.355	1690	25920	1.7	2.8	1.8	48	32	50	Central African Rep.
44	180	700	0.5	44	22	34	0.288	1989	30030	1.8	2.2	2.6	65	38	38	Chad
51	4160	9520	6.1	8	34	58	0.891	2582	942	6.5	2.9	3.8	5	5	11	Chile
90	620	2920	8	21	48	31	0.626	2727	1063	3.8	2.6	5.7	27	10	3	China
63	1910	6130	2.8	14	32	54	0.848	2677	1105	7.4	3.7	2	9	9	6	Colombia
84	680	2050	-3.2	10	38	52	0.5	2296	3713	6.8	8.3	1.7	33	17	50	Congo
13	120	490	-8.5	51	16	33	0.381	2060	15150	2.4	1	2	32	13	4	Congo (Zaïre)
34	2610	5850	2.9	17	24	59	0.889	2883	1133	8.5	4.7	0.3	5	5	8	Costa Rica
08	3250	3960	-20	12	25	63	0.76	...	500	10.1	...	12.6	5	1	...	Croatia
00	1250	3000	-10	...	...	...	0.723	2833	275	7.9	6.6	2.8	5	4	6	Cuba
10	11500	13000	4.6	6	43	51	0.907	3779	450	3.9	4.3	4.5	7	2	30	Cyprus
90	3870	9770	-1.8	6	39	55	0.882	...	273	9.9	5.9	2.8	0	0	5	Czech Rep.
27	29890	21230	1.5	4	29	67	0.927	3664	360	6.6	8.5	1.8	0	0	*273	Denmark
90	1460	3870	2.1	15	22	63	0.718	2286	949	5.3	1.9	1.3	18	18	16	Dominican Rep.
07	1390	4220	0.8	12	36	52	0.775	2583	652	5.3	3	3.4	12	8	21	Ecuador
07	790	3820	1.1	20	21	59	0.614	3335	1316	4.9	5	4.3	61	36	35	Egypt
57	1610	2610	2.9	14	22	64	0.592	2663	1515	5	1.6	1.8	30	27	54	El Salvador
52	2860	4220	-4.3	8	28	64	0.776	...	253	5.9	5.8	5.3	0	0	22	Estonia
22	100	450	-0.5	57	10	33	0.244	1610	32499	1.1	6.4	2.1	75	55	16	Ethiopia
74	20580	17760	-0.2	6	37	57	0.94	3018	406	8.3	8.4	2	0	0	*59	Finland
51	24990	21030	1.5	2	27	71	0.946	3633	334	9.7	5.8	3.1	1	1	*137	France
69	3490	3650	-1.6	9	59	32	0.562	2500	1987	0.5	3.2	1.7	47	26	138	Gabon
34	320	930	0.3	28	15	57	0.281	2360	14000	1.8	2.7	3.8	75	47	43	Gambia, The
68	440	1470	-17	67	22	11	0.637	...	182	0.3	1.9	3.4	1	0	106	Georgia
13	27510	20070	1.9	1	30	69	0.924	3344	367	9.5	4.8	2	0	0	*81	Germany
19	390	1990	1.5	46	16	38	0.468	2199	22970	3.5	3.1	1.2	47	24	38	Ghana
85	8210	11710	1.2	21	36	43	0.923	3815	312	6.4	3	4.6	7	2	...	Greece
55	1340	3340	0.3	25	19	56	0.572	2255	3999	2.7	1.6	1.4	51	38	21	Guatemala
13	550	1100	1.4	24	31	45	0.271	2389	7445	0.9	2.2	1.4	78	50	62	Guinea
5	250	790	1.8	46	24	30	0.291	2556	3500	1.1	2.8	3	58	32	113	Guinea-Bissau
3	590	2420	0.8	50	35	15	0.649	2384	3000	10.4	5	1.1	2	1	...	Guyana
7	250	910	-5.2	44	12	44	0.338	1706	10855	3.6	1.4	2.1	58	52	104	Haiti
6	600	1900	0.2	21	33	46	0.575	2305	1266	5.6	4	1.3	27	27	75	Honduras
9	4120	6410	-1	8	33	59	0.857	3503	306	7.3	6.7	1.4	1	1	7	Hungary
6	24950	20460	0.3	13	29	58	0.942	3058	360	6.9	5.4	...	0	0	...	Iceland
0	340	1400	3.1	29	29	42	0.446	2395	2459	3.5	3.8	2.5	62	35	2	India
0	980	3800	6	17	42	41	0.668	2752	7028	1.5	1.3	1.6	22	10	7	Indonesia
0	4800	5470	0.5	25	34	41	0.78	2860	3142	4.5	5.9	3.9	24	22	3	Iran
0	1800	3150	...	28	20	52	0.531	2121	1659	...	5.1	14.8	55	29	16	Iraq

	Population									Land and Agriculture					Energy	Trade	
	Population Total 1997	Population Density 1997	Average Annual Change 1970-80	Average Annual Change 1990-97	Birth Rate 1997	Death Rate 1997	Fertility Rate 1995	Life Expectancy Average 1997	Urban Population 1995	Land Area	Arable and Permanent Crops	Permanent grassland	Forest	Agriculture Population 1995	Consumption per capita 1994	Imports per capita 1995	Exports per capita 1995
	millions	persons per km²	%	%	births per thousand population	deaths per thousand population	children	years	%	thousand km²	% of land area	% of land area	% of land area	% of economically active pop.	tonnes of coal	US $	US $
Ireland	3.6	53	1.4	0.5	13	9	1.9	76	58	68.9	19	45	5	13	4.31	9237	12469
Israel	5.9	286	2.7	3.6	20	6	2.4	78	91	20.6	21	7	6	3	3.26	5337	3436
Italy	57.8	196	0.5	0.2	10	10	1.2	78	67	294	38	15	23	7	3.95	3562	4038
Ivory Coast	15.1	47	4	3.4	42	17	5.3	45	46	318	12	41	34	57	0.26	231	301
Jamaica	2.6	240	1.3	0.8	22	6	2.4	75	53	10.8	20	24	17	24	1.66	1089	545
Japan	125.9	334	1.1	0.3	10	8	1.5	80	78	377	12	2	66	6	4.98	2684	3540
Jordan	5.6	63	2.4	4.9	36	4	4.8	73	72	88.9	5	9	1	15	1.01	680	325
Kazakstan	17	6	1.3	0.2	19	10	2.3	64	58	2670	13	70	4	21	5.93	40	70
Kenya	31.9	56	3.8	4.1	32	11	4.7	54	25	570	8	37	30	78	0.12	98	63
Korea, North	24.5	203	2.2	1.7	22	5	2.2	71	61	120	17	0	61	34	4.21	75	41
Korea, South	46.1	466	1.8	1.1	16	6	1.8	74	75	98.7	21	1	65	14	3.77	3013	2788
Kyrgyzstan	4.7	24	2	0.8	26	9	3.3	64	40	191	7	44	4	31	0.76	71	76
Laos	5.2	23	1.7	3.3	41	13	6.5	53	22	231	4	3	54	77	0.04	40	20
Latvia	2.5	38	0.7	-1.3	12	15	1.3	67	72	64.1	28	13	46	14	2.3	697	520
Lebanon	3.2	313	0.8	2.5	28	6	2.8	70	87	10.2	30	1	8	4	1.83	2058	197
Lesotho	2.1	69	2.3	2.7	32	14	4.6	52	23	30.4	11	66	0	39	...	520	58
Liberia	3	30	3.1	2.9	42	12	6.5	59	45	96.8	4	21	48	70	0.06	116	197
Libya	5.5	3	4.4	2.8	44	7	6.1	65	86	1760	1	8	0	6	3.34	1240	2596
Lithuania	3.7	57	0.9	-0.1	14	13	1.5	68	71	65.2	47	7	31	18	3.04	696	545
Luxembourg	0.4	163.5	0.7	1.9	13	8	1.7	79	88	2.6	...	...	...	...	12.82	20295	16096
Macedonia	2.2	86	1.6	0.9	13	9	2.2	72	60	24.9	26	25	39	17	1.9	600	500
Madagascar	15.5	27	2.7	4.8	42	14	5.8	53	27	582	5	41	40	76	0.04	36	25
Malawi	10.3	109	3.2	3.1	41	25	6.6	35	13	94.1	18	20	39	86	0.04	49	4
Malaysia	20.9	64	2.4	2.2	26	5	3.4	70	52	329	23	1	68	23	2.29	3751	3560
Mali	11	9	2.3	4.4	51	19	6.8	47	27	1220	2	25	10	84	0.02	70	4
Malta	0.4	1172	1.1	0.9	15	7	1.9	79	88	0.32	41	0	0	2	1.97	7951	5170
Mauritania	2.4	2	2.4	2.5	47	15	5.2	50	54	1025	0	38	4	49	0.61	284	22
Mauritius	1.2	569	1.6	1.1	19	7	2.2	71	44	2.03	52	3	22	12	0.7	1797	1410
Mexico	97.4	51	2.9	1.8	26	5	3	74	75	1909	13	39	26	24	2.03	508	52
Moldova	4.5	132	1.1	0.3	17	12	2	65	50	33.7	66	13	13	31	1.55	185	16
Mongolia	2.5	2	2.8	1.9	25	8	3.4	61	60	1567	1	75	9	29	1.55	158	20
Morocco	28.1	63	2.4	1.6	27	6	3.4	70	52	446	21	47	20	41	0.47	315	17
Mozambique	19.1	24	2.6	4.3	44	18	6.2	45	32	784	4	56	22	81	0.03	45	1
Namibia	1.7	2	2.5	2	37	8	5	65	34	823	1	46	15	45	...	916	88
Nepal	22.1	162	2.6	2.1	37	12	5.3	54	13	137	17	15	42	93	0.03	64	1
Netherlands	15.9	469	0.8	0.9	12	9	1.6	78	89	33.9	28	31	10	4	7.22	11419	12688
New Zealand	3.7	14	1	1.1	15	8	2.1	77	86	268	14	50	28	10	5.47	3951	3882
Nicaragua	4.6	39	3	2.5	33	6	4.1	66	63	119	10	45	26	23	0.36	212	118
Niger	9.7	8	3	3.3	54	24	7.4	41	16	1267	3	8	2	89	0.06	37	2
Nigeria	118	130	2.2	3.1	43	12	5.5	55	38	911	36	44	12	38	0.21	71	9
Norway	4.4	14	0.5	0.8	11	11	1.9	78	73	307	3	0	27	5	7.44	7563	9637
Cman	2.4	11	4.2	6.9	38	4	7	71	13	212	0	5	0	42	5.41	1994	2688
Pakistan	136	176	2.6	2.8	35	11	5.2	59	34	771	28	6	5	48	0.33	88	6
Panama	2.7	37	2.5	1.7	22	5	2.7	74	55	74.4	9	20	44	22	1.2	955	23
Papua New Guinea	4.4	10	2.5	1.8	33	10	4.8	58	16	453	1	0	93	78	0.29	357	65
Paraguay	5.2	13	3	2.8	30	4	4	74	52	397	6	55	32	35	0.38	669	19
Peru	24.5	19	2.7	1.3	24	6	3.1	70	72	1280	3	21	66	33	0.46	392	23
Philippines	73.5	247	2.6	2.4	29	7	3.7	66	52	298	31	4	46	42	0.43	403	24
Poland	38.8	127	0.9	0.1	12	10	1.6	72	64	304	48	13	29	26	3.51	753	59
Portugal	10.1	110	0.8	-0.3	11	10	1.4	76	36	92	32	11	36	14	2.13	3261	228
Puerto Rico	3.8	432	1.7	1.4	18	8	2.1	75	77	8.86	9	26	16	3	3.07	4300	590
Romania	22.6	98	0.9	-0.3	10	12	1.4	70	55	230	43	21	29	19	2.54	453	34
Russia	147.8	9	0.6	0	11	16	1.4	64	75	16996	8	5	45	12	6	261	42
Rwanda	7	284	3.3	-0.4	39	21	6.2	39	6	24.7	47	28	10	91	0.03	46	
Saudi Arabia	19.1	9	5	4.4	38	5	6.2	70	79	2150	2	56	1	14	5.77	1539	233
Senegal	8.9	46	2.9	2.8	45	11	5.7	57	42	193	12	30	39	74	0.16	156	10
Sierra Leone	4.6	64	2.1	1.5	47	18	6.5	48	35	71.6	8	31	28	67	0.05	30	
Singapore	3.2	5246	1	2.5	16	5	1.7	79	100	0.61	2	0	5	1	9.67	41639	39552
Slovak Rep.	5.4	112	1.7	0.3	13	9	1.5	73	58	48.1	34	17	41	12	4.07	1250	102
Slovenia	2	99	0.9	0.2	8	10	1.3	75	50	20.3	14	25	54	5	3.11	4793	419
Somalia	9.9	16	3.8	1.9	44	13	7	56	27	627	2	69	26	74	0.05	26	
South Africa	42.3	35	2.3	1.6	27	12	3.9	56	57	1221	11	67	7	11	2.73	718	68
Spain	39.3	79	1.1	0	10	9	1.2	79	77	499	40	21	32	9	3.01	2890	233
Sri Lanka	18.7	289	1.7	1.2	18	6	2.3	73	22	64.6	29	7	32	47	0.16	290	2
Sudan	31	13	3	3	41	11	4.8	56	35	2376	5	46	18	68	0.06	44	

'ealth							Social Indicators								Aid	
NP 995	GNP per capita 1995	Real GDP per capita 1995	Average Annual growth of Real GNP per capita 1985-95	GDP share Agriculture 1995	GDP share Industry 1995	GDP share services 1995	HDI Human Development Index 1994	Food Intake	Population per doctor 1993	% of GNP spent on health 1990-95	% of GNP spent on education 1993-94	%o GNP spent on military 1995	Adult Illiteracy		given (*) and received per capita 1994	
'lion US $	US $	US $	%	%	%	%		calories per day	persons	%	%	%	Female %	Male %	US $	
765	14710	15680	5.2	9	37	54	0.929	3847	632	7.9	6.4	1.2	0	0	*35	Ireland
375	15920	16490	2.5	3	32	65	0.913	3050	220	4.1	6	9.2	7	3	226	Israel
085	19020	19870	1.7	3	31	66	0.921	3561	207	8.3	5.2	1.8	4	2	*37	Italy
648	660	1580	-4.3	31	20	49	0.368	2491	11739	3.4	...	1	70	50	87	Ivory Coast
303	1510	3540	3.7	9	38	53	0.736	2607	6420	5.4	4.7	0.6	11	19	43	Jamaica
587	39640	22110	2.9	2	38	60	0.94	2903	608	7	4.7	1.1	0	0	*106	Japan
354	1510	4060	-2.8	8	27	65	0.73	3022	554	7.9	3.8	6.7	21	7	127	Jordan
43	1330	3010	-8.6	12	30	58	0.709	...	254	2.2	5.4	3	4	1	2	Kazakstan
683	280	1380	0.1	29	17	54	0.463	2075	21970	1.9	6.8	2.3	30	14	42	Kenya
000	1000	4000	-8	...	...	...	0.765	2833	370	...	...	25.2	5	5	1	Korea, North
37	9700	11450	7.6	7	43	50	0.89	3285	951	5.4	4.5	3.4	2	2	1	Korea, South
58	700	1800	-6.9	44	24	32	0.635	...	303	3.5	6.8	3.5	4	1	19	Kyrgyzstan
94	350	2500	2.7	52	18	30	0.459	2259	4446	2.6	2.3	4.2	56	31	66	Laos
08	2270	3370	-6.6	9	31	60	0.711	...	278	3.7	6.5	3.2	0	0	14	Latvia
73	2660	4800	2.7	7	24	69	0.794	3317	537	5.3	2	5.3	10	5	48	Lebanon
19	770	1780	1.5	10	56	34	0.457	2201	24095	3.5	4.8	5.5	38	19	57	Lesotho
00	850	1000	1.5	...	...	...	...	1640	25000	8.2	...	4.8	78	46	23	Liberia
00	7000	6000	1	8	48	44	0.801	3308	957	...	9.6	5.5	37	12	1	Libya
70	1900	4120	-11.7	11	36	53	0.762	...	235	4.8	4.5	2.4	2	1	14	Lithuania
76	41210	37930	1	1	33	66	0.899	...	460	6.3	3.1	0.9	0	0	*148	Luxembourg
13	860	4000	-15	19	44	37	0.748	...	427	7.7	5.6	...	16	6	...	Macedonia
78	230	640	-2	34	13	53	0.35	2135	8385	1	1.9	1.1	27	12	23	Madagascar
23	170	750	-0.7	42	27	31	0.32	1825	44205	2.3	3.4	1.2	58	28	40	Malawi
21	3890	9020	5.7	13	43	44	0.832	2888	2441	1.4	5.3	4.5	22	11	6	Malaysia
10	250	550	0.6	46	17	37	0.229	2278	18376	1.3	2.1	2.4	77	61	57	Mali
70	11000	13000	5.1	3	28	69	0.887	3486	410	12.1	5.1	1.1	4	4	...	Malta
49	460	1540	0.5	27	30	43	0.355	2685	15772	1.5	...	1.9	74	50	99	Mauritania
15	3380	13210	5.7	9	33	58	0.831	...	1165	2.2	3.7	0.5	21	13	21	Mauritius
96	3320	6400	0.1	8	26	66	0.853	3146	615	5.3	5.8	0.9	13	8	4	Mexico
96	920	1600	-8.2	50	28	22	0.612	...	250	5.1	5.5	3.7	6	1	5	Moldova
67	310	1950	-3.8	21	46	33	0.661	1899	371	4.7	5.2	2.4	23	11	88	Mongolia
45	1110	3340	0.8	14	33	53	0.566	2984	4665	3.4	5.4	4.3	69	43	19	Morocco
53	80	810	3.6	33	21	46	0.281	1680	36225	4.6	6.2	3.7	77	42	66	Mozambique
98	2000	4150	2.8	14	29	57	0.57	2134	4328	7.6	8.7	2.7	26	22	125	Namibia
91	200	1170	2.4	42	22	36	0.347	1957	13634	5	2.9	1	86	59	21	Nepal
39	24000	19950	1.8	3	27	70	0.94	3222	399	8.8	5.5	2.2	0	0	*172	Netherlands
55	14340	16360	0.6	7	25	68	0.937	3669	518	7.5	7.3	1.7	1	1	*31	New Zealand
59	380	2000	-5.8	33	20	47	0.53	2293	2039	7.8	3.8	1.8	33	35	155	Nicaragua
61	220	750	-2.1	39	18	43	0.206	2257	53986	2.2	3.1	0.9	93	79	30	Niger
11	260	1220	1.2	43	27	30	0.393	2124	5208	2.7	1.3	2.9	53	33	2	Nigeria
77	31250	21940	1.6	3	36	61	0.943	3244	308	7.3	9.2	2.6	0	0	*255	Norway
78	4820	8140	0.3	3	48	49	0.718	...	1131	2.5	4.5	15.1	76	42	29	Oman
91	460	2230	1.2	26	24	50	0.445	2315	1923	0.8	2.7	6.5	76	50	6	Pakistan
35	2750	5980	-0.4	11	18	71	0.864	2242	562	7.5	5.2	1.3	10	9	19	Panama
76	1160	2420	2.1	26	38	36	0.525	2613	12754	2.8	...	1.3	37	19	88	Papua New Guinea
58	1690	3650	1.1	24	22	54	0.706	2670	1231	4.3	2.9	1.4	9	7	30	Paraguay
19	2310	3770	-1.6	7	38	55	0.717	1882	939	4.9	1.5	1.6	17	6	18	Peru
65	1050	2850	1.5	22	32	46	0.672	2257	8273	2.4	2.4	1.6	6	5	109	Philippines
29	2790	5400	-0.4	6	39	55	0.834	3301	451	4.6	5.5	2.5	2	1	40	Poland
89	9740	12670	3.7	6	40	54	0.89	3634	353	7.6	5.4	2.9	13	13	*27	Portugal
0	7500	7000	2.1	1	42	57	...	...	350	...	...	...	10	10	...	Puerto Rico
8	1480	4360	-4	21	49	30	0.748	3051	538	3.3	3.1	3.1	5	1	3	Romania
8	2240	4480	-5.1	7	38	55	0.792	...	222	4.8	4.4	7.4	3	0	12	Russia
8	180	540	-5	37	17	46	0.187	1821	24967	1.9	3.8	4.4	48	30	92	Rwanda
0	7040	9500	-1.9	6	51	43	0.774	2735	749	2.2	6.4	10.6	50	29	1	Saudi Arabia
0	600	1780	-1.2	20	18	62	0.326	2262	18192	1.6	4.2	1.9	77	57	82	Senegal
2	180	580	-3.4	42	27	31	0.176	1694	11000	1.6	1.4	5.7	82	55	45	Sierra Leone
1	26730	22770	6.2	0	36	64	0.9	...	714	3.5	3.3	5.9	14	4	6	Singapore
8	2950	3610	-2.6	6	33	61	0.873	...	287	6.3	4.9	2.8	0	0	6	Slovak Rep.
8	8200	10400	-1	5	39	56	0.886	...	500	7.9	6.2	1.5	0	0	...	Slovenia
5	500	1000	-2.3	65	9	26	...	1499	13300	1.5	0.4	0.9	52	39	61	Somalia
8	3160	5030	-1	5	31	64	0.716	2695	1500	7.9	7.1	2.9	18	18	10	South Africa
7	13580	14520	2.6	3	31	66	0.934	3708	261	7.4	4.7	1.5	6	2	*31	Spain
6	700	3250	2.7	23	25	52	0.711	2273	6843	1.9	3.2	4.9	13	7	31	Sri Lanka
0	750	1050	0.6	36	18	46	0.333	2202	10000	0.3	...	4.3	65	42	8	Sudan

	Population									Land and Agriculture					Energy	Trade	
	Population Total 1997	Population Density 1997	Average Annual Change 1970-80	Average Annual Change 1990-97	Birth Rate 1997	Death Rate 1997	Fertility Rate 1995	Life Expectancy Average 1997	Urban Population 1995	Land Area	Arable and Permanent Crops	Permanent grassland	Forest	Agriculture Population 1995	Consumption per capita 1994	Imports per capita 1995	Exports per cap 1995
	millions	persons per km²	%	%	births per thousand population	deaths per thousand population	children	years	%	thousand km²	% of land area	% of land area	% of land area	% of economically active pop.	tonnes of coal	US $	US $
Surinam	0.5	3	-0.6	1.5	24	6	2.6	70	52	156	0	0	96	20	2.01	1565	87:
Swaziland	1	55	3	3.1	43	10	4.6	58	29	17.2	11	62	7	34	...	1090	85
Sweden	8.9	22	0.3	0.7	11	11	1.7	78	84	412	7	1	68	4	6.79	7299	905
Switzerland	7.1	180	0.2	1	11	10	1.5	78	61	39.6	11	29	32	5	4.5	10938	1108
Syria	15.3	83	3.5	2.9	39	6	4.8	67	52	184	30	45	3	33	1.28	325	28
Taiwan	21.7	603	2	0.9	15	6	1.8	76	76	36	26	11	52	19	2.5	4868	523
Tajikistan	6	42	3	1.8	34	8	4.2	65	32	143	6	25	4	38	0.58	93	8
Tanzania	31.2	35	3.4	2.8	41	20	5.8	42	24	884	4	40	38	83	0.04	55	2
Thailand	60.8	119	2.7	0.9	17	7	1.8	69	19	511	41	2	26	60	1.07	1236	94
Togo	4.5	82	2.6	3.4	46	10	6.4	58	31	54.4	45	4	17	62	0.08	94	5
Trinidad & Tobago	1.3	253	1.1	0.2	16	7	2.1	70	70	5.13	24	2	46	9	7.53	1329	190
Tunisia	9.2	59	2.2	1.9	24	5	2.9	73	57	155	32	20	4	24	0.75	886	61
Turkey	63.5	83	2.3	1.1	22	5	2.7	72	65	770	36	16	26	51	1.16	579	35
Turkmenistan	4.8	10	2.7	3.9	29	9	3.8	62	47	488	3	64	9	36	3.68	250	53
Uganda	20.8	104	3	2.4	45	21	6.7	40	12	200	34	9	32	83	0.03	50	2
Ukraine	51.5	85	0.6	-0.1	12	15	1.5	67	69	604	59	13	18	18	4.39	192	18
United Kingdom	58.6	243	0.1	0.3	13	11	1.7	77	90	242	25	46	10	2	5.33	4527	413
United States	268	28	1.1	1	15	9	2.1	76	77	9573	20	25	30	3	11.39	2929	222
Uruguay	3.3	19	0.4	0.7	17	9	2.2	75	90	175	7	77	5	14	0.78	899	66
Uzbekistan	23.8	56	2.9	2.1	29	8	3.7	65	42	425	11	50	3	34	2.94	111	13
Venezuela	22.5	26	3.5	1.9	24	5	3.1	72	92	882	4	20	34	11	3.75	553	85
Vietnam	77.1	237	2.3	2.1	22	7	3.1	67	20	325	21	1	30	69	0.16	30	3
Yemen	16.5	31	1.9	5.6	45	9	7.4	60	34	528	3	30	4	57	0.33	165	7
Yugoslavia	10.5	103	1	0.3	14	10	1.9	72	54	102	40	21	26	20	1.22	533	45
Zambia	9.5	13	3.2	2.4	44	24	5.7	45	45	743	7	40	43	74	0.19	12	9
Zimbabwe	12.1	31	3.1	3.7	32	19	3.8	60	32	387	7	44	23	67	0.7	231	18

	Land area thousand sq km	Population 1997 thousands		Land area thousand sq km	Population 1997 thousands		Land area thousand sq km
American Samoa	0.2	62	French Polynesia	3.66	226	Pitcairn I.	0.05
Andorra	0.45	75	Gaza Strip	0.36	900	Qatar	11
Anguilla	0.1	10	Gibraltar	0.01	28	Réunion	2.5
Antigua & Barbuda	0.44	66	Greenland	342	57	St Kitts-Nevis	0.36
Aruba	0.19	70	Grenada	0.34	99	St Helena	0.3
Ascension I.	0.09	1.1	Guadeloupe	1.69	440	St Lucia	0.61
Bahrain	0.68	605	Guam	0.55	161	St Pierre & Miquelon	0.23
Belize	22.8	228	Kiribati	0.73	85	St Vincent & the Grenadines	0.39
Bermuda	0.05	65	Kuwait	17.8	2050	San Marino	0.06
Bhutan	47	1790	Liechtenstein	0.16	32	São Tomé & Principe	0.96
British Virgin Is.	0.15	13	Macau	0.02	450	Seychelles	0.45
Brunei	5.27	300	Maldives	0.3	275	Solomon Is.	28
Cape Verde Is.	4.03	410	Marshall Is.	0.18	60	Svalbard	63
Cayman Is.	0.26	35	Martinique	1.06	405	Tokelau	0.01
Cocos Is.	0.01	1	Mayotte	0.37	105	Tonga	0.72
Comoros	2.23	630	Micronesia	0.7	127	Turks & Caicos Is.	0.43
Cook Is.	0.23	20	Monaco	0.002	33	Tuvalu	0.03
Djibouti	23.2	650	Montserrat	0.1	12	United Arab Emirates	83.6
Dominica	0.75	78	Nauru	0.02	53	US Virgin Is.	0.34
Equatorial Guinea	28.1	420	Netherlands Antilles	0.8	12	Vanuatu	12.2
Eritrea	101	3500	New Caledonia	18.3	210	Vatican City	0.0004
Falkland Is.	12.2	2	Niue	0.26	192	Wallis & Futuna Is.	0.2
Faroe Is.	1.4	45	Norfolk I.	0.04	2	West Bank	5.9
Fiji	18.3	800	Northern Marianas	0.48	2	Western Sahara	267
French Guiana	88.2	155	Palau	0.49	17	Western Samoa	2.83

ealth							Social Indicators								Aid	
NP 1995	GNP per capita 1995	Real GDP per capita 1995	Average Annual growth of Real GNP per capita 1985-95	GDP share Agriculture 1995	GDP share Industry 1995	GDP share services 1995	HDI Human Development Index 1994	Food Intake	Population per doctor 1993	% of GNP spent on health 1990-95	% of GNP spent on education 1993-94	%o GNP spent on military 1995	Adult Illiteracy		given (*) and received per capita 1994	
lion US $	US $	US $	%	%	%	%		calories per day	persons	%	%	%	Female %	Male %	US $	
360	880	2250	0.7	22	23	55	0.792	2547	1200	2.9	3.6	3.9	9	5	183	Surinam
)51	1170	2880	0.6	10	25	65	0.582	2706	9250	7.2	6.8	...	24	22	59	Swaziland
720	23750	18540	-0.1	2	32	66	0.936	2972	394	7.7	8.4	2.9	0	0	*189	Sweden
)14	40630	25860	0.2	3	32	65	0.93	3379	580	9.6	5.6	1.9	0	0	*135	Switzerland
780	1120	5320	1	18	43	39	0.755	3175	1159	2.1	4.2	6.8	44	14	25	Syria
)00	12000	13000	7	3	42	55	...	3048	800	4.3		4.8	10	3	...	Taiwan
976	340	920	-13	27	45	28	0.58	...	424	6.4	9.5	6.9	3	1	5	Tajikistan
703	120	640	0.9	58	17	25	0.357	2018	22000	2.8	5	2.7	43	21	30	Tanzania
530	2740	7540	8.4	11	40	49	0.833	2432	4416	5.3	3.8	2.5	8	4	15	Thailand
266	310	1130	-2.8	38	21	41	0.365	2242	11385	1.7	6.1	2.5	63	33	47	Togo
351	3770	8610	-1.6	3	42	55	0.88	2585	1520	3.9	4.5	1.3	3	1	20	Trinidad & Tobago
369	1820	5000	1.8	12	29	59	0.748	3330	1549	5.9	6.3	2	45	21	8	Tunisia
152	2780	5580	2.2	16	31	53	0.772	3429	976	4.2	3.3	3.6	28	8	5	Turkey
25	920	3500	-9.6	31	31	38	0.723	...	306	2.8	7.9	1.9	3	1	3	Turkmenistan
68	240	1470	2.8	50	14	36	0.328	2159	22399	3.9	1.9	2.6	50	26	43	Uganda
84	1630	2400	-9.2	18	42	40	0.689	...	227	5.4	8.2	3	3	0	5	Ukraine
34	18700	19260	1.4	2	32	66	0.931	3317	300	6.9	5.4	3.1	0	0	*53	United Kingdom
07	26980	26980	1.4	2	26	72	0.942	3732	421	14.3	5.5	3.8	5	4	*33	United States
58	5170	6630	3.3	9	26	65	0.883	2750	500	8.5	2.5	2.6	2	3	26	Uruguay
79	970	2370	-3.9	33	34	33	0.662	...	282	3.5	11	3.6	4	1	1	Uzbekistan
82	3020	7900	0.5	5	38	57	0.861	2618	633	7.1	5.1	1.1	10	8	4	Venezuela
34	240	1200	4.2	28	30	42	0.557	2250	2279	5.2	...	4.3	9	4	8	Vietnam
44	260	850	3.1	22	27	51	0.361	2203	4498	2.6	4.6	3.9	74	47	13	Yemen
50	1400	4000	1.8	26	36	38	...	...	232	5.1	...	...	11	2	...	Yugoslavia
05	400	930	-1	22	40	38	0.369	1931	10917	3.3	2.6	1.9	29	14	221	Zambia
33	540	2030	-0.6	15	36	49	0.513	1985	7384	2.1	8.3	4.2	20	10	45	Zimbabwe

igures for Luxembourg are included in those gium.

ergy, the figures for South Africa include those swana, Lesotho, Swaziland and Namibia.

n ... means that figures are not available.

ation Total. This is an estimate for the mid-997.

ation Density. This is the total population l by the land area, both quoted in the table.

ation Change. This shows the average percentage change for the two periods, 0 and 1990-97.

and Death Rates and Life Expectancy. are estimates from the US Census Bureau. th and Death rates are the number of those nces per year, per thousand population. Life ancy is the number of years that a child born an expect to live if the levels of mortality of ast throughout its life. The figure is the e of that for men and women.

y Rate. This is the average number of n born to a woman in her lifetime.

Population. This is the percentage of the pulation living in urban areas. The definition n is that of the individual nations and often s quite small towns.

Land Area. This is the total area of the country less the area covered by major lakes and rivers.

Arable Land and Permanent Crops. This excludes fallow land but includes temporary pasture.

Forest and Woodland. This includes natural and planted woodland and land recently cleared of timber which will be replanted.

Agricultural Population. This is the percentage of the economically active population working in agriculture. It includes those working in forestry, hunting and fishing.

Energy. All forms of energy have been expressed in an approximate equivalent of tonnes of coal per person.

Trade. The trade figures are for 1994 or 1995. In a few cases the figure is older than this but is the latest available. The total Import and Export figures have been divided by the population to give a figure in US $ per capita.

Gross National Product (GNP). This figure is an estimate of the value of a country's production and the average production per person for 1995, in US $. The GNP measures the value of goods and services produced in a country, plus the balance, positive or negative, of income from abroad, for example, from investments, interest on capital, money returned from workers abroad, etc. The Gross Domestic Product (GDP), is the GNP less the foreign balances. The adjoining three columns show the percentage contribution to the GDP made by the

agricultural, mining and manufacturing and service sectors of the economy. The average annual rate of change is for the GNP per capita in PPP $ during the period 1985-95

Real GDP per capita. Using official exchange rates to convert national currencies into US $ makes no attempt to reflect the varying domestic purchasing powers of the local currency. The UN has made these estimates of Real GDP taking into account these local purchasing values and they are called Purchasing Power Parity $.

Human Development Index. This is a calculation made by the UN Development Programme, using 1994 data and takes into account not only national income, but also life expectancy, adult literacy and the years in education. It is a measure of national human progress. The wealthy developed countries have an index approaching 1, and the figures range down to some of the poorer with an index of less than 0.1.

Food Intake. The figures are the average intake per person in calories per day. They are for 1992 and are the latest estimates that are available.

Adult Illiteracy. This is the percentage of the male and female population aged 15 and over who cannot read or write a simple sentence.

Aid. The bulk of the table is concerned with aid received but aid given is shown by an asterisk.

To convert square kilometres to square miles multiply by 0.39.

AZIMUTHAL OR ZENITHAL PROJECTIONS

These are constructed by the projection of part of the graticule from the globe onto a plane tangential to any single point on it. This plane may be tangential to the equator (equatorial case), the poles (polar case) or any other point (oblique case). Any straight line drawn from the point at which the plane touches the globe is the shortest distance from that point and is known as a great circle. In its Gnomonic construction any straight line on the map is a great circle, but there is great exaggeration towards the edges and this reduces its general uses. There are five different ways of transferring the graticule onto the plane and these are shown below. The diagrams below also show how the graticules vary, using the polar case as the example.

Equidistant	Equal-Area	Orthographic	Gnomonic	Stereographic (conformal)

Polar Case

The polar case is the simplest to construct and the diagram on the right shows the differing effects of all five methods of construction comparing their coverage, distortion etc., using North America as the example.

Oblique Case

The plane touches the globe at any point between the equator and poles. The oblique orthographic uses the distortion in azimuthal projections away from the centre to give a graphic depiction of the earth as seen from any desired point in space.

Equatorial Case

The example shown here is Lambert's Equivalent Azimuthal. It is the only projection which is both equal area and where bearing is true from the centre.

MAP PROJECTIONS

A map projection is the systematic depiction of the imaginary grid of lines of latitude and longitude from a globe onto a flat surface. The grid of lines is called the graticule and it can be constructed either by graphical means or by mathematical formulae to form the basis of a map. As a globe is three dimensional it is not possible to depict its surface on a flat map without some form of distortion. Preservation of one of the basic properties listed below can only be secured at the expense of the others and the choice of projection is often a compromise solution.

Correct Area
In these projections the areas from the globe are to scale on the map. This is particularly useful in the mapping of densities and distributions. Projections with this property are termed Equal Area, Equivalent or Homolographic.

Correct Distance
In these projections the scale is correct along the meridians, or in the case of the Azimuthal Equidistant scale is true along any line drawn from the centre of the projection. They are called Equidistant.

Correct Shape
This property can only be true within small areas as it is achieved only by having a uniform scale distortion along both x and y axes of the projection. The projections are called Conformal or Orthomorphic.

Map projections can be divided into three broad categories - azimuthal, conic and cylindrical. Cartographers use different projections from these categories depending on the map scale, the size of the area to be mapped, and what they want the map to show.

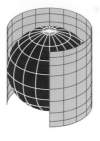

CONICAL PROJECTIONS

These use the projection of the graticule from the globe onto a cone which is tangential to a line of latitude (termed the standard parallel). This line is always an arc and scale is always true along it. Because of its method of construction it is used mainly for depicting the temperate latitudes around the standard parallel i.e. where there is least distortion. To reduce the distortion and include a larger range of latitudes, the projection may be constructed with the cone bisecting the surface of the globe so that there are two standard parallels each of which is true to scale. The distortion is thus spread more evenly between the two chosen parallels.

Simple Conical with one standard parallel

Bonne
This is a modification of the simple conic whereby the true scale along the meridians is sacrificed to enable the accurate representation of areas. However scale is true along each parallel but shapes are distorted at the edges.

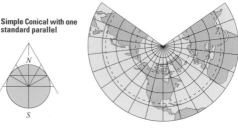

Albers Conical Equal Area
This projection uses two standard parallels. The selection of these relative to the land area to be mapped is very important. It is equal area and is especially useful for large land masses oriented East-West, for example the U.S.A.

CYLINDRICAL AND OTHER WORLD PROJECTIONS

This group of projections are those which permit the whole of the Earth's surface to be depicted on one map. They are a very large group of projections and the following are only a few of them. Cylindrical projections are constructed by the projection of the graticule from the globe onto a cylinder tangential to the globe. Although cylindrical projections can depict all the main land masses, there is considerable distortion of shape and area towards the poles. One cylindrical projection, Mercator overcomes this shortcoming by possesing the unique navigational property that any straight line drawn on it is a line of constant bearing (loxodrome). It is used for maps and charts between 15° either side of the equator. Beyond this enlargement of area is a serious drawback, although it is used for navigational charts at all latitudes.

Simple Cylindrical		Cylindrical with two standard parallels	

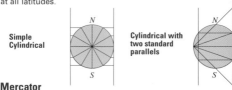

Mercator

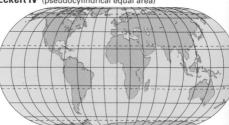

Eckert IV (pseudocylindrical equal area)

Hammer (polyconic equal area)

INDEX TO WORLD MAPS

The index contains the names of all the principal places and features shown on the World Maps. Each name is followed by an additional entry in italics giving the country or region within which it is located. The alphabetical order of names composed of two or more words is governed primarily by the first word and then by the second. This is an example of the rule:

New South Wales □, *Australia*.. **34 G8**   33 0S   146 0E
New York □, *U.S.A.* **43 D10** 42 40N   76 0W
New York City, *U.S.A.* **43 E11** 40 45N   74 0W
New Zealand ■, *Oceania*............. **35 J13** 40 0S   176 0E
Newark, *U.S.A.* **43 F10** 39 42N 75 45W

Physical features composed of a proper name (Erie) and a description (Lake) are positioned alphabetically by the proper name. The description is positioned after the proper name and is usually abbreviated:

Erie, L., *N. Amer.* **42 D7**   42 15N   81 0W

Where a description forms part of a settlement or administrative name, however, it is always written in full and put in its true alphabetical position:

Mount Isa, *Australia*...................... **34 E6**   20 42S   139 26E

Names beginning with M' and Mc are indexed as if they were spelt Mac. Names beginning St. are alphabetized under Saint, but Santa and San are all spelt in full and are alphabetized accordingly. If the same placename occurs two or more times in the index and all are in the same country, each is followed by the name of the administrative subdivision in which it is located.   The names are placed in the alphabetical order of the subdivision. For example:

Columbus, Ga., *U.S.A.* **41 D10** 32 30N 84 58W
Columbus, Ind., *U.S.A.* **42 F5** 39 14N 85 55W
Columbus, Ohio, *U.S.A.* **42 F6** 39 57N   83 1W

The number in bold type which follows each name in the index refers to the number of the map page where that feature or place will be found. This is usually the largest scale at which the place or feature appears.

The letter and figure which are in bold type immediately after the page number give the grid square on the map page, within which the feature is situated. The letter represents the latitude and the figure the longitude. In some cases the feature itself may fall within the specified square, while the name is outside.

For a more precise location, the geographical co-ordinates which follow the letter-figure references give the latitude and the longitude of each place. The first set of figures represent the latitude, which is the distance north or south of the Equator measured as an angle at the centre of the Earth. The Equator is latitude 0°, the North Pole is 90°N, and the South Pole 90°S.

The second set of figures represent the longitude, which is the distance east or west of the prime meridian, which runs through Greenwich, England. Longitude is also measured as an angle at the centre of the Earth and is given east or west of the prime meridian, from 0° to 180° in either direction.

The unit of measurement for latitude and longitude is the degree, which is subdivided into 60 minutes. Each index entry states the position of a place in degrees and minutes, a space being left between the degrees and the minutes. The latitude is followed by N(orth) or S(outh) and the longitude by E(ast) or W(est).

Rivers are indexed to their mouths or confluences, and carry the symbol ⤳ after their names. A solid square ■ follows the name of a country, while an open square □ refers to a first order administrative area.

ABBREVIATIONS USED IN THE INDEX

Afghan. – Afghanistan
Ala. – Alabama
Alta. – Alberta
Amer. – America(n)
Arch. – Archipelago
Ariz. – Arizona
Ark. – Arkansas
Atl. Oc. – Atlantic Ocean
B. – Baie, Bahia, Bay, Bucht, Bugt
B.C. – British Columbia
Bangla. – Bangladesh
C. – Cabo, Cap, Cape, Coast
C.A.R. – Central African Republic
C. Prov. – Cape Province
Calif. – California
Cent. – Central
Chan. – Channel
Colo. – Colorado

Conn. – Connecticut
Cord. – Cordillera
Cr. – Creek
D.C. – District of Columbia
Del. – Delaware
Domin. – Dominica
Dom. Rep. – Dominican Republic
E. – East
El Salv. – El Salvador
Eq. Guin. – Equatorial Guinea
Fla. – Florida
Falk. Is. – Falkland Is.
G. – Golfe, Golfo, Gulf
Ga. – Georgia
Guinea-Biss. – Guinea–Bissau
Hd. – Head
Hts. – Heights
I.(s). – Ile, Ilha, Insel,

Isla, Island, Isle(s)
Ill. – Illinois
Ind. – Indiana
Ind. Oc. – Indian Ocean
Ivory C. – Ivory Coast
Kans. – Kansas
Ky. – Kentucky
L. – Lac, Lacul, Lago, Lagoa, Lake, Limni, Loch, Lough
La. – Louisiana
Lux. – Luxembourg
Madag. – Madagascar
Man. – Manitoba
Mass. – Massachusetts
Md. – Maryland
Me. – Maine
Medit. S. – Mediterranean Sea
Mich. – Michigan
Minn. – Minnesota
Miss. – Mississippi

Mo. – Missouri
Mont. – Montana
Mozam.– Mozambique
Mt.(s).– Mont, Monte, Monti, Montaña, Mountain
N. – Nord, Norte, North, Northern
N.B. – New Brunswick
N.C. – North Carolina
N. Cal. – New Caledonia
N. Dak. – North Dakota
N.H. – New Hampshire
N.J. – New Jersey
N. Mex. – New Mexico
N.S. – Nova Scotia
N.S.W. – New South Wales
N.W.T. – North West Territory
N.Y. – New York
N.Z. – New Zealand

Nebr. – Nebraska
Neths. – Netherlands
Nev. – Nevada
Nfld. – Newfoundland
Nic. – Nicaragua

Okla. – Oklahoma
Ont. – Ontario
Oreg. – Oregon
P.E.I. – Prince Edward Island
Pa. – Pennsylvania
Pac. Oc. – Pacific Ocean
Papua N.G. – Papua New Guinea
Pen. – Peninsula, Peninsule
Phil. – Philippines
Pk. – Park, Peak
Plat. – Plateau
Prov. – Province,

Provincial
Pt. – Point
Pta. – Ponta, Punta
Pte. – Pointe
Qué. – Québec
Queens. – Queensland
R. – Rio, River
R.I. – Rhode Island
Ra.(s). – Range(s)
Reg. – Region
Rep. – Republic
Res. – Reserve, Reservoir
S. – San, South
Si. Arabia – Saudi Arabia
S.C. – South Carolina
S. Dak. – South Dakota
S. Leone – Sierra Leone
Sa. – Serra, Sierra
Sask. – Saskatchewan
Scot. – Scotland
Sd. – Sound

Sib. – Siberia
St. – Saint, Sankt, Sint
Str. – Strait, Stretto
Switz. – Switzerland
Tas. – Tasmania
Tenn. – Tennessee
Tex. – Texas
Trin. & Tob. – Trinidad & Tobago
U.A.E. – United Arab Emirates
U.K. – United Kingdom
U.S.A. – United States of America
Va. – Virginia
Vic. – Victoria
Vol. – Volcano
Vt. – Vermont
W. – West
W. Va. – West Virginia
Wash. – Washington
Wis. – Wisconsin

88 INDEX TO WORLD MAPS

Aachen — Banda Aceh

A

Aachen, *Germany* **10 C4** 50 45N 6 6 E
Aalborg, *Denmark* **6 G9** 57 2N 9 54 E
Aarau, *Switz.* **10 E5** 47 23N 8 4 E
Aare ➝, *Switz.* **10 E5** 47 33N 8 14 E
Aarhus, *Denmark* **6 G10** 56 8N 10 11 E
Abadan, *Iran* **24 B3** 30 22N 48 20 E
Abbeville, *France* **8 A4** 50 6N 1 49 E
Abéché, *Chad* **29 F9** 13 50N 20 35 E
Abeokuta, *Nigeria* **30 C2** 7 3N 3 19 E
Aberdeen, *U.K.* **7 C5** 57 9N 2 5W
Abidjan, *Ivory C.* **28 G4** 5 26N 3 58W
Abitibi L., *Canada* **42 A8** 48 40N 79 40W
Abkhazia □, *Georgia* **15 F7** 43 12N 41 5 E
Abohar, *India* **23 D5** 30 10N 74 10 E
Abu Dhabi, *U.A.E.* **24 C4** 24 28N 54 22 E
Abuja, *Nigeria* **30 C3** 9 16N 7 2 E
Acapulco, *Mexico* **44 D5** 16 51N 99 56W
Accomac, *U.S.A.* **43 G10** 37 43N 75 40W
Accra, *Ghana* **30 C1** 5 35N 0 6W
Acklins I., *Bahamas* **45 C10** 22 30N 74 0W
Aconcagua, *Argentina* **47 F3** 32 39S 70 0W
Acre □, *Brazil* **46 C2** 9 1S 71 0W
Adamawa Highlands, *Cameroon* **29 G7** 7 20N 12 20 E
Adana, *Turkey* **15 G6** 37 0N 35 16 E
Adapazarı, *Turkey* **15 F5** 40 48N 30 25 E
Addis Ababa, *Ethiopia* **29 G12** 9 2N 38 42 E
Adelaide, *Australia* **34 G6** 34 52S 138 30 E
Adelaide, *S. Africa* **31 C4** 32 42S 26 20 E
Aden, *Yemen* **24 D3** 12 45N 45 0 E
Aden, G. of, *Asia* **24 D3** 12 30N 47 30 E
Adirondack Mts., *U.S.A.* **43 D10** 44 0N 74 0W
Admiralty Is., *Papua N. G.* **36 H6** 2 0S 147 0 E
Ado-Ekiti, *Nigeria* **30 C3** 7 38N 5 12 E
Adoni, *India* **25 D6** 15 33N 77 18 E
Adour ➝, *France* **8 E3** 43 32N 1 32W
Adrar, *Algeria* **28 C4** 27 51N 0 11W
Adrian, *U.S.A.* **42 E5** 41 54N 84 2W
Adriatic Sea, *Medit. S.* **12 C6** 43 0N 16 0 E
Ægean Sea, *Medit. S.* **13 E11** 38 30N 25 0 E
Afghanistan ■, *Asia* **24 B5** 33 0N 65 0 E
'Afif, *Si. Arabia* **24 C3** 23 53N 42 56 E
Agadès, *Niger* **30 A3** 16 58N 7 59 E
Agadir, *Morocco* **28 B3** 30 28N 9 55W
Agartala, *India* **23 H13** 23 50N 91 23 E
Agen, *France* **8 D4** 44 12N 0 38 E
Agra, *India* **23 F6** 27 17N 77 58 E
Agrigento, *Italy* **12 F5** 37 19N 13 34 E
Aguascalientes, *Mexico* **44 C4** 21 53N 102 12W
Agulhas, C., *S. Africa* **31 C3** 34 52S 20 0 E
Ahmadabad, *India* **23 H4** 23 0N 72 40 E
Ahmadnagar, *India* **25 D6** 19 7N 74 46 E
Ahmadpur, *Pakistan* **23 E3** 29 12N 71 10 E
Ahvaz, *Iran* **24 B3** 31 20N 48 40 E
Ahvenanmaa Is., *Finland* **6 F11** 60 15N 20 0 E
Aïr, *Niger* **28 E6** 18 30N 8 0 E
Aisne ➝, *France* **8 B5** 49 26N 2 50 E
Aix-en-Provence, *France* **8 E6** 43 32N 5 27 E
Aix-les-Bains, *France* **8 D6** 45 41N 5 53 E
Ajaccio, *France* **8 F8** 41 55N 8 40 E
Ajanta Ra., *India* **23 J5** 20 28N 75 50 E
Ajaria □, *Georgia* **15 F7** 41 30N 42 0 E
Ajmer, *India* **23 F5** 26 28N 74 37 E
Akashi, *Japan* **19 B4** 34 45N 134 58 E
Akita, *Japan* **19 A7** 39 45N 140 7 E
Akola, *India* **23 J6** 20 42N 77 2 E
Akranes, *Iceland* **6 B2** 64 19N 22 5W
Akron, *U.S.A.* **42 E7** 41 5N 81 31W
Aktyubinsk, *Kazakstan* **15 D10** 50 17N 57 10 E
Akure, *Nigeria* **30 C3** 7 15N 5 5 E
Akureyri, *Iceland* **6 B4** 65 40N 18 6W
Al Ḥudaydah, *Yemen* **24 D3** 14 50N 43 0 E
Al Hufūf, *Si. Arabia* **24 C3** 25 25N 49 45 E
Al Jawf, *Si. Arabia* **24 C2** 29 55N 39 40 E
Al Kut, *Iraq* **24 B3** 32 30N 46 0 E
Al Qatif, *Si. Arabia* **24 C3** 26 35N 50 0 E
Al 'Ula, *Si. Arabia* **24 C2** 26 35N 38 0 E
Alabama □, *U.S.A.* **41 D9** 33 0N 87 0W
Aland Is. = Ahvenanmaa Is., *Finland* **6 F11** 60 15N 20 0 E
Alaska □, *U.S.A.* **38 B5** 64 0N 154 0W
Alaska, G. of, *Pac. Oc.* **38 C5** 58 0N 145 0W
Alaska Peninsula, *U.S.A.* **38 C4** 56 0N 159 0W
Alaska Range, *U.S.A.* **38 B4** 62 50N 151 0W
Alba-Iulia, *Romania* **11 E12** 46 8N 23 39 E
Albacete, *Spain* **9 C5** 39 0N 1 50W
Albania ■, *Europe* **13 D9** 41 0N 20 0 E
Albany, *Australia* **34 H2** 35 1S 117 58 E
Albany, *Ga., U.S.A.* **41 D10** 31 35N 84 10W
Albany, *N.Y., U.S.A.* **43 D11** 42 39N 73 45W
Albany ➝, *Canada* **39 C11** 52 17N 81 31W
Albert L., *Africa* **32 D6** 1 30N 31 0 E
Alberta □, *Canada* **38 C8** 54 40N 115 0W
Albertville, *France* **8 D7** 45 40N 6 22 E
Albi, *France* **8 E5** 43 56N 2 9 E
Albion, *U.S.A.* **42 D5** 42 15N 84 45W
Albuquerque, *U.S.A.* **40 C5** 35 5N 106 39W
Albury, *Australia* **34 H8** 36 3S 146 56 E
Alcalá de Henares, *Spain* **9 B4** 40 28N 3 22W
Aldabra Is., *Seychelles* **27 G8** 9 22S 46 28 E
Aldan ➝, *Russia* **18 C14** 63 28N 129 35 E
Aleksandrovsk-Sakhalinskiy, *Russia* **18 D16** 50 50N 142 20 E
Alençon, *France* **8 B4** 48 27N 0 4 E
Alès, *France* **8 D6** 44 9N 4 5 E
Alessándria, *Italy* **12 B3** 44 54N 8 37 E
Ålesund, *Norway* **6 F9** 62 28N 6 12 E
Aleutian Is., *Pac. Oc.* **36 B10** 52 0N 175 0W
Alexander Arch., *U.S.A.* **38 C6** 56 0N 136 0W
Alexandria, *Egypt* **29 B10** 31 13N 29 58 E
Alexandria, *La., U.S.A.* **41 D8** 31 18N 92 27W
Alexandria, *Va., U.S.A.* **42 F9** 38 48N 77 3W
Algarve, *Portugal* **9 D1** 36 58N 8 20W
Algeciras, *Spain* **9 D3** 36 9N 5 28W
Algeria ■, *Africa* **28 C5** 28 30N 2 0 E
Algiers, *Algeria* **28 A5** 36 42N 3 8 E
Alicante, *Spain* **9 C5** 38 23N 0 30W
Alice Springs, *Australia* **34 E5** 23 40S 133 50 E
Aligarh, *India* **23 F7** 27 55N 78 10 E
Alipur Duar, *India* **23 F12** 26 30N 89 35 E
Aliquippa, *U.S.A.* **42 E7** 40 37N 80 15W
Aliwal North, *S. Africa* **31 C4** 30 45S 26 45 E
Alkmaar, *Neths.* **10 B3** 52 37N 4 45 E
Allahabad, *India* **23 G8** 25 25N 81 58 E
Allegan, *U.S.A.* **42 D5** 42 32N 85 51W
Allegheny ➝, *U.S.A.* **42 E8** 40 27N 80 1W
Allegheny Plateau, *U.S.A.* **42 G7** 38 0N 80 0W
Allentown, *U.S.A.* **43 E10** 40 37N 75 29W
Alleppey, *India* **25 E6** 9 30N 76 28 E
Allier ➝, *France* **8 C5** 46 57N 3 4 E
Alma, *U.S.A.* **42 D5** 43 23N 84 39W
Almaty, *Kazakstan* **18 E9** 43 15N 76 57 E
Almelo, *Neths.* **10 B4** 52 22N 6 42 E
Almería, *Spain* **9 D4** 36 52N 2 27W
Alor, *Indonesia* **22 D4** 8 15S 124 30 E
Alpena, *U.S.A.* **42 C6** 45 4N 83 27W
Alps, *Europe* **10 E5** 46 30N 9 30 E
Alsace, *France* **8 B7** 48 15N 7 25 E
Altai, *Mongolia* **20 B4** 46 40N 92 45 E
Altay, *China* **20 B3** 47 48N 88 10 E
Altoona, *U.S.A.* **42 E8** 40 31N 78 24W
Altun Shan, *China* **20 C3** 38 30N 88 0 E
Alwar, *India* **23 F6** 27 38N 76 34 E
Amadjuak L., *Canada* **39 B12** 65 0N 71 8W
Amagasaki, *Japan* **19 B4** 34 42N 135 20 E
Amarillo, *U.S.A.* **40 C6** 35 13N 101 50W
Amazon ➝, *S. Amer.* **46 C4** 0 5S 50 0W
Ambala, *India* **23 D6** 30 23N 76 56 E
Ambikapur, *India* **23 H9** 23 15N 83 15 E
Ambon, *Indonesia* **22 D4** 3 35S 128 20 E
American Samoa □, *Pac. Oc.* **35 C17** 14 20S 170 40W
Amiens, *France* **8 B5** 49 54N 2 16 E
Amman, *Jordan* **24 B2** 31 57N 35 52 E
Amos, *Canada* **42 A8** 48 35N 78 5W
Amravati, *India* **23 J6** 20 55N 77 45 E
Amreli, *India* **23 J3** 21 35N 71 17 E
Amritsar, *India* **23 D5** 31 35N 74 57 E
Amroha, *India* **23 E7** 28 53N 78 30 E
Amsterdam, *Neths.* **10 B3** 52 23N 4 54 E
Amsterdam, *U.S.A.* **43 D10** 42 56N 74 11W
Amudarya ➝, *Uzbekistan* **18 E7** 43 58N 59 34 E
Amundsen Gulf, *Canada* **38 A7** 71 0N 124 0W
Amundsen Sea, *Antarctica* **48 E1** 72 0S 115 0W
Amur ➝, *Russia* **18 D16** 52 56N 141 10 E
An Najaf, *Iraq* **24 B3** 32 3N 44 15 E
An Nasiriyah, *Iraq* **24 B3** 31 0N 46 15 E
An Nhon, *Vietnam* **22 B2** 13 55N 109 7 E
Anadyr, *Russia* **18 C19** 64 35N 177 20 E
Anadyr, G. of, *Russia* **18 C20** 64 0N 180 0 E
Anaheim, *U.S.A.* **40 D3** 33 50N 117 55W
Anambas Is., *Indonesia* **22 C2** 3 20N 106 30 E
Anantnag, *India* **23 C5** 33 45N 75 10 E
Anar, *Iran* **24 B4** 30 55N 55 13 E
Anatolia, *Turkey* **15 G5** 39 0N 30 0 E
Anchorage, *U.S.A.* **38 B5** 61 13N 149 54W
Ancona, *Italy* **12 C5** 43 38N 13 30 E
Anda, *China* **21 B7** 46 24N 125 19 E
Andalucía □, *Spain* **9 D3** 37 35N 5 0W
Andaman Is., *Ind. Oc.* **25 D8** 12 30N 92 30 E
Anderson, *U.S.A.* **42 E5** 40 10N 85 41W
Andes, *S. Amer.* **46 E3** 20 0S 68 0W
Andhra Pradesh □, *India* **25 D6** 18 0N 79 0 E
Andorra ■, *Europe* **9 A6** 42 30N 1 30 E
Andreanof Is., *U.S.A.* **38 C2** 52 0N 178 0W
Ándria, *Italy* **12 D7** 41 13N 16 17 E
Andros I., *Bahamas* **45 C9** 24 30N 78 0W
Angara ➝, *Russia* **18 D11** 58 5N 94 20 E
Ånge, *Sweden* **6 F11** 62 31N 15 35 E
Angel Falls, *Venezuela* **46 B3** 5 57N 62 30W
Angerman ➝, *Sweden* **6 F11** 62 40N 18 0 E
Angers, *France* **8 C3** 47 30N 0 35W
Anglesey, *U.K.* **7 E4** 53 17N 4 20W
Angola ■, *Africa* **33 G3** 12 0S 18 0 E
Angoulême, *France* **8 D4** 45 39N 0 10 E
Angoumois, *France* **8 D3** 45 50N 0 25 E
Anguilla ■, *W. Indies* **44 J18** 18 14N 63 5W
Anhui □, *China* **21 C6** 32 0N 117 0 E
Anjou, *France* **8 C3** 47 20N 0 15W
Ankara, *Turkey* **15 G5** 39 57N 32 54 E
Ann, C., *U.S.A.* **43 D12** 42 38N 70 35W
Ann Arbor, *U.S.A.* **42 D6** 42 17N 83 45W
Annaba, *Algeria* **28 A6** 36 50N 7 46 E
Annapolis, *U.S.A.* **42 F9** 38 59N 76 30W
Annecy, *France* **8 D7** 45 55N 6 8 E
Annobón, *Atl. Oc.* **27 G4** 1 25S 5 36 E
Anshun, *China* **20 D5** 26 18N 105 57 E
Antalya, *Turkey* **15 G5** 36 52N 30 45 E
Antananarivo, *Madag.* **33 H9** 18 55S 47 31 E
Antarctic Pen., *Antarctica* **48 D4** 67 0S 60 0W
Antibes, *France* **8 E7** 43 34N 7 6 E
Anticosti I., *Canada* **43 A16** 49 30N 63 0W
Antigua & Barbuda ■, *W. Indies* **44 K20** 17 20N 61 48W
Antofagasta, *Chile* **47 E2** 23 50S 70 30W
Antsiranana, *Madag.* **33 G9** 12 25S 49 20 E
Antwerp, *Belgium* **10 C3** 51 13N 4 25 E
Anyang, *China* **21 C6** 36 5N 114 21 E
Aomori, *Japan* **19 F12** 40 45N 140 45 E
Aparri, *Phil.* **22 B4** 18 22N 121 38 E
Apeldoorn, *Neths.* **10 B3** 52 13N 5 57 E
Apennines, *Italy* **12 B4** 44 0N 10 0 E
Apia, *W. Samoa* **35 C16** 13 50S 171 50W
Appalachian Mts., *U.S.A.* **42 G7** 38 0N 80 0W
Appleton, *U.S.A.* **42 C3** 44 16N 88 25W
Aqmola, *Kazakstan* **18 D9** 51 10N 71 30 E
Ar Ramadi, *Iraq* **24 B3** 33 25N 43 20 E
Arabian Desert, *Egypt* **29 C11** 27 30N 32 30 E
Arabian Gulf = Gulf, The, *Asia* **24 C4** 27 0N 50 0 E
Arabian Sea, *Ind. Oc.* **24 D5** 16 0N 65 0 E
Aracaju, *Brazil* **46 D6** 10 55S 37 4W
Arad, *Romania* **11 E11** 46 10N 21 20 E
Arafura Sea, *E. Indies* **22 D5** 9 0S 135 0 E
Aragón □, *Spain* **9 B5** 41 25N 0 40W
Araguaia ➝, *Brazil* **46 C5** 5 21S 48 41W
Arak, *Iran* **24 B3** 34 0N 49 40 E
Arakan Yoma, *Burma* **25 C8** 20 0N 94 40 E
Aral, *Kazakstan* **18 E8** 46 41N 61 45 E
Aral Sea, *Asia* **18 E8** 44 30N 60 0 E
Arcachon, *France* **8 D3** 44 40N 1 10W
Arctic Ocean, *Arctic* **48 B17** 78 0N 160 0W
Arctic Red River, *Canada* **38 B6** 67 15N 134 0W
Ardabil, *Iran* **24 B3** 38 15N 48 18 E
Ardennes, *Belgium* **10 D3** 49 50N 5 5 E
Arendal, *Norway* **6 G9** 58 28N 8 46 E
Arequipa, *Peru* **46 D2** 16 20S 71 30W
Argentan, *France* **8 B3** 48 45N 0 1W
Argentina ■, *S. Amer.* **47 F3** 35 0S 66 0W
Arima, *Trin. & Tob.* **44 S20** 10 38N 61 17W
Arizona □, *U.S.A.* **40 D4** 34 0N 112 0W
Arkansas □, *U.S.A.* **41 D8** 35 0N 92 30W
Arkansas ➝, *U.S.A.* **41 D8** 33 47N 91 4W
Arkhangelsk, *Russia* **14 B7** 64 38N 40 36 E
Arles, *France* **8 E6** 43 41N 4 40 E
Arlington, *U.S.A.* **42 F9** 38 53N 77 7W
Arlon, *Belgium* **10 D3** 49 42N 5 49 E
Armenia ■, *Asia* **15 F7** 40 20N 45 0 E
Arnhem, *Neths.* **10 C3** 51 58N 5 55 E
Arnhem Land, *Australia* **34 C5** 13 10S 134 30 E
Arnprior, *Canada* **42 C9** 45 26N 76 21W
Arrah, *India* **23 G10** 25 35N 84 32 E
Arran, *U.K.* **7 D4** 55 34N 5 12W
Arras, *France* **8 A5** 50 17N 2 46 E
Artois, *France* **8 A5** 50 20N 2 30 E
Aru Is., *Indonesia* **22 D5** 6 0S 134 30 E
Arunachal Pradesh □, *India* **25 C8** 28 0N 95 0 E
Arusha, *Tanzania* **32 E7** 3 20S 36 40 E
Arviat, *Canada* **38 B10** 61 10N 94 15W
Asab, *Namibia* **31 B2** 25 30S 18 0 E
Asahigawa, *Japan* **19 F12** 43 46N 142 22 E
Asansol, *India* **23 H11** 23 40N 87 1 E
Asbestos, *Canada* **43 C12** 45 47N 71 58W
Asbury Park, *U.S.A.* **43 E10** 40 13N 74 1W
Ascension I., *Atl. Oc.* **27 G2** 8 0S 14 15W
Ashkhabad, *Turkmenistan* **18 F7** 38 0N 57 50 E
Ashland, *Ky., U.S.A.* **42 F6** 38 28N 82 38W
Ashland, *Ohio, U.S.A.* **42 E6** 40 52N 82 19W
Ashtabula, *U.S.A.* **42 E7** 41 52N 80 47W
Asifabad, *India* **23 K7** 19 20N 79 24 E
Asir □, *Si. Arabia* **24 D3** 18 40N 42 30 E
Asmara, *Eritrea* **29 E12** 15 19N 38 55 E
Assam □, *India* **23 F13** 26 0N 93 0 E
Assen, *Neths.* **10 B4** 53 0N 6 35 E
Assisi, *Italy* **12 C5** 43 4N 12 37 E
Asti, *Italy* **12 B3** 44 54N 8 12 E
Astrakhan, *Russia* **15 E8** 46 25N 48 5 E
Asturias □, *Spain* **9 A3** 43 15N 6 0W
Asunción, *Paraguay* **47 E4** 25 10S 57 30W
Aswân, *Egypt* **29 D11** 24 4N 32 57 E
Atacama Desert, *Chile* **47 E3** 24 0S 69 20W
Atbara, *Sudan* **29 E11** 17 42N 33 59 E
Atbara ➝, *Sudan* **29 E11** 17 40N 33 56 E
Athabasca ➝, *Canada* **38 C8** 58 40N 110 50W
Athabasca, L., *Canada* **38 C9** 59 15N 109 15W
Athens, *Greece* **13 F10** 37 58N 23 46 E
Athens, *U.S.A.* **42 F6** 39 20N 82 6W
Atikokan, *Canada* **42 A2** 48 45N 91 37W
Atlanta, *U.S.A.* **41 D10** 33 45N 84 23W
Atlantic City, *U.S.A.* **43 F10** 39 21N 74 27W
Atlantic Ocean **2 E9** 0 0 20 0W
Atyraū, *Kazakstan* **18 E7** 47 5N 52 0 E
Au Sable ➝, *U.S.A.* **42 C6** 44 25N 83 20W
Aube ➝, *France* **8 B5** 48 34N 3 43 E
Auburn, *Ind., U.S.A.* **42 E5** 41 22N 85 4W
Auburn, *N.Y., U.S.A.* **42 D9** 42 56N 76 34W
Aubusson, *France* **8 D5** 45 57N 2 11 E
Auch, *France* **8 E4** 43 39N 0 36 E
Auckland, *N.Z.* **35 H13** 36 52S 174 46 E
Aude ➝, *France* **8 E5** 43 13N 3 14 E
Augrabies Falls, *S. Africa* **31 B3** 28 35S 20 20 E
Augsburg, *Germany* **10 D6** 48 25N 10 52 E
Augusta, *Ga., U.S.A.* **41 D10** 33 28N 81 58W
Augusta, *Maine, U.S.A.* **43 C13** 44 19N 69 47W
Aunis, *France* **8 C3** 46 5N 0 50W
Aurangabad, *Bihar, India* **23 G10** 24 45N 84 18 E
Aurangabad, *Maharashtra, India* **23 K5** 19 50N 75 23 E
Aurillac, *France* **8 D5** 44 55N 2 26 E
Aurora, *U.S.A.* **42 E3** 41 45N 88 19W
Austin, *U.S.A.* **40 D7** 30 17N 97 45W
Australia ■, *Oceania* **34 E5** 23 0S 135 0 E
Australian Alps, *Australia* **34 H8** 36 30S 148 30 E
Australian Capital Territory □, *Australia* **34 H8** 35 30S 149 0 E
Austria ■, *Europe* **10 E8** 47 0N 14 0 E
Autun, *France* **8 C6** 46 58N 4 17 E
Auvergne, *France* **8 D5** 45 20N 3 15 E
Auxerre, *France* **8 C5** 47 48N 3 32 E
Avallon, *France* **8 C5** 47 30N 3 53 E
Avellino, *Italy* **12 D6** 40 54N 14 47 E
Avignon, *France* **8 E6** 43 57N 4 50 E
Ávila, *Spain* **9 B3** 40 39N 4 43W
Avranches, *France* **8 B3** 48 40N 1 20W
Axiós ➝, *Greece* **13 D10** 40 57N 22 35 E
Ayers Rock, *Australia* **34 F5** 25 23S 131 5 E
Ayr, *U.K.* **7 D4** 55 28N 4 38W
Azamgarh, *India* **23 F9** 26 5N 83 13 E
Azerbaijan ■, *Asia* **15 F8** 40 20N 48 0 E
Azores, *Atl. Oc.* **2 C8** 38 44N 29 0W
Azov, Sea of, *Europe* **15 E6** 46 0N 36 30 E
Azuero Pen., *Panama* **45 F8** 7 30N 80 30W

B

Babol, *Iran* **24 B4** 36 40N 52 50 E
Babuyan Chan., *Phil.* **22 B4** 18 40N 121 30 E
Bacău, *Romania* **11 E14** 46 35N 26 55 E
Bacolod, *Phil.* **22 B4** 10 40N 122 57 E
Bad Axe, *U.S.A.* **42 D6** 43 48N 83 0W
Badajoz, *Spain* **9 C2** 38 50N 6 59W
Badalona, *Spain* **9 B7** 41 26N 2 15 E
Baden-Württemberg □, *Germany* **10 D5** 48 20N 8 40 E
Baffin I., *Canada* **39 B12** 68 0N 75 0W
Baghdad, *Iraq* **24 B3** 33 20N 44 30 E
Baguio, *Phil.* **22 B4** 16 26N 120 34 E
Bahamas ■, *N. Amer.* **45 C10** 24 0N 75 0W
Baharampur, *India* **23 G12** 24 2N 88 27 E
Bahawalpur, *Pakistan* **23 E3** 29 24N 71 40 E
Bahía = Salvador, *Brazil* **46 D6** 13 0S 38 30W
Bahía □, *Brazil* **46 D5** 12 0S 42 0W
Bahía Blanca, *Argentina* **47 F3** 38 35S 62 13W
Bahraich, *India* **23 F8** 27 38N 81 37 E
Bahrain ■, *Asia* **24 C4** 26 0N 50 35 E
Baia Mare, *Romania* **11 E12** 47 40N 23 35 E
Baie-St-Paul, *Canada* **43 B12** 47 28N 70 32W
Baikal, L., *Russia* **18 D12** 53 0N 108 0 E
Baja California, *Mexico* **44 B2** 31 10N 115 12W
Bakersfield, *U.S.A.* **40 C3** 35 23N 119 1W
Bakhtaran, *Iran* **24 B3** 34 23N 47 0 E
Baku, *Azerbaijan* **15 F8** 40 29N 49 56 E
Balabac Str., *E. Indies* **22 C3** 7 53N 117 5 E
Balaghat, *India* **23 J8** 21 49N 80 12 E
Balaton, *Hungary* **11 E9** 46 50N 17 40 E
Balboa, *Panama* **44 H14** 8 57N 79 34W
Baldwin, *U.S.A.* **42 D5** 43 54N 85 51W
Balearic Is., *Spain* **9 C7** 39 30N 3 0 E
Baleshwar, *India* **23 J11** 21 35N 87 3 E
Bali, *Indonesia* **22 D3** 8 20S 115 0 E
Balikeşir, *Turkey* **13 E12** 39 35N 27 58 E
Balikpapan, *Indonesia* **22 D3** 1 10S 116 55 E
Balkan Mts., *Bulgaria* **13 C10** 43 15N 23 0 E
Balkhash, L., *Kazakstan* **18 E9** 46 0N 74 50 E
Ballarat, *Australia* **34 H7** 37 33S 143 50 E
Balqash, *Kazakstan* **18 E9** 46 50N 74 50 E
Balrampur, *India* **23 F9** 27 30N 82 20 E
Balsas ➝, *Mexico* **44 D4** 17 55N 102 10W
Baltic Sea, *Europe* **6 G11** 57 0N 19 0 E
Baltimore, *U.S.A.* **42 F9** 39 17N 76 37W
Bam, *Iran* **24 C4** 29 7N 58 14 E
Bamako, *Mali* **28 F3** 12 34N 7 55W
Bamberg, *Germany* **10 D6** 49 54N 10 54 E
Bamenda, *Cameroon* **30 C4** 5 57N 10 11 E
Bancroft, *Canada* **42 C9** 45 3N 77 51W
Banda, *India* **23 G8** 25 30N 80 26 E
Banda Aceh, *Indonesia* **22 C1** 5 35N 95 20 E

Place names on the yellow-coded large scale map section are to be found in the index at the end of that section

INDEX TO WORLD MAPS 89

Banda Is. Brussels

Banda Is., Indonesia 22 D4 4 37S 129 50 E
Banda Sea, Indonesia 22 D4 6 0S 130 0 E
Bandar Abbas, Iran 24 C4 27 15N 56 15 E
Bandar Khomeyni, Iran 24 B3 30 30N 49 5 E
Bandar Seri Begawan, Brunei 22 C3 4 52N 115 0 E
Bandundu, Congo (Zaïre) 32 E3 3 15S 17 22 E
Bandung, Indonesia 22 D2 6 54S 107 36 E
Bangalore, India 25 D6 12 59N 77 40 E
Banggai Arch., Indonesia 22 D4 1 40S 123 30 E
Bangka, Indonesia 22 D2 2 0S 105 50 E
Bangka Str., Indonesia 22 D2 2 30S 105 30 E
Bangkok, Thailand 22 B2 13 45N 100 35 E
Bangladesh ■, Asia 23 H13 24 0N 90 0 E
Bangor, U.S.A. 43 C13 44 48N 68 46W
Bangui, C.A.R. 32 D3 4 23N 18 35 E
Bangweulu, L., Zambia 32 G6 11 0S 30 0 E
Banja Luka, Bos.-H. 12 B7 44 49N 17 11 E
Banjarmasin, Indonesia 22 D3 3 20S 114 35 E
Banjul, Gambia 28 F1 13 28N 16 40W
Banks I., Canada 38 A7 73 15N 121 30W
Bankura, India 23 H11 23 11N 87 18 E
Bannu, Pakistan 23 C3 33 0N 70 18 E
Banská Bystrica, Slovak Rep. 11 D10 48 46N 19 14 E
Banyak Is., Indonesia 22 C1 2 10N 97 10 E
Baoding, China 21 C6 38 50N 115 28 E
Baoji, China 20 C5 34 20N 107 5 E
Baotou, China 21 B6 40 32N 110 2 E
Bar Harbor, U.S.A. 43 C13 44 23N 68 13W
Bar-le-Duc, France 8 B6 48 47N 5 10 E
Baracaldo, Spain 9 A4 43 18N 2 59W
Baramula, India 23 B5 34 15N 74 20 E
Baran, India 23 G6 25 9N 76 40 E
Baranovichi, Belarus 11 B14 53 10N 26 0 E
Barbados ■, W. Indies 44 P22 13 10N 59 30W
Barberton, S. Africa 31 B5 25 42S 31 2 E
Barberton, U.S.A. 42 E7 41 0N 81 39W
Barcelona, Spain 9 B7 41 21N 2 10 E
Barddhaman, India 23 H11 23 14N 87 39 E
Bardstown, U.S.A. 42 G5 37 49N 85 28W
Bareilly, India 23 E7 28 22N 79 27 E
Barents Sea, Arctic 48 B8 73 0N 39 0 E
Barhi, India 23 G10 24 15N 85 25 E
Bari, Italy 12 D7 41 8N 16 51 E
Bari Doab, Pakistan 23 D4 30 20N 73 0 E
Barisal, Bangla. 23 H13 22 45N 90 20 E
Barito →, Indonesia 22 D3 4 0S 114 50 E
Barkly Tableland, Australia 34 D6 17 50S 136 40 E
Barkly West, S. Africa 31 B3 28 5S 24 31 E
Barletta, Italy 12 D7 41 19N 16 17 E
Barmer, India 23 G3 25 45N 71 20 E
Barnaul, Russia 18 D10 53 20N 83 40 E
Barques, Pt. Aux, U.S.A. 42 C6 44 4N 82 58W
Barquísimeto, Venezuela 46 A3 10 4N 69 19W
Barrancabermeja, Colombia 46 B2 7 0N 73 50W
Barranquilla, Colombia 46 A2 11 0N 74 50W
Barre, U.S.A. 43 C11 44 12N 72 30W
Barrie, Canada 42 C8 44 24N 79 40W
Barry's Bay, Canada 42 C9 45 29N 77 41W
Bashkortostan □, Russia 14 D10 54 0N 57 0 E
Basilan, Phil. 22 C4 6 35N 122 0 E
Baskatong, Rés., Canada 43 B10 46 46N 75 50W
Basle, Switz. 10 E4 47 35N 7 35 E
Basque Provinces = País Vasco □, Spain 9 A4 42 50N 2 45W
Basra, Iraq 24 B3 30 30N 47 50 E
Bass Str., Australia 34 H8 39 15S 146 30 E
Basse-Terre, Guadeloupe 44 M20 16 0N 61 44W
Bassein, Burma 25 D8 16 45N 94 30 E
Basseterre, St. Kitts & Nevis 44 K19 17 17N 62 43W
Basti, India 23 F9 26 52N 82 55 E
Bastia, France 8 E8 42 40N 9 30 E
Bata, Eq. Guin. 32 D1 1 57N 9 50 E
Batangas, Phil. 22 B4 13 35N 121 10 E
Batavia, U.S.A. 42 D8 43 0N 78 11W
Bath, U.K. 7 F5 51 23N 2 22W
Bath, Maine, U.S.A. 43 D13 43 55N 69 49W
Bath, N.Y., U.S.A. 42 D9 42 20N 77 19W
Bathurst, Australia 34 G8 33 25S 149 31 E
Bathurst, Canada 43 B15 47 37N 65 43W
Batna, Algeria 28 A6 35 34N 6 15 E
Baton Rouge, U.S.A. 41 D8 30 27N 91 11W
Battambang, Cambodia 22 B2 13 7N 103 12 E
Batticaloa, Sri Lanka 25 E7 7 43N 81 45 E
Battle Creek, U.S.A. 42 D5 42 19N 85 11W
Batu Is., Indonesia 22 D1 0 30S 98 25 E
Batu Pahat, Malaysia 22 C2 1 50N 102 56 E
Batumi, Georgia 15 F7 41 39N 41 44 E
Bavaria = Bayern □, Germany 10 D6 48 50N 12 0 E
Bawean, Indonesia 22 D3 5 46S 112 35 E
Bay City, U.S.A. 42 D6 43 36N 83 54W
Bayamo, Cuba 45 C9 20 20N 76 40W
Bayan Har Shan, China 20 C4 34 0N 98 0 E
Bayern □, Germany 10 D6 48 50N 12 0 E
Bayeux, France 8 B3 49 17N 0 42W
Bayonne, France 8 E3 43 30N 1 28W
Bayrūt, Lebanon 24 B2 33 53N 35 31 E
Beacon, U.S.A. 43 E11 41 30N 73 58W
Beagle, Canal, S. Amer. 47 H3 55 0S 68 30W
Béarn, France 8 E3 43 20N 0 30W
Beauce, Plaine de la, France 8 B4 48 10N 1 45 E
Beaufort Sea, Arctic 48 B18 72 0N 140 0W
Beaufort West, S. Africa 31 C3 32 18S 22 36 E
Beauharnois, Canada 43 C11 45 20N 73 52W
Beaumont, U.S.A. 41 D8 30 5N 94 6W
Beaune, France 8 C6 47 2N 4 50 E
Beauvais, France 8 B5 49 25N 2 8 E
Beaver Falls, U.S.A. 42 E7 40 46N 80 20W
Beaver I., U.S.A. 42 C5 45 40N 85 33W
Beawar, India 23 F5 26 3N 74 18 E
Béchar, Algeria 28 B4 31 38N 2 18W
Beckley, U.S.A. 42 G7 37 47N 81 11W
Bedford, Ind., U.S.A. 42 F4 38 52N 86 29W
Bedford, Va., U.S.A. 42 G8 37 20N 79 31W
Bei'an, China 21 B7 48 10N 126 20 E
Beijing, China 21 C6 39 55N 116 20 E
Beira, Mozam. 33 H6 19 50S 34 52 E
Békéscsaba, Hungary 11 E11 46 40N 21 5 E
Bela, Pakistan 23 F1 26 12N 66 20 E
Belarus ■, Europe 11 B14 53 30N 27 0 E
Belau = Palau ■, Pac. Oc. 36 G5 7 30N 134 30 E
Belaya Tserkov, Ukraine 11 D16 49 45N 30 10 E
Belcher Is., Canada 39 C12 56 15N 78 45W
Belém, Brazil 46 C5 1 20S 48 30W
Belfast, S. Africa 31 B5 25 42S 30 2 E
Belfast, U.K. 7 D4 54 37N 5 56W
Belfast, U.S.A. 43 C13 44 26N 69 1W
Belfort, France 8 C7 47 38N 6 50 E
Belgaum, India 25 D6 15 55N 74 35 E
Belgium ■, Europe 10 C3 50 30N 5 0 E
Belgorod, Russia 15 D6 50 35N 36 35 E
Belgrade, Serbia, Yug. 13 B9 44 50N 20 37 E
Beliton Is., Indonesia 22 D2 3 10S 107 50 E
Belize ■, Cent. Amer. 44 D7 17 0N 88 30W
Belize City, Belize 44 D7 17 25N 88 0W
Bellaire, U.S.A. 42 E7 40 1N 80 45W
Bellary, India 25 D6 15 10N 76 56 E
Belle-Ile, France 8 C2 47 20N 3 10W
Belle Isle, Str. of, Canada 39 C14 51 30N 56 30W
Bellefontaine, U.S.A. 42 E6 40 22N 83 46W
Belleville, Canada 42 C9 44 10N 77 23W
Bellingshausen Sea, Antarctica 48 D3 66 0S 80 0W
Bellinzona, Switz. 10 E5 46 11N 9 1 E
Belmopan, Belize 44 D7 17 18N 88 30W
Belo Horizonte, Brazil 46 D5 19 55S 43 56W
Belonia, India 23 H13 23 15N 91 30 E
Belorussia = Belarus ■, Europe 11 B14 53 30N 27 0 E
Beltsy, Moldova 11 E14 47 48N 28 0 E
Belukha, Russia 18 E10 49 50N 86 50 E
Ben Nevis, U.K. 7 C4 56 48N 5 1W
Benares = Varanasi, India 23 G9 25 22N 83 0 E
Bendigo, Australia 34 H7 36 40S 144 15 E
Benevento, Italy 12 D6 41 8N 14 45 E
Bengal, Bay of, Ind. Oc. 23 K12 15 0N 90 0 E
Bengbu, China 21 C6 32 58N 117 20 E
Benghazi, Libya 29 B9 32 11N 20 3 E
Bengkulu, Indonesia 22 D2 3 50S 102 12 E
Beni Suef, Egypt 29 C11 29 5N 31 6 E
Benidorm, Spain 9 C5 38 33N 0 9W
Benin ■, Africa 30 C2 10 0N 2 0 E
Benin, Bight of, W. Afr. 30 C2 5 0N 3 0 E
Benin City, Nigeria 30 C3 6 20N 5 31 E
Benoni, S. Africa 31 B4 26 11S 28 18 E
Benton Harbor, U.S.A. 42 D4 42 6N 86 27W
Benue →, Nigeria 30 C3 7 48N 6 46 E
Benxi, China 21 B7 41 20N 123 48 E
Berbérati, C.A.R. 32 D3 4 15N 15 40 E
Berea, U.S.A. 42 G5 37 34N 84 17W
Bérgamo, Italy 12 B3 45 41N 9 43 E
Bergen, Norway 6 F9 60 20N 5 20 E
Bergerac, France 8 D4 44 51N 0 30 E
Berhala Str., Indonesia 22 D2 1 0S 104 15 E
Berhampur = Brahmapur, India 23 K10 19 15N 84 54 E
Bering Sea, Pac. Oc. 36 B9 58 0N 171 0 E
Bering Strait, U.S.A. 38 B3 65 30N 169 0W
Berlin, Germany 10 B7 52 30N 13 25 E
Berlin, U.S.A. 43 C12 44 28N 71 11W
Bermuda ■, Atl. Oc. 45 A12 32 45N 65 0W
Berne, Switz. 10 E4 46 57N 7 28 E
Berry, France 8 C5 46 50N 2 0 E
Berwick, U.S.A. 42 E9 41 3N 76 14W
Berwick-upon-Tweed, U.K. 7 D5 55 46N 2 0W
Besançon, France 8 C7 47 15N 6 2 E
Bethal, S. Africa 31 B4 26 27S 29 28 E
Bethlehem, S. Africa 31 B4 28 14S 28 18 E
Bethlehem, U.S.A. 43 E10 40 37N 75 23W
Béthune, France 8 A5 50 30N 2 38 E
Bettiah, India 23 F10 26 48N 84 33 E
Betul, India 23 J6 21 58N 77 59 E
Béziers, France 8 E5 43 20N 3 12 E
Bhagalpur, India 23 G11 25 10N 87 0 E
Bhandara, India 23 J7 21 5N 79 42 E
Bhanrer Ra., India 23 H7 23 40N 79 45 E
Bharatpur, India 23 F6 27 15N 77 30 E
Bhatinda, India 23 D5 30 15N 74 57 E
Bhatpara, India 23 H12 22 50N 88 25 E
Bhavnagar, India 23 J4 21 45N 72 10 E
Bhilwara, India 23 G5 25 25N 74 38 E
Bhima →, India 25 D6 16 25N 77 17 E
Bhiwani, India 23 E6 28 50N 76 9 E
Bhopal, India 23 H6 23 20N 77 30 E
Bhubaneshwar, India 23 J10 20 15N 85 50 E
Bhuj, India 23 H2 23 15N 69 49 E
Bhusaval, India 23 J5 21 3N 75 46 E
Bhutan ■, Asia 23 F13 27 25N 90 30 E
Biafra, B. of, Africa 26 F4 3 30N 9 20 E
Biała Podlaska, Poland 11 B12 52 4N 23 6 E
Białystok, Poland 11 B12 53 10N 23 10 E
Biarritz, France 8 E3 43 29N 1 33W
Biddeford, U.S.A. 43 D12 43 30N 70 28W
Bié Plateau, Angola 33 G3 12 0S 16 0 E
Biel, Switz. 10 E4 47 8N 7 14 E
Bielefeld, Germany 10 B5 52 1N 8 33 E
Bielsko-Biała, Poland 11 D10 49 50N 19 2 E
Bien Hoa, Vietnam 22 B2 10 57N 106 49 E
Big Rapids, U.S.A. 42 D5 43 42N 85 29W
Bighorn Mts., U.S.A. 40 B5 44 30N 107 30W
Bihar, India 23 G10 25 5N 85 40 E
Bihar □, India 23 G10 25 0N 86 0 E
Bikaner, India 23 E4 28 2N 73 18 E
Bikini Atoll, Pac. Oc. 36 F8 12 0N 167 30 E
Bilaspur, India 23 H9 22 2N 82 15 E
Bilbao, Spain 9 A4 43 16N 2 56W
Billings, U.S.A. 40 A5 45 47N 108 30W
Bina-Etawah, India 23 G7 24 13N 78 14 E
Binghamton, U.S.A. 43 D10 42 6N 75 55W
Binjai, Indonesia 22 C1 3 20N 98 30 E
Bioko, Eq. Guin. 30 D3 3 30N 8 40 E
Birmingham, U.K. 7 E6 52 29N 1 52W
Birmingham, U.S.A. 41 D9 33 31N 86 48W
Biscay, B. of, Atl. Oc. 8 D1 45 0N 2 0W
Bishkek, Kyrgyzstan 18 E9 42 54N 74 46 E
Bisho, S. Africa 31 C4 32 50S 27 23 E
Biskra, Algeria 28 B6 34 50N 5 44 E
Bismarck Arch., Papua N. G. 34 A9 2 30S 150 0 E
Bissau, Guinea-Biss. 28 F1 11 45N 15 45W
Bitolj, Macedonia 13 D9 41 5N 21 10 E
Bitterfontein, S. Africa 31 C2 31 1S 18 32 E
Biwa-Ko, Japan 19 B5 35 15N 136 10 E
Biysk, Russia 18 D10 52 40N 85 0 E
Black Forest = Schwarzwald, Germany 10 D5 48 30N 8 20 E
Black Sea, Eurasia 15 F6 43 30N 35 0 E
Black Volta →, Africa 30 C1 8 41N 1 33W
Blackburn, U.K. 7 E5 53 45N 2 29W
Blackpool, U.K. 7 E5 53 49N 3 3W
Blacksburg, U.S.A. 42 G7 37 14N 80 25W
Blagoveshchensk, Russia 18 D14 50 20N 127 30 E
Blanc, Mont, Alps 8 D7 45 48N 6 50 E
Blantyre, Malawi 33 H6 15 45S 35 0 E
Blenheim, N.Z. 35 J13 41 38S 173 57 E
Blitar, Indonesia 22 D3 8 5S 112 11 E
Bloemfontein, S. Africa 31 B4 29 6S 26 7 E
Bloemhof, S. Africa 31 B4 27 38S 25 32 E
Blois, France 8 C4 47 35N 1 20 E
Bloomington, U.S.A. 42 F4 39 10N 86 32W
Bloomsburg, U.S.A. 42 E9 41 0N 76 27W
Blue Mts., Oreg., U.S.A. 40 A3 45 15N 119 0W
Blue Mts., Pa., U.S.A. 42 E9 40 30N 76 30W
Blue Nile →, Sudan 29 E11 15 38N 32 31 E
Blue Ridge Mts., U.S.A. 41 C10 36 30N 80 15W
Bluefield, U.S.A. 42 G7 37 15N 81 17W
Bobcaygeon, Canada 42 C8 44 33N 78 33W
Bobo-Dioulasso, Burkina Faso 28 F4 11 8N 4 13W
Bóbr →, Poland 10 B8 52 4N 15 4 E
Bobruysk, Belarus 11 B15 53 10N 29 15 E
Bochum, Germany 10 C4 51 28N 7 13 E
Boden, Sweden 6 E12 65 50N 21 42 E
Bodø, Norway 6 E10 67 17N 14 24 E
Bodrog →, Hungary 11 D11 48 11N 21 22 E
Bogor, Indonesia 22 D2 6 36S 106 48 E
Bogotá, Colombia 46 B2 4 34N 74 0W
Bogra, Bangla. 23 G12 24 51N 89 22 E
Bohemian Forest = Böhmerwald, Germany 10 D7 49 8N 13 14 E
Böhmerwald, Germany 10 D7 49 8N 13 14 E
Bohol, Phil. 22 C4 9 50N 124 10 E
Bohol Sea, Phil. 22 C4 9 0N 124 0 E
Boise, U.S.A. 40 B3 43 37N 116 13W
Bolgatanga, Ghana 30 B1 10 44N 0 53W
Bolivia ■, S. Amer. 46 D3 17 6S 64 0W
Bolivian Plateau, S. Amer. 46 D3 20 0S 67 30W
Bologna, Italy 12 B4 44 29N 11 20 E
Bolshevik I., Russia 18 B12 78 30N 102 0 E
Bolton, U.K. 7 E5 53 35N 2 26W
Bolzano, Italy 12 A4 46 31N 11 22 E
Boma, Congo (Zaïre) 32 F2 5 50S 13 4 E
Bombay = Mumbai, India 25 D6 18 55N 72 50 E
Bonifacio, France 8 F8 41 24N 9 10 E
Bonn, Germany 10 C4 50 46N 7 6 E
Boonville, U.S.A. 42 F4 38 3N 87 16W
Boothia, Gulf of, Canada 39 A11 71 0N 90 0W
Boothia Pen., Canada 38 A10 71 0N 94 0W
Borås, Sweden 6 G10 57 43N 12 56 E
Bordeaux, France 8 D3 44 50N 0 36W
Borisov, Belarus 11 A15 54 17N 28 28 E
Borneo, E. Indies 22 C3 1 0N 115 0 E
Bornholm, Denmark 6 G11 55 10N 15 0 E
Bosnia-Herzegovina ■, Europe 12 B7 44 0N 17 0 E
Bosporus, Turkey 13 D13 41 10N 29 10 E
Boston, U.S.A. 43 D12 42 22N 71 4W
Bothnia, G. of, Europe 6 F12 63 0N 20 15 E
Botletle →, Botswana 31 A3 20 10S 23 15 E
Botoşani, Romania 11 E14 47 42N 26 41 E
Botswana ■, Africa 31 A3 22 0S 24 0 E
Bouaké, Ivory C. 28 G3 7 40N 5 2W
Bouar, C.A.R. 32 C3 6 0N 15 40 E
Boulogne-sur-Mer, France 8 A4 50 42N 1 36 E
Bourbonnais, France 8 C5 46 28N 3 0 E
Bourg-en-Bresse, France 8 C6 46 13N 5 12 E
Bourges, France 8 C5 47 9N 2 25 E
Bourgogne, France 8 C6 47 0N 4 50 E
Bourke, Australia 34 G8 30 8S 145 55 E
Bournemouth, U.K. 7 F6 50 43N 1 52W
Bowling Green, Ky., U.S.A. 42 G4 36 59N 86 27W
Bowling Green, Ohio, U.S.A. 42 E6 41 23N 83 39W
Bracebridge, Canada 42 C8 45 2N 79 19W
Bräcke, Sweden 6 F11 62 45N 15 26 E
Bradford, U.K. 7 E6 53 47N 1 45W
Bradford, U.S.A. 42 E8 41 58N 78 38W
Braga, Portugal 9 B1 41 35N 8 25W
Brahamapur, India 23 K10 19 15N 84 54 E
Brahmanbaria, Bangla. 23 H13 23 58N 91 15 E
Brahmani →, India 23 J11 20 39N 86 46 E
Brahmaputra →, India 23 H12 23 58N 89 50 E
Brăila, Romania 11 F14 45 19N 27 59 E
Brampton, Canada 42 D8 43 45N 79 45W
Brandenburg, Germany 10 B7 52 25N 12 33 E
Brandenburg □, Germany 10 B6 52 50N 13 0 E
Brandon, Canada 38 D10 49 50N 99 57W
Brandvlei, S. Africa 31 C3 30 25S 20 30 E
Brantford, Canada 42 D7 43 10N 80 15W
Bras d'Or, L., Canada 43 C17 45 50N 60 50W
Brasília, Brazil 46 D5 15 47S 47 55W
Braşov, Romania 11 F13 45 38N 25 35 E
Brassey Ra., Malaysia 22 C3 5 0N 117 15 E
Bratislava, Slovak Rep. 11 D9 48 10N 17 7 E
Brattleboro, U.S.A. 43 D11 42 51N 72 34W
Brazil, U.S.A. 42 F4 39 32N 87 8W
Brazil ■, S. Amer. 46 D5 12 0S 50 0W
Brazzaville, Congo 32 E3 4 9S 15 12 E
Breda, Neths. 10 C3 51 35N 4 45 E
Bredasdorp, S. Africa 31 C3 34 33S 20 2 E
Bregenz, Austria 10 E5 47 30N 9 45 E
Breiðafjörður, Iceland 6 B2 65 15N 23 15W
Bremen, Germany 10 B5 53 4N 8 47 E
Bremerhaven, Germany 10 B5 53 33N 8 36 E
Brenner P., Austria 10 E6 47 2N 11 30 E
Bréscia, Italy 12 B3 45 33N 10 15 E
Brest, Belarus 11 B12 52 10N 23 40 E
Brest, France 8 B1 48 24N 4 31W
Bretagne, France 8 B2 48 10N 3 0W
Brewer, U.S.A. 43 C13 44 48N 68 46W
Breyten, S. Africa 31 B4 26 16S 30 0 E
Briançon, France 8 D7 44 54N 6 39 E
Bridgeport, U.S.A. 43 E11 41 11N 73 12W
Bridgeton, U.S.A. 43 F10 39 26N 75 14W
Bridgetown, Barbados 44 P22 13 5N 59 30W
Bridgewater, Canada 43 C15 44 25N 64 31W
Brighton, U.K. 7 F6 50 49N 0 7W
Brindisi, Italy 13 D7 40 39N 17 55 E
Brisbane, Australia 34 F9 27 25S 153 2 E
Bristol, U.K. 7 F5 51 26N 2 35W
Bristol Channel, U.K. 7 F4 51 18N 4 30W
British Columbia □, Canada 38 C7 55 0N 125 15W
British Isles, Europe 4 E5 54 0N 4 0W
Brits, S. Africa 31 B4 25 37S 27 48 E
Britstown, S. Africa 31 C3 30 37S 23 30 E
Brittany = Bretagne, France 8 B2 48 10N 3 0W
Brive-la-Gaillarde, France 8 D4 45 10N 1 32 E
Brno, Czech Rep. 11 D9 49 10N 16 35 E
Brocken, Germany 10 C6 51 47N 10 37 E
Brockville, Canada 43 C10 44 35N 75 41W
Broken Hill, Australia 34 G7 31 58S 141 29 E
Brooks Ra., U.S.A. 38 B5 68 40N 147 0W
Bruay-en-Artois, France 8 A5 50 29N 2 33 E
Bruce, Mt., Australia 34 E2 22 37S 118 8 E
Brugge, Belgium 10 C2 51 13N 3 13 E
Brunei ■, Asia 22 C3 4 50N 115 0 E
Brunswick, Germany 10 B6 52 15N 10 31 E
Brunswick, U.S.A. 43 D13 43 55N 69 58W
Brussels, Belgium 10 C3 50 51N 4 21 E

Place names on the yellow-coded large scale map section are to be found in the index at the end of that section

Bryan, *U.S.A.* **42 E5** 41 28N 84 33W
Bryansk, *Russia* **14 D5** 53 13N 34 25 E
Bucaramanga, *Colombia* **46 B2** 7 0N 73 0W
Bucharest, *Romania* **11 F14** 44 27N 26 10 E
Buckhannon, *U.S.A.* **42 F7** 39 0N 80 8W
Buckingham, *Canada* **43 C10** 45 37N 75 24W
Bucyrus, *U.S.A.* **42 E6** 40 48N 82 59W
Budapest, *Hungary* **11 E10** 47 29N 19 5 E
Buena Vista, *U.S.A.* **42 G8** 37 44N 79 21W
Buenos Aires, *Argentina* **47 F4** 34 30S 58 20W
Buffalo, *U.S.A.* **42 D8** 42 53N 78 53W
Bug →, *Poland* **11 B11** 52 31N 21 5 E
Buh →, *Ukraine* **15 E5** 46 59N 31 58 E
Bujumbura, *Burundi* **32 E5** 3 16S 29 18 E
Bukavu, *Congo (Zaïre)* **32 E5** 2 20S 28 52 E
Bukittinggi, *Indonesia* **22 D2** 0 20S 100 20 E
Bulandshahr, *India* **23 E6** 28 28N 77 51 E
Bulawayo, *Zimbabwe* **33 J5** 20 7S 28 32 E
Bulgaria ■, *Europe* **13 C11** 42 35N 25 30 E
Bunbury, *Australia* **34 G2** 33 20S 115 35 E
Bundaberg, *Australia* **34 E9** 24 54S 152 22 E
Bundi, *India* **23 G5** 25 30N 75 35 E
Buraydah, *Si. Arabia* **24 C3** 26 20N 44 8 E
Burgas, *Bulgaria* **13 C12** 42 33N 27 29 E
Burgersdorp, *S. Africa* **31 C4** 31 0S 26 20 E
Burgos, *Spain* **9 A4** 42 21N 3 41W
Burgundy = Bourgogne, *France* **8 C6** 47 0N 4 50 E
Burkina Faso ■, *Africa* **30 B1** 12 0N 1 0W
Burlington, *Vt., U.S.A.* **43 C11** 44 29N 73 12W
Burlington, *Wis., U.S.A.* **42 D3** 42 41N 88 17W
Burlyu-Tyube, *Kazakstan* **18 E9** 46 30N 79 10 E
Burma ■, *Asia* **25 C8** 21 0N 96 30 E
Burnie, *Australia* **34 J8** 41 4S 145 56 E
Bursa, *Turkey* **13 D13** 40 15N 29 5 E
Buru, *Indonesia* **22 D4** 3 30S 126 30 E
Burundi ■, *Africa* **32 E5** 3 15S 30 0 E
Bushehr, *Iran* **24 C4** 28 55N 50 55 E
Butler, *U.S.A.* **42 E8** 40 52N 79 54W
Buton, *Indonesia* **22 D4** 5 0S 122 45 E
Butterworth, *Malaysia* **22 C2** 5 24N 100 23 E
Butuan, *Phil.* **22 C4** 8 57N 125 33 E
Buzău, *Romania* **11 F14** 45 10N 26 50 E
Bydgoszcz, *Poland* **11 B9** 53 10N 18 0 E
Byelorussia = Belarus ■, *Europe* **11 B14** 53 30N 27 0 E
Bytom, *Poland* **11 C10** 50 25N 18 54 E

C

Cabinda □, *Angola* **32 F2** 5 0S 12 30 E
Cabonga, Réservoir, *Canada* **42 B9** 47 20N 76 40W
Čačak, *Serbia, Yug.* **13 C9** 43 54N 20 20 E
Cáceres, *Spain* **9 C2** 39 26N 6 23W
Cadillac, *U.S.A.* **42 C5** 44 15N 85 24W
Cádiz, *Spain* **9 D2** 36 30N 6 20W
Caen, *France* **8 B3** 49 10N 0 22W
Cagayan de Oro, *Phil.* **22 C4** 8 30N 124 40 E
Cágliari, *Italy* **12 E3** 39 13N 9 7 E
Cahors, *France* **8 D4** 44 27N 1 27 E
Caicos Is., *W. Indies* **45 C10** 21 40N 71 40W
Cairns, *Australia* **34 D8** 16 57S 145 45 E
Cairo, *Egypt* **29 B11** 30 1N 31 14 E
Calabar, *Nigeria* **30 D3** 4 57N 8 20 E
Calábria □, *Italy* **12 E7** 39 0N 16 30 E
Calais, *France* **8 A4** 50 57N 1 56 E
Calais, *U.S.A.* **43 C14** 45 11N 67 17W
Calamian Group, *Phil.* **22 B3** 11 50N 119 55 E
Calapan, *Phil.* **22 B4** 13 25N 121 7 E
Calcutta, *India* **23 H12** 22 36N 88 24 E
Caledon, *S. Africa* **31 C2** 34 14S 19 26 E
Caledon →, *S. Africa* **31 C4** 30 31S 26 5 E
Calgary, *Canada* **38 C8** 51 0N 114 10W
Cali, *Colombia* **46 B2** 3 25N 76 35W
Calicut, *India* **25 D6** 11 15N 75 43 E
California □, *U.S.A.* **40 C2** 37 30N 119 30W
California, G. of, *Mexico* **44 B2** 27 0N 111 0W
Calitzdorp, *S. Africa* **31 C3** 33 33S 21 42 E
Callao, *Peru* **46 D2** 12 0S 77 0W
Caltanissetta, *Italy* **12 F6** 37 29N 14 4 E
Calvi, *France* **8 E8** 42 34N 8 45 E
Calvinia, *S. Africa* **31 C2** 31 28S 19 45 E
Camagüey, *Cuba* **45 C9** 21 20N 78 0W
Camargue, *France* **8 E6** 43 34N 4 34 E
Cambay, G. of, *India* **23 J4** 20 45N 72 30 E
Cambodia ■, *Asia* **22 B2** 12 15N 105 0 E
Cambrai, *France* **8 A5** 50 11N 3 14 E
Cambrian Mts., *U.K.* **7 E5** 52 3N 3 57W
Cambridge, *U.K.* **7 E7** 52 12N 0 8 E
Cambridge, *Mass., U.S.A.* **43 D12** 42 22N 71 6W
Cambridge, *Md., U.S.A.* **43 F9** 38 34N 76 5W
Cambridge, *Ohio, U.S.A.* **42 E7** 40 2N 81 35W
Cambridge Bay = Ikaluktutiak, *Canada* **38 B9** 69 10N 105 0W
Camden, *U.S.A.* **43 F10** 39 56N 75 7W
Cameroon ■, *Africa* **30 C4** 6 0N 12 30 E
Cameroun, Mt., *Cameroon* **30 D3** 4 13N 9 10 E
Campánia □, *Italy* **12 D6** 41 0N 14 30 E
Campbellsville, *U.S.A.* **42 G5** 37 21N 85 20W
Campbellton, *Canada* **43 B14** 47 57N 66 43W
Campeche, *Mexico* **44 D6** 19 50N 90 32W
Campeche, G. of, *Mexico* **44 D6** 19 30N 93 0W
Campina Grande, *Brazil* **46 C6** 7 20S 35 47W
Campinas, *Brazil* **47 E5** 22 50S 47 0W
Campo Grande, *Brazil* **46 E4** 20 25S 54 40W
Campos, *Brazil* **46 E5** 21 50S 41 20W
Camrose, *Canada* **38 C8** 53 0N 112 50W
Can Tho, *Vietnam* **22 B2** 10 2N 105 46 E
Canada ■, *N. Amer.* **38 C10** 60 0N 100 0W
Canadian Shield, *Canada* **39 C10** 53 0N 75 0W
Canandaigua, *U.S.A.* **42 D9** 42 54N 77 17W
Canary Is., *Atl. Oc.* **28 C1** 28 30N 16 0W
Canaveral, C., *U.S.A.* **41 E10** 28 27N 80 32W
Canberra, *Australia* **34 H8** 35 15S 149 8 E
Cannes, *France* **8 E7** 43 32N 7 1 E
Canso, *Canada* **43 C17** 45 20N 61 0W
Cantabria □, *Spain* **9 A4** 43 10N 4 0W
Cantabrian Mts., *Spain* **9 A3** 43 0N 5 10W
Canterbury, *U.K.* **7 F7** 51 16N 1 6 E
Canton, *N.Y., U.S.A.* **43 C10** 44 36N 75 10W
Canton, *Ohio, U.S.A.* **42 E7** 40 48N 81 23W
Cap-Chat, *Canada* **43 A14** 49 6N 66 40W
Cap-de-la-Madeleine, *Canada* **43 B11** 46 22N 72 31W
Cape Breton I., *Canada* **43 B17** 46 0N 60 30W
Cape Charles, *U.S.A.* **43 G10** 37 16N 76 1W
Cape Coast, *Ghana* **30 C1** 5 5N 1 15W
Cape May, *U.S.A.* **43 F10** 38 56N 74 56W
Cape Town, *S. Africa* **31 C2** 33 55S 18 22 E
Cape Verde Is. ■, *Atl. Oc.* **27 E1** 17 10N 25 20W
Cape York Peninsula, *Australia* **34 C7** 12 0S 142 30 E
Capreol, *Canada* **42 B7** 46 43N 80 56W
Capri, *Italy* **12 D6** 40 33N 14 14 E
Caracas, *Venezuela* **46 A3** 10 30N 66 55W
Carbondale, *U.S.A.* **43 E10** 41 35N 75 30W
Carcassonne, *France* **8 E5** 43 13N 2 20 E
Cardiff, *U.K.* **7 F5** 51 29N 3 10W
Caribbean Sea, *W. Indies* **45 E10** 15 0N 75 0W
Caribou, *U.S.A.* **43 B13** 46 52N 68 1W
Carleton Place, *Canada* **43 C9** 45 8N 76 9W
Carletonville, *S. Africa* **31 B4** 26 23S 27 22 E
Carlisle, *U.S.A.* **42 E9** 40 12N 77 12W
Carmaux, *France* **8 D5** 44 3N 2 10 E
Carmi, *U.S.A.* **42 F3** 38 5N 88 10W
Carnarvon, *Australia* **34 E1** 24 51S 113 42 E
Carnarvon, *S. Africa* **31 C3** 30 56S 22 8 E
Carnegie, L., *Australia* **34 F3** 26 5S 122 30 E
Caro, *U.S.A.* **42 D6** 43 29N 83 24W
Carolina, *S. Africa* **31 B5** 26 5S 30 6 E
Caroline Is., *Pac. Oc.* **36 G6** 8 0N 150 0 E
Carpathians, *Europe* **11 D11** 49 30N 21 0 E
Carpentaria, G. of, *Australia* **34 C6** 14 0S 139 0 E
Carpentras, *France* **8 D6** 44 3N 5 2 E
Cartagena, *Colombia* **46 A2** 10 25N 75 33W
Cartagena, *Spain* **9 D5** 37 38N 0 59W
Casablanca, *Morocco* **28 B3** 33 36N 7 36W
Cascade Ra., *U.S.A.* **40 A2** 47 0N 121 30W
Casper, *U.S.A.* **40 B5** 42 51N 106 19W
Caspian Sea, *Eurasia* **15 F9** 43 0N 50 0 E
Cass City, *U.S.A.* **42 D6** 43 36N 83 11W
Castellón de la Plana, *Spain* **9 C5** 39 58N 0 3W
Castelsarrasin, *France* **8 E4** 44 2N 1 7 E
Castilla La Mancha □, *Spain* **9 C4** 39 30N 3 30W
Castilla y Leon □, *Spain* **9 B3** 42 0N 5 0W
Castres, *France* **8 E5** 43 37N 2 13 E
Castries, *St. Lucia* **44 N21** 14 2N 60 58W
Cataluña □, *Spain* **9 B6** 41 40N 1 15 E
Catanduanes, *Phil.* **22 B4** 13 50N 124 20 E
Catánia, *Italy* **12 F6** 37 30N 15 6 E
Catanzaro, *Italy* **12 E7** 38 54N 16 35 E
Catskill, *U.S.A.* **43 D11** 42 14N 73 52W
Catskill Mts., *U.S.A.* **43 D10** 42 10N 74 25W
Caucasus Mountains, *Eurasia* **15 F7** 42 50N 44 0 E
Caxias do Sul, *Brazil* **47 E4** 29 10S 51 10W
Cayenne, *Fr. Guiana* **46 B4** 5 5N 52 18W
Cayuga L., *U.S.A.* **42 D9** 42 41N 76 41W
Cedar Rapids, *U.S.A.* **41 B8** 41 59N 91 40W
Cegléd, *Hungary* **11 E10** 47 11N 19 47 E
Celebes Sea, *Indonesia* **22 C4** 3 0N 123 0 E
Celina, *U.S.A.* **42 E5** 40 33N 84 35W
Central African Rep. ■, *Africa* **32 C4** 7 0N 20 0 E
Central Makran Range, *Pakistan* **24 C5** 26 30N 64 15 E
Cephalonia = Kefallinía, *Greece* **13 E9** 38 20N 20 30 E
Ceram, *Indonesia* **22 D4** 3 10S 129 0 E
Ceram Sea, *Indonesia* **22 D4** 2 30S 128 30 E
Ceres, *S. Africa* **31 C2** 33 21S 19 18 E
Cerignola, *Italy* **12 D6** 41 17N 15 53 E
České Budějovice, *Czech Rep.* **10 D8** 48 55N 14 25 E
Ceuta, *N. Afr.* **9 E3** 35 52N 5 18W
Cévennes, *France* **8 D5** 44 10N 3 50 E
Chad ■, *Africa* **29 E8** 15 0N 17 15 E
Chakradharpur, *India* **23 H10** 22 45N 85 40 E
Chaleur B., *Canada* **43 B15** 47 55N 65 30W
Chalisgaon, *India* **23 J5** 20 30N 75 10 E
Chalon-sur-Saône, *France* **8 C6** 46 48N 4 50 E
Châlons-en-Champagne, *France* **8 B6** 48 58N 4 20 E
Chamba, *India* **23 C6** 32 35N 76 10 E
Chambal →, *India* **23 F7** 26 29N 79 15 E
Chambersburg, *U.S.A.* **42 F9** 39 56N 77 40W
Chambéry, *France* **8 D6** 45 34N 5 55 E
Champagne, *France* **8 B6** 48 40N 4 20 E
Champaign, *U.S.A.* **42 E3** 40 7N 88 15W
Champlain, L., *U.S.A.* **43 C11** 44 40N 73 20W
Chandigarh, *India* **23 D6** 30 43N 76 47 E
Chandpur, *Bangla.* **23 H13** 23 8N 90 45 E
Changchun, *China* **21 B7** 43 57N 125 17 E
Changde, *China* **21 D6** 29 4N 111 35 E
Changsha, *China* **21 D6** 28 12N 113 0 E
Changzhou, *China* **21 C6** 31 47N 119 58 E
Chanthaburi, *Thailand* **22 B2** 12 38N 102 12 E
Chapleau, *Canada* **42 B6** 47 50N 83 24W
Chapra, *India* **23 G10** 25 48N 84 44 E
Chardzhou, *Turkmenistan* **18 F8** 39 6N 63 34 E
Chārīkār, *Afghan.* **23 B2** 35 0N 69 10 E
Charleroi, *Belgium* **10 C3** 50 24N 4 27 E
Charles, C., *U.S.A.* **43 G10** 37 7N 75 58W
Charleston, *Ill., U.S.A.* **42 F3** 39 30N 88 10W
Charleston, *S.C., U.S.A.* **41 D11** 32 46N 79 56W
Charleston, *W. Va., U.S.A.* **42 F7** 38 21N 81 38W
Charleville, *Australia* **34 F8** 26 24S 146 15 E
Charleville-Mézières, *France* **8 B6** 49 44N 4 40 E
Charlevoix, *U.S.A.* **42 C5** 45 19N 85 16W
Charlotte, *Mich., U.S.A.* **42 D5** 42 34N 84 50W
Charlotte, *N.C., U.S.A.* **41 C10** 35 13N 80 51W
Charlottesville, *U.S.A.* **42 F8** 38 2N 78 30W
Charlottetown, *Canada* **43 B16** 46 14N 63 8W
Charolles, *France* **8 C6** 46 27N 4 16 E
Charters Towers, *Australia* **34 E8** 20 5S 146 13 E
Chartres, *France* **8 B4** 48 29N 1 30 E
Châteaubriant, *France* **8 C3** 47 43N 1 23W
Châteaulin, *France* **8 B1** 48 11N 4 8W
Châteauroux, *France* **8 C4** 46 50N 1 40 E
Châtellerault, *France* **8 C4** 46 50N 0 30 E
Chatham, *N.B., Canada* **43 B15** 47 2N 65 28W
Chatham, *Ont., Canada* **42 D6** 42 24N 82 11W
Chattanooga, *U.S.A.* **41 C9** 35 3N 85 19W
Chaumont, *France* **8 B6** 48 7N 5 8 E
Cheb, *Czech Rep.* **10 C7** 50 9N 12 28 E
Cheboksary, *Russia* **14 C8** 56 8N 47 12 E
Cheboygan, *U.S.A.* **42 C5** 45 39N 84 29W
Chechenia □, *Russia* **15 F8** 43 30N 45 29 E
Chedabucto B., *Canada* **43 C17** 45 25N 61 8W
Chełm, *Poland* **11 C12** 51 8N 23 30 E
Chelyabinsk, *Russia* **18 D8** 55 10N 61 24 E
Chelyuskin, C., *Russia* **18 B12** 77 30N 103 0 E
Chemnitz, *Germany* **10 C7** 50 51N 12 54 E
Chenab →, *Pakistan* **23 D3** 30 23N 71 2 E
Chengdu, *China* **20 C5** 30 38N 104 2 E
Chennai, *India* **25 D7** 13 8N 80 19 E
Cher →, *France* **8 C4** 47 21N 0 29 E
Cherbourg, *France* **8 B3** 49 39N 1 40W
Cheremkhovo, *Russia* **18 D12** 53 8N 103 1 E
Cherepovets, *Russia* **14 C6** 59 5N 37 55 E
Cherkassy, *Ukraine* **15 E5** 49 27N 32 4 E
Chernigov, *Ukraine* **14 D5** 51 28N 31 20 E
Chernobyl, *Ukraine* **11 C16** 51 20N 30 15 E
Chernovtsy, *Ukraine* **11 D13** 48 15N 25 52 E
Cherski Ra., *Russia* **18 C16** 65 0N 143 0 E
Chesapeake B., *U.S.A.* **42 F9** 38 0N 76 10W
Chester, *U.S.A.* **43 F10** 39 51N 75 22W
Chesterfield Inlet = Igluligaarjuk, *Canada* **38 B10** 63 30N 90 45W
Chesuncook L., *U.S.A.* **43 B13** 46 0N 69 21W
Chhatarpur, *India* **23 G7** 24 55N 79 35 E
Chiai, *Taiwan* **21 D7** 23 29N 120 25 E
Chiba, *Japan* **19 B7** 35 30N 140 7 E
Chibougamau, *Canada* **43 A10** 49 56N 74 24W
Chibougamau L., *Canada* **43 A10** 49 50N 74 20W
Chicago, *U.S.A.* **42 E4** 41 53N 87 38W
Chiclayo, *Peru* **46 C2** 6 42S 79 50W
Chicopee, *U.S.A.* **43 D11** 42 9N 72 37W
Chicoutimi, *Canada* **43 A12** 48 28N 71 5W
Chidley, C., *Canada* **39 B13** 60 23N 64 26W
Chieti, *Italy* **12 C6** 42 21N 14 10 E
Chihli, G. of, *China* **21 C6** 39 0N 119 0 E
Chihuahua, *Mexico* **44 B3** 28 40N 106 3W
Chile ■, *S. Amer.* **47 F2** 35 0S 72 0W
Chilka L., *India* **23 K10** 19 40N 85 25 E
Chillán, *Chile* **47 F2** 36 40S 72 10W
Chillicothe, *U.S.A.* **42 F6** 39 20N 82 59W
Chilpancingo, *Mexico* **44 D5** 17 30N 99 30W
Chilton, *U.S.A.* **42 C3** 44 2N 88 10W
Chilung, *Taiwan* **21 D7** 25 3N 121 45
Chimborazo, *Ecuador* **46 C2** 1 29S 78 55W
Chimbote, *Peru* **46 C2** 9 0S 78 35W
Chimkent, *Kazakstan* **18 E8** 42 18N 69 36
China ■, *Asia* **21 C6** 30 0N 110 0
Chindwin →, *Burma* **25 C8** 21 26N 95 15
Chingola, *Zambia* **33 G5** 12 31S 27 53
Chinon, *France* **8 C4** 47 10N 0 15
Chíos, *Greece* **13 E12** 38 27N 26 9
Chipata, *Zambia* **33 G6** 13 38S 32 28
Chipman, *Canada* **43 B15** 46 6N 65 53W
Chita, *Russia* **18 D13** 52 0N 113 35
Chitral, *Pakistan* **23 B3** 35 50N 71 56
Chittagong, *Bangla.* **23 H13** 22 19N 91 48
Cholet, *France* **8 C3** 47 4N 0 52W
Chŏngjin, *N. Korea* **21 B7** 41 47N 129 50
Chongqing, *China* **20 D5** 29 35N 106 25
Chorzów, *Poland* **11 C10** 50 18N 18 57
Choybalsan, *Mongolia* **21 B6** 48 4N 114 30
Christchurch, *N.Z.* **35 J13** 43 33S 172 47
Christiana, *S. Africa* **31 B4** 27 52S 25 8
Chukot Ra., *Russia* **18 C19** 68 0N 175 0
Chumphon, *Thailand* **22 B1** 10 35N 99 14
Chur, *Switz.* **10 E5** 46 52N 9 32
Churchill →, *Man., Canada* **38 C10** 58 47N 94 12W
Churchill →, *Nfld., Canada* **39 C13** 53 19N 60 10W
Churu, *India* **23 E5** 28 20N 74 50
Chushal, *India* **23 C7** 33 40N 78 40
Chuvashia □, *Russia* **14 C8** 55 30N 47 0
Cicero, *U.S.A.* **42 E4** 41 48N 87 48W
Ciechanów, *Poland* **11 B11** 52 52N 20 38
Ciénaga, *Colombia* **46 A2** 11 1N 74 15W
Cienfuegos, *Cuba* **45 C8** 22 10N 80 30W
Cincinnati, *U.S.A.* **42 F5** 39 6N 84 31W
Cinto, Mte., *France* **8 E8** 42 24N 8 54
Circleville, *U.S.A.* **42 F6** 39 36N 82 57W
Cirebon, *Indonesia* **22 D2** 6 45S 108 32
Citlaltépetl, *Mexico* **44 D5** 19 0N 97 20W
Ciudad Bolívar, *Venezuela* **46 B3** 8 5N 63 36W
Ciudad Guayana, *Venezuela* **46 B3** 8 0N 62 30W
Ciudad Juárez, *Mexico* **44 A3** 31 40N 106 28W
Ciudad Madero, *Mexico* **44 C5** 22 19N 97 50W
Ciudad Obregón, *Mexico* **44 B3** 27 28N 109 59W
Ciudad Real, *Spain* **9 C4** 38 59N 3 55W
Ciudad Victoria, *Mexico* **44 C5** 23 41N 99 9W
Clanwilliam, *S. Africa* **31 C2** 32 11S 18 52
Claremont, *U.S.A.* **43 D11** 43 23N 72 20W
Clarksburg, *U.S.A.* **42 F7** 39 17N 80 30W
Clarksville, *U.S.A.* **41 C9** 36 32N 87 21W
Clearfield, *U.S.A.* **42 E8** 41 2N 78 27W
Clermont-Ferrand, *France* **8 D5** 45 46N 3 4
Cleveland, *U.S.A.* **42 E7** 41 30N 81 42W
Clifton Forge, *U.S.A.* **42 G8** 37 49N 79 50W
Cluj-Napoca, *Romania* **11 E12** 46 47N 23 38
Clyde →, *U.K.* **7 D4** 55 55N 4 30W
Coast Mts., *Canada* **38 C7** 55 0N 129 20W
Coast Ranges, *U.S.A.* **40 B2** 39 0N 123 0W
Coaticook, *Canada* **43 C12** 45 10N 71 46W
Coatzacoalcos, *Mexico* **44 D6** 18 7N 94 25W
Cobourg, *Canada* **42 D8** 43 58N 78 10W
Cochabamba, *Bolivia* **46 D3** 17 26S 66 10W
Cochin, *India* **25 E6** 9 59N 76 22
Cochrane, *Canada* **42 A7** 49 0N 81 0W
Cockburn I., *Canada* **42 C6** 45 55N 83 22W
Cod, C., *U.S.A.* **41 B13** 42 5N 70 10W
Cognac, *France* **8 D3** 45 41N 0 20W
Coimbatore, *India* **25 D6** 11 2N 76 59
Coimbra, *Portugal* **9 B1** 40 15N 8 27W
Colebrook, *U.S.A.* **43 C12** 44 54N 71 30W
Colesberg, *S. Africa* **31 C4** 30 45S 25 5
Colima, *Mexico* **44 D4** 19 14N 103 43W
Collingwood, *Canada* **42 C7** 44 29N 80 13W
Colmar, *France* **8 B7** 48 5N 7 20
Cologne, *Germany* **10 C4** 50 56N 6 57
Colombia ■, *S. Amer.* **46 B2** 3 45N 73 0W
Colombo, *Sri Lanka* **25 E6** 6 56N 79 58
Colón, *Panama* **44 H14** 9 20N 79 54W
Colonial Heights, *U.S.A.* **42 G9** 37 15N 77 25W
Colorado □, *U.S.A.* **40 C5** 39 30N 105 30W
Colorado →, *N. Amer.* **40 D4** 31 45N 114 40W
Colorado →, *U.S.A.* **41 E7** 28 36N 95 59W
Colorado Plateau, *U.S.A.* **40 C4** 37 0N 111 0W
Colorado Springs, *U.S.A.* **40 C6** 38 50N 104 49W
Columbia, *U.S.A.* **41 D10** 34 0N 81 2W
Columbia →, *U.S.A.* **40 A2** 46 15N 124 5W
Columbia, District of □, *U.S.A.* **42 F9** 38 55N 77 0W
Columbus, *Ga., U.S.A.* **41 D10** 32 28N 84 59W
Columbus, *Ind., U.S.A.* **42 F5** 39 13N 85 55W
Columbus, *Ohio, U.S.A.* **42 F6** 39 58N 83 0W
Comilla, *Bangla.* **23 H13** 23 28N 91 10
Communism Pk., *Tajikistan* **18 F9** 39 0N 72 2
Como, *Italy* **12 B3** 45 47N 9 5
Como, L. di, *Italy* **12 B3** 46 0N 9 11

Place names on the yellow-coded large scale map section are to be found in the index at the end of that section

Comodoro Rivadavia   **Eskilstuna**

Place names on the yellow-coded large scale map section are to be found in the index at the end of that section

Eskimo Pt. = Arviat, Canada 38 B10 61 10N 94 15W
Eskişehir, Turkey 15 G5 39 50N 30 35 E
Esperance, Australia 34 G3 33 45S 121 55 E
Essen, Germany 10 C4 51 28N 7 0 E
Estcourt, S. Africa 31 B4 29 0S 29 53 E
Estonia ■, Europe 14 C4 58 30N 25 30 E
Etawah, India 23 F7 26 48N 79 6 E
Ethiopia ■, Africa 32 C7 8 0N 40 0 E
Ethiopian Highlands, Ethiopia 26 E7 10 0N 37 0 E
Etna, Italy 12 F6 37 50N 14 55 E
Euclid, U.S.A. 42 E7 41 34N 81 32W
Eugene, U.S.A. 40 B2 44 5N 123 4W
Euphrates →, Asia 24 B3 31 0N 47 25 E
Evanston, U.S.A. 42 D4 42 3N 87 41W
Evansville, U.S.A. 42 G4 37 58N 87 35W
Everest, Mt., Nepal 23 E11 28 5N 86 58 E
Évora, Portugal 9 C2 38 33N 7 57W
Évreux, France 8 B4 49 3N 1 8 E
Évvoia, Greece 13 E11 38 30N 24 0 E
Exeter, U.K. 7 F5 50 43N 3 31W
Extremadura □, Spain 9 C2 39 30N 6 5W
Eyre, L., Australia 34 F6 29 30S 137 26 E

F

Færoe Is., Atl. Oc. 5 C4 62 0N 7 0W
Fairbanks, U.S.A. 38 B5 64 51N 147 43W
Fairfield, U.S.A. 42 F3 38 23N 88 22W
Fairmont, U.S.A. 42 F7 39 29N 80 9W
Faisalabad, Pakistan 23 D4 31 30N 73 5 E
Faizabad, India 23 F9 26 45N 82 10 E
Fakfak, Indonesia 22 D5 3 0S 132 15 E
Falkland Is. □, Atl. Oc. 47 H4 51 30S 59 0W
Fall River, U.S.A. 43 E12 41 43N 71 10W
Falmouth, U.S.A. 42 F5 38 41N 84 20W
Falun, Sweden 6 F11 60 37N 15 37 E
Farah, Afghan. 24 B5 32 20N 62 7 E
Farmville, U.S.A. 42 G8 37 18N 78 24W
Fatehgarh, India 23 F7 27 25N 79 35 E
Fatehpur, India 23 G8 25 56N 81 13 E
Faya-Largeau, Chad 29 E8 17 58N 19 6 E
Fayetteville, U.S.A. 41 C11 35 3N 78 53W
Fazilka, India 23 D5 30 27N 74 2 E
Fdérik, Mauritania 28 D2 22 40N 12 45W
Fécamp, France 8 B4 49 45N 0 22 E
Fehmarn, Germany 10 A6 54 27N 11 7 E
Feira de Santana, Brazil 46 D6 12 15S 38 57W
Fernando Póo = Bioko, Eq. Guin. 30 D3 3 30N 8 40 E
Ferrara, Italy 12 B4 44 50N 11 35 E
Ferret, C., France 8 D3 44 38N 1 15W
Fès, Morocco 28 B4 34 0N 5 0W
Fianarantsoa, Madag. 33 J9 21 26S 47 5 E
Ficksburg, S. Africa 31 B4 28 51S 27 53 E
Figeac, France 8 D5 44 37N 2 2 E
Fiji ■, Pac. Oc. 35 D14 17 20S 179 0 E
Findlay, U.S.A. 42 E6 41 2N 83 39W
Finisterre, C., Spain 9 A1 42 50N 9 19W
Finland ■, Europe 6 F13 63 0N 27 0 E
Finland, G. of, Europe 6 G12 60 0N 26 0 E
Firozabad, India 23 F7 27 10N 78 25 E
Firozpur, India 23 D5 30 55N 74 40 E
Fish →, Namibia 31 B2 28 7S 17 10 E
Fitchburg, U.S.A. 43 D12 42 35N 71 48W
Flandre, Europe 10 C2 51 0N 3 0 E
Flensburg, Germany 10 A5 54 47N 9 27 E
Flers, France 8 B3 48 47N 0 33W
Flinders →, Australia 34 D7 17 36S 140 36 E
Flinders Ras., Australia 34 G6 31 30S 138 30 E
Flint, U.S.A. 42 D6 43 1N 83 41W
Flint →, U.S.A. 41 D10 30 57N 84 34W
Flora, U.S.A. 42 F3 38 40N 88 29W
Florence, Italy 12 C4 43 46N 11 15 E
Flores, Indonesia 22 D4 8 35S 121 0 E
Florianópolis, Brazil 47 E5 27 30S 48 30W
Florida □, U.S.A. 41 E10 28 0N 82 0W
Florida, Straits of, U.S.A. 45 C9 25 0N 80 0W
Florida Keys, U.S.A. 41 F10 24 40N 81 0W
Florø, Norway 6 F9 61 35N 5 1 E
Focşani, Romania 11 F14 45 41N 27 15 E
Fóggia, Italy 12 D6 41 27N 15 34 E
Foix, France 8 E4 42 58N 1 38 E
Fontainebleau, France 8 B5 48 24N 2 40 E
Fontenay-le-Comte, France 8 C3 46 28N 0 48W
Forlì, Italy 12 B5 44 13N 12 3 E
Fort Beaufort, S. Africa 31 C4 32 46S 26 40 E
Fort Collins, U.S.A. 40 B5 40 35N 105 5W
Fort-Coulonge, Canada 42 C9 45 50N 76 45W
Fort-de-France, Martinique 44 N20 14 36N 61 2W
Fort Kent, U.S.A. 43 B13 47 15N 68 36W
Fort Lauderdale, U.S.A. 41 E10 26 7N 80 8W
Fort McMurray, Canada 38 C8 56 44N 111 7W
Fort Sandeman, Pakistan 23 D2 31 20N 69 31 E
Fort Smith, U.S.A. 41 C8 35 23N 94 25W
Fort Wayne, U.S.A. 42 E5 41 4N 85 9W
Fort Worth, U.S.A. 41 D7 32 45N 97 18W
Fortaleza, Brazil 46 C6 3 45S 38 35W
Foshan, China 21 D6 23 4N 113 5 E
Fostoria, U.S.A. 42 E6 41 10N 83 25W
Fougères, France 8 B3 48 21N 1 14W
Foxe Chan., Canada 39 B11 65 0N 80 0W
France ■, Europe 8 C5 47 0N 3 0 E
Franche-Comté, France 8 C6 46 50N 5 55 E
Francistown, Botswana 31 A4 21 7S 27 33 E
Frankfort, S. Africa 31 B4 27 17S 28 30 E
Frankfort, Ind., U.S.A. 42 E4 40 17N 86 31W
Frankfort, Ky., U.S.A. 42 F5 38 12N 84 52W
Frankfort, Mich., U.S.A. 42 C4 44 38N 86 14W
Frankfurt, Brandenburg, Germany 10 B8 52 20N 14 32 E
Frankfurt, Hessen, Germany 10 C5 50 7N 8 41 E
Franklin, N.H., U.S.A. 43 D12 43 27N 71 39W
Franklin, Pa., U.S.A. 42 E8 41 24N 79 50W
Franz Josef Land, Russia 18 A7 82 0N 55 0 E
Fraser →, Canada 38 D7 49 7N 123 11W
Fraserburg, S. Africa 31 C3 31 55S 21 30 E
Frederick, U.S.A. 42 F9 39 25N 77 25W
Fredericksburg, U.S.A. 42 F9 38 18N 77 28W
Fredericton, Canada 43 C14 45 57N 66 40W
Fredonia, U.S.A. 42 D8 42 26N 79 20W
Fredrikstad, Norway 6 G10 59 13N 10 57 E
Free State □, S. Africa 31 B4 28 30S 27 0 E
Freetown, S. Leone 28 G2 8 30N 13 17W
Freiburg, Germany 10 E4 47 59N 7 51 E
Fremont, U.S.A. 42 E6 41 21N 83 7W
French Creek →, U.S.A. 42 E8 41 24N 79 50W
French Guiana □, S. Amer. 46 B4 4 0N 53 0W
French Polynesia □, Pac. Oc. 37 J13 20 0S 145 0W
Fresnillo, Mexico 44 C4 23 10N 103 0W
Fresno, U.S.A. 40 C3 36 44N 119 47W
Frobisher B., Canada 39 B13 62 30N 66 0W
Front Royal, U.S.A. 42 F8 38 55N 78 12W
Frunze = Bishkek, Kyrgyzstan 18 E9 42 54N 74 46 E
Frýdek-Místek, Czech Rep. 11 D10 49 40N 18 20 E
Fuji-San, Japan 19 B6 35 22N 138 44 E
Fujian □, China 21 D6 26 0N 118 0 E
Fukui, Japan 19 A5 36 5N 136 10 E
Fukuoka, Japan 19 C2 33 39N 130 21 E
Fukushima, Japan 19 A7 37 44N 140 28 E
Fukuyama, Japan 19 B3 34 35N 133 20 E
Fulda, Germany 10 C5 50 32N 9 40 E
Fulda →, Germany 10 C5 51 25N 9 39 E
Fulton, U.S.A. 42 D9 43 19N 76 25W
Funafuti, Pac. Oc. 35 B14 8 30S 179 0 E
Fundy, B. of, Canada 43 C15 45 0N 66 0W
Furneaux Group, Australia 34 J8 40 10S 147 50 E
Fürth, Germany 10 D6 49 28N 10 59 E
Fury and Hecla Str., Canada 39 B11 69 56N 84 0W
Fushun, China 21 B7 41 50N 123 56 E
Fuxin, China 21 B7 42 5N 121 48 E
Fuzhou, China 21 D6 26 5N 119 16 E
Fyn, Denmark 6 G10 55 20N 10 30 E

G

Gabès, Tunisia 28 B7 33 53N 10 2 E
Gabon ■, Africa 32 E2 0 10S 10 0 E
Gaborone, Botswana 31 A4 24 45S 25 57 E
Gabrovo, Bulgaria 13 C11 42 52N 25 19 E
Gadag, India 25 D6 15 30N 75 45 E
Gadarwara, India 23 H7 22 50N 78 50 E
Gainesville, U.S.A. 41 E10 29 40N 82 20W
Galápagos, Pac. Oc. 37 H18 0 0 91 0W
Galaţi, Romania 11 F15 45 27N 28 2 E
Galdhøpiggen, Norway 6 F9 61 38N 8 18 E
Galicia □, Spain 9 A2 42 43N 7 45W
Galle, Sri Lanka 25 E7 6 5N 80 10 E
Gallipoli, Turkey 13 D12 40 28N 26 43 E
Gallipolis, U.S.A. 42 F6 38 49N 82 12W
Gällivare, Sweden 6 E12 67 9N 20 40 E
Galveston, U.S.A. 41 E8 29 18N 94 48W
Galway, Ireland 7 E2 53 17N 9 3W
Gambia ■, W. Afr. 28 F1 13 25N 16 0W
Gan Jiang →, China 21 D6 29 15N 116 0 E
Gananoque, Canada 43 C9 44 20N 76 10W
Gandak →, India 23 G10 25 39N 85 13 E
Gandhi Sagar Dam, India 23 G5 24 40N 75 40 E
Ganganagar, India 23 E4 29 56N 73 56 E
Gangdisê Shan, China 23 D8 31 20N 81 0 E
Ganges →, India 23 H13 23 20N 90 30 E
Gangtok, India 23 F12 27 20N 88 37 E
Gansu □, China 20 C5 36 0N 104 0 E
Gap, France 8 D7 44 33N 6 5 E
Garda, L. di, Italy 12 B4 45 40N 10 41 E
Gardēz, Afghan. 23 C2 33 37N 69 9 E
Garies, S. Africa 31 C2 30 32S 17 59 E
Garonne →, France 8 D3 45 2N 0 36W
Garoua, Cameroon 30 C4 9 19N 13 21 E
Gary, U.S.A. 42 E4 41 36N 87 20W
Garzê, China 20 C5 31 38N 100 1 E
Gascogne, France 8 E4 43 45N 0 20 E
Gascogne, G. de, Europe 8 D2 44 0N 2 0W
Gaspé, Canada 43 A15 48 52N 64 30W
Gaspé, C., Canada 43 A15 48 48N 64 7W
Gaspé Pen., Canada 43 A15 48 45N 65 40W
Gatineau →, Canada 43 C10 45 27N 75 42W
Gatun, Panama 44 H14 9 16N 79 55W
Gatun, L., Panama 44 H14 9 7N 79 56W
Gauhati, India 23 F13 26 10N 91 45 E
Gävle, Sweden 6 F11 60 40N 17 9 E
Gawilgarh Hills, India 23 J6 21 15N 76 45 E
Gaya, India 23 G10 24 47N 85 4 E
Gaylord, U.S.A. 42 C5 45 2N 84 41W
Gaziantep, Turkey 15 G6 37 6N 37 23 E
Gcuwa, S. Africa 31 C4 32 20S 28 11 E
Gdańsk, Poland 11 A10 54 22N 18 40 E
Gdynia, Poland 11 A10 54 35N 18 33 E
Gebe, Indonesia 22 C4 0 5N 129 25 E
Gedser, Denmark 6 H10 54 35N 11 55 E
Geelong, Australia 34 H7 38 10S 144 22 E
Gejiu, China 20 D5 23 20N 103 10 E
Gelsenkirchen, Germany 10 C4 51 32N 7 1 E
Geneva, Switz. 10 E4 46 12N 6 9 E
Geneva, U.S.A. 42 D9 42 52N 76 59W
Geneva, L. = Léman, L., Europe 10 E4 46 26N 6 30 E
Gennargentu, Mti. del, Italy 12 D3 40 1N 9 19 E
Genoa, Italy 12 B3 44 25N 8 57 E
Gent, Belgium 10 C2 51 2N 3 42 E
George, S. Africa 31 C3 33 58S 22 29 E
George Town, Malaysia 22 C2 5 25N 100 15 E
Georgetown, Guyana 46 B4 6 50N 58 12W
Georgetown, U.S.A. 42 F5 38 13N 84 33W
Georgia □, U.S.A. 41 D10 32 50N 83 15W
Georgia ■, Asia 15 F7 42 0N 43 0 E
Georgian B., Canada 42 C7 45 15N 81 0W
Gera, Germany 10 C7 50 53N 12 4 E
Geraldton, Australia 34 F1 28 48S 114 32 E
Geraldton, Canada 42 A4 49 44N 86 59W
Germany ■, Europe 10 C6 51 0N 10 0 E
Germiston, S. Africa 31 B4 26 15S 28 10 E
Gerona, Spain 9 B7 41 58N 2 46 E
Getafe, Spain 9 B4 40 18N 3 44W
Ghaghara →, India 23 G10 25 45N 84 40 E
Ghana ■, W. Afr. 30 C1 8 0N 1 0W
Ghanzi, Botswana 31 A3 21 50S 21 34 E
Ghazâl, Bahr el →, Sudan 32 C6 9 31N 30 25 E
Ghaziabad, India 23 E6 28 42N 77 26 E
Ghazipur, India 23 G9 25 38N 83 35 E
Ghazni, Afghan. 23 C2 33 30N 68 28 E
Ghent = Gent, Belgium 10 C2 51 2N 3 42 E
Gibraltar □, Europe 9 D3 36 7N 5 22W
Gibraltar, Str. of, Medit. S. 9 E3 35 55N 5 40W
Gibson Desert, Australia 34 E4 24 0S 126 0 E
Gifu, Japan 19 B5 35 30N 136 45 E
Gijón, Spain 9 A3 43 32N 5 42W
Gilgit, India 23 B5 35 50N 74 15 E
Giridih, India 23 G11 24 10N 86 21 E
Gironde →, France 8 D3 45 32N 1 7W
Gisborne, N.Z. 35 H14 38 39S 178 5 E
Giza, Egypt 29 C11 30 0N 31 10 E
Gizhiga, Russia 18 C18 62 3N 160 30 E
Glace Bay, Canada 43 B18 46 11N 59 58W
Gladstone, Australia 34 E9 23 52S 151 16 E
Gladstone, U.S.A. 42 C4 45 51N 87 1W
Gladwin, U.S.A. 42 D5 43 59N 84 29W
Glasgow, U.K. 7 D4 55 51N 4 15W
Glasgow, U.S.A. 42 G5 37 0N 85 55W
Glencoe, S. Africa 31 B5 28 11S 30 11 E
Glendale, U.S.A. 40 D3 34 9N 118 15W
Glens Falls, U.S.A. 43 D11 43 19N 73 39W
Gliwice, Poland 11 C10 50 22N 18 41 E
Głogów, Poland 10 C9 51 37N 16 5 E
Glomma →, Norway 6 G10 59 12N 10 57 E
Gloversville, U.S.A. 43 D10 43 3N 74 21W
Gniezno, Poland 11 B9 52 30N 17 35 E
Go Cong, Vietnam 22 B2 10 22N 106 40 E
Goa □, India 25 D6 15 33N 73 59 E
Gobabis, Namibia 31 A2 22 30S 19 0 E
Gobi, Asia 21 B6 44 0N 111 0 E
Godavari →, India 25 D7 16 25N 82 18 E
Goderich, Canada 42 D7 43 45N 81 41W
Godhra, India 23 H4 22 49N 73 40 E
Godthåb, Greenland 48 C4 64 10N 51 35W
Gogama, Canada 42 B7 47 35N 81 43W
Goiânia, Brazil 46 D5 16 43S 49 20W
Gold Coast, Australia 34 F9 28 0S 153 25 E
Gomel, Belarus 11 B16 52 28N 31 0 E
Gómez Palacio, Mexico 44 B4 25 40N 104 0W
Gonabad, Iran 24 B4 34 15N 58 45 E
Gonda, India 23 F8 27 9N 81 58 E
Gonder, Ethiopia 29 F12 12 39N 37 30 E
Gondia, India 23 J8 21 23N 80 10 E
Good Hope, C. of, S. Africa 31 C2 34 24S 18 30 E
Gorakhpur, India 23 F9 26 47N 83 23 E
Gorkiy = Nizhniy Novgorod, Russia 14 C7 56 20N 44 0 E
Görlitz, Germany 10 C8 51 9N 14 58 E
Gorontalo, Indonesia 22 C4 0 35N 123 5 E
Gorzów Wielkopolski, Poland 10 B8 52 43N 15 15 E
Gota Canal, Sweden 6 G11 58 30N 15 58 E
Gotha, Germany 10 C6 50 56N 10 42 E
Gothenburg, Sweden 6 G10 57 43N 11 59 E
Gotland, Sweden 6 G11 57 30N 18 33 E
Göttingen, Germany 10 C5 51 31N 9 55 E
Gouda, Neths. 10 B3 52 1N 4 42 E
Gouin Res., Canada 43 A10 48 35N 74 40W
Goulburn, Australia 34 G8 34 44S 149 44 E
Governador Valadares, Brazil 46 D5 18 15S 41 57W
Gozo, Malta 12 F6 36 3N 14 13 E
Graaff-Reinet, S. Africa 31 C3 32 13S 24 32 E
Grahamstown, S. Africa 31 C4 33 19S 26 31 E
Grampian Mts., U.K. 7 C4 56 50N 4 0W
Gran Canaria, Canary Is. 28 C1 27 55N 15 35W
Gran Chaco, S. Amer. 47 E3 25 0S 61 0W
Granada, Spain 9 D4 37 10N 3 35W
Granby, Canada 43 C11 45 25N 72 45W
Grand Bahama I., Bahamas 45 B9 26 40N 78 30W
Grand Canyon, U.S.A. 40 C4 36 3N 112 9W
Grand Canyon National Park, U.S.A. 40 C4 36 15N 112 30W
Grand Cayman, Cayman Is. 45 D8 19 20N 81 20W
Grand Haven, U.S.A. 42 D4 43 4N 86 13W
Grand L., Canada 43 C14 45 57N 66 7W
Grand Manan I., Canada 43 C14 44 45N 66 52W
Grand-Mère, Canada 43 B11 46 36N 72 40W
Grand Rapids, U.S.A. 42 D4 42 58N 85 40W
Grand St.-Bernard, Col du, Europe 10 F4 45 50N 7 10 E
Grande, Rio →, U.S.A. 41 E7 25 58N 97 9W
Grande de Santiago →, Mexico 44 C3 21 36N 105 26W
Grande Prairie, Canada 38 C8 55 10N 118 50W
Granville, U.S.A. 43 D11 43 24N 73 16W
Grasse, France 8 E7 43 38N 6 56 E
Graulhet, France 8 E4 43 45N 1 59 E
Grayling, U.S.A. 42 C5 44 40N 84 43W
Graz, Austria 10 E8 47 4N 15 27 E
Great Abaco I., Bahamas 45 B9 26 25N 77 10W
Great Australian Bight, Australia 34 G4 33 30S 130 0 E
Great Barrier Reef, Australia 34 D8 18 0S 146 50 E
Great Basin, U.S.A. 40 B3 40 0N 117 0W
Great Bear L., Canada 38 B7 65 30N 120 0W
Great Belt, Denmark 6 G10 55 20N 11 0 E
Great Dividing Ra., Australia 34 E8 23 0S 146 0 E
Great Falls, U.S.A. 40 A4 47 30N 111 17W
Great Inagua I., Bahamas 45 C10 21 0N 73 20W
Great Karoo, S. Africa 31 C3 31 55S 21 0 E
Great Plains, N. Amer. 40 A6 47 0N 105 0W
Great Salt L., U.S.A. 40 B4 41 15N 112 40W
Great Sandy Desert, Australia 34 E3 21 0S 124 0 E
Great Sangi, Indonesia 22 C4 3 45N 125 30 E
Great Slave L., Canada 38 B8 61 23N 115 38W
Great Victoria Desert, Australia 34 F4 29 30S 126 30 E
Greater Antilles, W. Indies 45 D10 17 40N 74 0W
Greece ■, Europe 13 E9 40 0N 23 0 E
Greeley, U.S.A. 40 B6 40 25N 104 42W
Green →, U.S.A. 42 G4 37 54N 87 30W
Green B., U.S.A. 42 C4 45 0N 87 30W
Green Bay, U.S.A. 42 C4 44 31N 88 0W
Greencastle, U.S.A. 42 F4 39 38N 86 52W
Greenfield, Ind., U.S.A. 42 F5 39 47N 85 46W
Greenfield, Mass., U.S.A. 43 D11 42 35N 72 36W
Greenland □, N. Amer. 48 C4 66 0N 45 0W
Greensboro, U.S.A. 41 C11 36 4N 79 48W
Greensburg, Ind., U.S.A. 42 F5 39 20N 85 29W
Greensburg, Pa., U.S.A. 42 E8 40 18N 79 33W
Greenville, Maine, U.S.A. 43 C13 45 28N 69 35W
Greenville, Mich., U.S.A. 42 D5 43 11N 85 15W
Greenville, Ohio, U.S.A. 42 E5 40 6N 84 38W
Grenada ■, W. Indies 44 Q20 12 10N 61 40W
Grenoble, France 8 D6 45 12N 5 42
Grey Ra., Australia 34 F7 27 0S 143 30
Greymouth, N.Z. 35 J13 42 29S 171 13
Greytown, S. Africa 31 B5 29 1S 30 36
Gris-Nez, C., France 8 A4 50 52N 1 35
Grodno, Belarus 11 B12 53 42N 23 52
Groningen, Neths. 10 B4 53 15N 6 35
Groot →, S. Africa 31 C3 33 45S 24 36

Place names on the yellow-coded large scale map section are to be found in the index at the end of that section

INDEX TO WORLD MAPS 93

Groot Vis — James B.

Groot Vis →, S. Africa 31 C4 33 28S 27 5 E
Gross Glockner, Austria 10 E7 47 5N 12 40 E
Groundhog →, Canada 42 A6 48 45N 82 58W
Groznyy, Russia 15 F8 43 20N 45 45 E
Grudziądz, Poland 11 B10 53 30N 18 47 E
Guadalajara, Mexico 44 C4 20 40N 103 20W
Guadalajara, Spain 9 B4 40 37N 3 12W
Guadalete →, Spain 9 D2 36 35N 6 13W
Guadalquivir →, Spain 9 D2 36 47N 6 22W
Guadarrama, Sierra de, Spain 9 B4 41 0N 4 0W
Guadeloupe □, W. Indies 44 L20 16 20N 61 40W
Guadiana →, Portugal 9 D2 37 14N 7 22W
Guadix, Spain 9 D4 37 18N 3 11W
Guam ■, Pac. Oc. 36 F6 13 27N 144 45 E
Guangdong □, China 21 D6 23 0N 113 0 E
Guangxi Zhuangzu Zizhiqu □, China 21 D5 24 0N 109 0 E
Guangzhou, China 21 D6 23 5N 113 10 E
Guantánamo, Cuba 45 C9 20 10N 75 14W
Guaporé →, Brazil 46 D3 11 55S 65 4W
Guatemala, Guatemala 44 E6 14 40N 90 22W
Guatemala ■, Cent. Amer. 44 D6 15 40N 90 30W
Guayaquil, Ecuador 46 C2 2 15S 79 52W
Guaymas, Mexico 44 B2 27 59N 110 54W
Guelph, Canada 42 D7 43 35N 80 20W
Guéret, France 8 C4 46 11N 1 51 E
Guilin, China 21 D6 25 18N 110 15 E
Guinea ■, W. Afr. 28 F2 10 20N 11 30W
Guinea, Gulf of, Atl. Oc. 26 F3 3 0N 2 30 E
Guinea-Bissau ■, Africa 28 F2 12 0N 15 0W
Guingamp, France 8 B2 48 34N 3 10W
Guiyang, China 20 D5 26 32N 106 40 E
Guizhou □, China 20 D5 27 0N 107 0 E
Gujarat □, India 23 H3 23 20N 71 0 E
Gujranwala, Pakistan 23 C5 32 10N 74 12 E
Gujrat, Pakistan 23 C5 32 40N 74 2 E
Gulbarga, India 25 D6 17 20N 76 50 E
Gulf, The, Asia 24 C4 27 0N 50 0 E
Guna, India 23 G6 24 40N 77 19 E
Guntur, India 25 D7 16 23N 80 30 E
Gurgaon, India 23 E6 28 27N 77 1 E
Gurkha, Nepal 23 E10 28 5N 84 40 E
Guyana ■, S. Amer. 46 B4 5 0N 59 0W
Guyenne, France 8 D4 44 30N 0 40 E
Gwadar, Pakistan 24 C5 25 10N 62 18 E
Gwalior, India 23 F7 26 12N 78 10 E
Gweru, Zimbabwe 33 H5 19 28S 29 45 E
Gyandzha, Azerbaijan 15 F8 40 45N 46 20 E
Gympie, Australia 34 F9 26 11S 152 38 E
Györ, Hungary 11 E9 47 41N 17 40 E
Gyumri, Armenia 15 F7 40 47N 43 50 E

H

Haarlem, Neths. 10 B3 52 23N 4 39 E
Hachinohe, Japan 19 F12 40 30N 141 29 E
Hadd, Ras al, Oman 24 C4 22 35N 59 50 E
Haeju, N. Korea 21 C7 38 3N 125 45 E
Hafizabad, Pakistan 23 C4 32 5N 73 40 E
Hafnarfjörður, Iceland 6 B3 64 4N 21 57W
Hagen, Germany 10 C4 51 21N 7 27 E
Hagerstown, U.S.A. 42 F9 39 39N 77 43W
Hague, C. de la, France 8 B3 49 44N 1 56W
Haguenau, France 8 B7 48 49N 7 47 E
Haifa, Israel 24 B2 32 46N 35 0 E
Haikou, China 21 D6 20 1N 110 16 E
Hail, Si. Arabia 24 C3 27 28N 41 45 E
Hailar, China 21 B6 49 10N 119 38 E
Haileybury, Canada 42 B8 47 30N 79 38W
Hainan □, China 21 E5 19 0N 109 30 E
Haiphong, Vietnam 20 D5 20 47N 106 41 E
Haiti ■, W. Indies 45 D10 19 0N 72 30W
Hakodate, Japan 19 F12 41 45N 140 44 E
Halab, Syria 24 B2 36 10N 37 15 E
Halberstadt, Germany 10 C6 51 54N 11 3 E
Halden, Norway 6 G10 59 9N 11 23 E
Haldwani, India 23 E7 29 31N 79 30 E
Halifax, Canada 43 C16 44 38N 63 35W
Halle, Germany 10 C6 51 30N 11 56 E
Halmahera, Indonesia 22 C4 0 40N 128 0 E
Halmstad, Sweden 6 G10 56 41N 12 52 E
Hama, Syria 24 B2 35 5N 36 40 E
Hamadan, Iran 24 B3 34 52N 48 32 E
Hamamatsu, Japan 19 B5 34 45N 137 45 E
Hamar, Norway 6 F10 60 48N 11 7 E
Hamburg, Germany 10 B5 53 33N 9 59 E
Hämeenlinna, Finland 6 F12 61 0N 24 28 E
Hameln, Germany 10 B5 52 6N 9 21 E
Hamersley Ra., Australia 34 E2 22 0S 117 45 E
Hamilton, Bermuda 45 A12 32 15N 64 45W
Hamilton, Canada 42 D8 43 15N 79 50W
Hamilton, N.Z. 35 H14 37 47S 175 19 E
Hamilton, U.S.A. 42 F5 39 24N 84 34W
Hamm, Germany 10 C4 51 40N 7 50 E
Hammerfest, Norway 6 D12 70 39N 23 41 E
Hammond, U.S.A. 42 E4 41 38N 87 30W
Hammonton, U.S.A. 43 F10 39 39N 74 48W
Hancock, U.S.A. 42 B3 47 8N 88 35W
Hangzhou, China 21 C7 30 18N 120 11 E
Hannover, Germany 10 B5 52 22N 9 46 E
Hanoi, Vietnam 20 D5 21 5N 105 55 E
Hanover, U.S.A. 42 F9 39 48N 76 59W
Haora, India 23 H12 22 37N 88 20 E
Haparanda, Sweden 6 E12 65 52N 24 8 E
Happy Valley-Goose Bay, Canada 39 C13 53 15N 60 20W
Hapur, India 23 E6 28 45N 77 45 E
Harare, Zimbabwe 33 H6 17 43S 31 2 E
Harbin, China 21 B7 45 48N 126 40 E
Harbor Beach, U.S.A. 42 D6 43 51N 82 39W
Hardanger Fjord, Norway 6 F9 60 5N 6 0 E
Harding, S. Africa 31 C4 30 35S 29 55 E
Hari →, Indonesia 22 D2 1 16S 104 5 E
Haridwar, India 23 E7 29 58N 78 9 E
Haringhata →, Bangla. 23 J12 22 0N 89 58 E
Härnösand, Sweden 6 F11 62 38N 17 55 E
Harrisburg, U.S.A. 42 E9 40 16N 76 53W
Harrismith, S. Africa 31 B4 28 15S 29 8 E
Harrisonburg, U.S.A. 42 F8 38 27N 78 52W
Harrisville, U.S.A. 42 C6 44 39N 83 17W
Hart, U.S.A. 42 D4 43 42N 86 22W
Hartford, Conn., U.S.A. 43 E11 41 46N 72 41W
Hartford, Ky., U.S.A. 42 G4 37 27N 86 55W
Harts →, S. Africa 31 B3 28 24S 24 17 E
Harvey, U.S.A. 42 E4 41 36N 87 50W
Haryana □, India 23 E6 29 0N 76 10 E
Harz, Germany 10 C6 51 38N 10 44 E
Hasa, Si. Arabia 24 C3 26 0N 49 0 E
Hastings, U.S.A. 42 D5 42 39N 85 17W
Hathras, India 23 F7 27 36N 78 6 E
Hatteras, C., U.S.A. 41 C11 35 14N 75 32W
Haugesund, Norway 6 G9 59 23N 5 13 E
Havana, Cuba 45 C8 23 8N 82 22W
Havel →, Germany 10 B7 52 50N 12 3 E
Haverhill, U.S.A. 43 D12 42 47N 71 5W
Hawaiian Is., Pac. Oc. 40 H17 20 30N 156 0W
Hawkesbury, Canada 43 C10 45 37N 74 37W
Hay River, Canada 38 B8 60 51N 115 44W
Hazard, U.S.A. 42 G6 37 15N 83 12W
Hazaribag, India 23 H10 23 58N 85 26 E
Hazleton, U.S.A. 42 E10 40 57N 75 59W
Hearst, Canada 42 A6 49 40N 83 41W
Heath Pt., Canada 43 A17 49 8N 61 40W
Hebei □, China 21 C6 39 0N 116 0 E
Hechuan, China 20 C5 30 2N 106 12 E
Heerlen, Neths. 10 C3 50 55N 5 58 E
Hefei, China 21 C6 31 52N 117 18 E
Hegang, China 21 B8 47 20N 130 19 E
Heidelberg, Germany 10 D5 49 24N 8 42 E
Heilbron, S. Africa 31 B4 27 16S 27 59 E
Heilbronn, Germany 10 D5 49 9N 9 13 E
Heilongjiang □, China 21 B7 48 0N 126 0 E
Hejaz, Si. Arabia 24 C2 26 0N 37 30 E
Helgoland, Germany 10 A4 54 10N 7 53 E
Helmand →, Afghan. 24 B5 31 12N 61 34 E
Helsingborg, Sweden 6 G10 56 3N 12 42 E
Helsinki, Finland 6 F13 60 15N 25 3 E
Henan □, China 21 C6 34 0N 114 0 E
Henderson, U.S.A. 42 G4 37 50N 87 35W
Hengyang, China 21 D6 26 52N 112 33 E
Henlopen, C., U.S.A. 43 F10 38 48N 75 6W
Herat, Afghan. 24 B5 34 20N 62 7 E
Herford, Germany 10 B5 52 7N 8 39 E
Hermanus, S. Africa 31 C2 34 27S 19 12 E
Hermosillo, Mexico 44 B2 29 10N 111 0W
Hernád →, Hungary 11 D11 47 56N 21 8 E
's-Hertogenbosch, Neths. 10 C3 51 42N 5 17 E
Hessen □, Germany 10 C5 50 30N 9 0 E
High Atlas, Morocco 28 B3 32 30N 5 0W
Hildesheim, Germany 10 B5 52 9N 9 56 E
Hillsdale, U.S.A. 42 E5 41 56N 84 38W
Hilo, U.S.A. 40 J17 19 44N 155 5W
Hilversum, Neths. 10 B3 52 14N 5 10 E
Himachal Pradesh □, India 23 D6 31 30N 77 0 E
Himalaya, Asia 23 E10 29 0N 84 0 E
Himeji, Japan 19 B4 34 50N 134 40 E
Hindu Kush, Asia 23 B2 36 0N 71 0 E
Hingoli, India 23 K6 19 41N 77 15 E
Hinton, U.S.A. 42 G7 37 40N 80 54W
Hiroshima, Japan 19 B3 34 24N 132 30 E
Hisar, India 23 E5 29 12N 75 45 E
Hispaniola, W. Indies 45 D10 19 0N 71 0W
Hjälmaren, Sweden 6 G11 59 18N 15 40 E
Ho Chi Minh City, Vietnam 22 B2 10 58N 106 40 E
Hobart, Australia 34 J8 42 50S 147 21 E
Hódmezövásárhely, Hungary 11 E11 46 28N 20 22 E
Hoggar, Algeria 28 D6 23 0N 6 30 E
Hohhot, China 21 B6 40 52N 111 40 E
Hokkaidō □, Japan 19 F12 43 30N 143 0 E
Holguín, Cuba 45 C9 20 50N 76 20W
Hollams Bird I., Namibia 31 A1 24 40S 14 30 E
Holland, U.S.A. 42 D4 42 47N 86 7W
Homs, Syria 24 B2 34 40N 36 45 E
Honduras ■, Cent. Amer. 44 E7 14 40N 86 30W
Honduras, G. de, Caribbean 44 D7 16 50N 87 0W
Hong Kong, China 21 D6 22 11N 114 14 E
Hongha →, Vietnam 20 D5 22 0N 104 0 E
Honiara, Solomon Is. 35 B10 9 27S 159 57 E
Honolulu, U.S.A. 40 H16 21 19N 157 52W
Honshū, Japan 19 B6 36 0N 138 0 E
Hooghly →, India 23 J12 21 56N 88 4 E
Hoopeston, U.S.A. 42 E4 40 28N 87 40W
Hoorn, Neths. 10 B3 52 38N 5 4 E
Hopetown, S. Africa 31 B3 29 34S 24 3 E
Hopkinsville, U.S.A. 42 G4 36 52N 87 29W
Hormuz, Str. of, The Gulf 24 C4 26 30N 56 30 E
Horn, C., Chile 47 H3 55 50S 67 30W
Hornavan, Sweden 6 E11 66 15N 17 30 E
Hornell, U.S.A. 42 D9 42 20N 77 40W
Hornepayne, Canada 42 A5 49 14N 84 48W
Horsham, Australia 34 H7 36 44S 142 13 E
Hospitalet de Llobregat, Spain 9 B7 41 21N 2 6 E
Hotan, China 20 C2 37 25N 79 55 E
Houghton, U.S.A. 42 B3 47 7N 88 34W
Houghton L., U.S.A. 42 C5 44 21N 84 44W
Houlton, U.S.A. 43 B14 46 8N 67 51W
Houston, U.S.A. 41 E7 29 46N 95 22W
Hovd, Mongolia 20 B4 48 2N 91 37 E
Hövsgöl Nuur, Mongolia 20 A5 51 0N 100 30 E
Howell, U.S.A. 42 D6 42 36N 83 56W
Howick, S. Africa 31 B5 29 28S 30 14 E
Howrah = Haora, India 23 H12 22 37N 88 20 E
Høyanger, Norway 6 F9 61 13N 6 4 E
Hradec Králové, Czech Rep. 10 C8 50 15N 15 50 E
Hron →, Slovak Rep. 11 E10 47 49N 18 45 E
Huainan, China 21 C6 32 38N 116 58 E
Huambo, Angola 33 G3 12 42S 15 54 E
Huancayo, Peru 46 D2 12 5S 75 12W
Huangshi, China 21 C6 30 10N 115 3 E
Hubei □, China 21 C6 31 0N 112 0 E
Hudiksvall, Sweden 6 F11 61 43N 17 10 E
Hudson →, U.S.A. 43 E10 40 42N 74 2W
Hudson Bay, Canada 39 C11 60 0N 86 0W
Hudson Falls, U.S.A. 43 D11 43 18N 73 35W
Hudson Str., Canada 39 B13 62 0N 70 0W
Hue, Vietnam 22 B2 16 30N 107 35 E
Huelva, Spain 9 D2 37 18N 6 57W
Huesca, Spain 9 A5 42 8N 0 25W
Hughenden, Australia 34 E7 20 52S 144 10 E
Hull = Kingston upon Hull, U.K. 7 E6 53 45N 0 21W
Hull, Canada 43 C10 45 25N 75 44W
Humboldt →, U.S.A. 40 B3 39 59N 118 36W
Húnaflói, Iceland 6 B3 65 50N 20 50W
Hunan □, China 21 D6 27 30N 112 0 E
Hungary ■, Europe 11 E10 47 20N 19 20 E
Hungnam, N. Korea 21 C7 39 49N 127 45 E
Hunsrück, Germany 10 D4 49 56N 7 27 E
Huntington, Ind., U.S.A. 42 E5 40 53N 85 30W
Huntington, W. Va., U.S.A. 42 F6 38 25N 82 27W
Huntsville, Canada 42 C8 45 20N 79 14W
Huntsville, U.S.A. 41 D9 34 44N 86 35W
Huron, L., U.S.A. 42 C6 44 30N 82 40W
Húsavík, Iceland 6 A5 66 3N 17 21W
Hwang-ho →, China 21 C6 37 55N 118 50 E
Hyderabad, India 25 D6 17 22N 78 29 E
Hyderabad, Pakistan 23 G2 25 23N 68 24 E
Hyères, France 8 E7 43 8N 6 9 E
Hyères, Is. d', France 8 E7 43 0N 6 20 E

I

Ialomiţa →, Romania 11 F14 44 42N 27 51 E
Iaşi, Romania 11 E14 47 10N 27 40 E
Ibadan, Nigeria 30 C2 7 22N 3 58 E
Ibagué, Colombia 46 B2 4 20N 75 20W
Iberian Peninsula, Europe 4 H5 40 0N 5 0W
Ibiza, Spain 9 C6 38 54N 1 26 E
Iceland ■, Europe 6 B4 64 45N 19 0W
Ichinomiya, Japan 19 B5 35 18N 136 48 E
Idaho □, U.S.A. 40 B4 45 0N 115 0W
Idar-Oberstein, Germany 10 D4 49 43N 7 16 E
Ife, Nigeria 30 C2 7 30N 4 31 E
Iglésias, Italy 12 E3 39 19N 8 32 E
Igluligaarjuk, Canada 38 B10 63 30N 90 45W
Ignace, Canada 42 A2 49 30N 91 40W
Iguaçu Falls, Brazil 47 E4 25 41S 54 26W
Iisalmi, Finland 6 F13 63 32N 27 10 E
IJsselmeer, Neths. 10 B3 52 45N 5 20 E
Ikaluktutiak, Canada 38 B9 69 10N 105 0W
Ikerre-Ekiti, Nigeria 30 C3 7 25N 5 19 E
Ila, Nigeria 30 C2 8 0N 4 39 E
Île-de-France, France 8 B5 49 0N 2 20 E
Ilesha, Nigeria 30 C2 7 37N 4 40 E
Ilhéus, Brazil 46 D6 14 49S 39 2W
Ili →, Kazakstan 18 E9 45 53N 77 10 E
Iller →, Germany 10 D6 48 23N 9 58 E
Illinois □, U.S.A. 41 C9 40 15N 89 30W
Iloilo, Phil. 22 B4 10 45N 122 33 E
Ilorin, Nigeria 30 C2 8 30N 4 35 E
Imperatriz, Brazil 46 C5 5 30S 47 29W
Imphal, India 25 C8 24 48N 93 56 E
Inari, L., Finland 6 E13 69 0N 28 0 E
Inchon, S. Korea 21 C7 37 27N 126 40 E
Incomáti →, Mozam. 31 B5 25 46S 32 43 E
Indals →, Sweden 6 F11 62 36N 17 30 E
India ■, Asia 23 K7 20 0N 78 0 E
Indiana, U.S.A. 42 E8 40 37N 79 9W
Indiana □, U.S.A. 42 E4 40 0N 86 0W
Indianapolis, U.S.A. 42 F4 39 46N 86 9W
Indigirka →, Russia 18 B16 70 48N 148 54 E
Indonesia ■, Asia 22 D3 5 0S 115 0 E
Indore, India 23 H5 22 42N 75 53 E
Indre →, France 8 C4 47 16N 0 11 E
Indus →, Pakistan 23 G1 24 20N 67 47 E
Ingolstadt, Germany 10 D6 48 46N 11 26 E
Inn →, Austria 10 D7 48 35N 13 28 E
Inner Mongolia □, China 21 B6 42 0N 112 0 E
Innsbruck, Austria 10 E6 47 16N 11 23 E
Inowrocław, Poland 11 B10 52 50N 18 12 E
Insein, Burma 25 D8 16 50N 96 5 E
Interlaken, Switz. 10 E4 46 41N 7 50 E
Inuvik, Canada 38 B6 68 16N 133 40W
Invercargill, N.Z. 35 K12 46 24S 168 24 E
Inverness, U.K. 7 C4 57 29N 4 13W
Ionia, U.S.A. 42 D5 42 59N 85 4W
Ionian Is., Greece 13 E9 38 40N 20 0 E
Ionian Sea, Medit. S. 13 E7 37 30N 17 30 E
Iowa □, U.S.A. 41 B8 42 18N 93 30W
Iowa City, U.S.A. 41 B8 41 40N 91 32W
Ipoh, Malaysia 22 C2 4 35N 101 5 E
Ipswich, U.K. 7 E7 52 4N 1 10 E
Iquique, Chile 46 E2 20 19S 70 5W
Iquitos, Peru 46 C2 3 45S 73 10W
Iráklion, Greece 13 G11 35 20N 25 12 E
Iran ■, Asia 24 B4 33 0N 53 0 E
Iran Ra., Malaysia 22 C3 2 20N 114 50 E
Irapuato, Mexico 44 C4 20 40N 101 30W
Iraq ■, Asia 24 B3 33 0N 44 0 E
Ireland ■, Europe 7 E2 53 50N 7 52W
Irian Jaya □, Indonesia 22 D5 4 0S 137 0 E
Iringa, Tanzania 32 F7 7 48S 35 43 E
Irish Sea, U.K. 7 E4 53 38N 4 48W
Irkutsk, Russia 18 D12 52 18N 104 20 E
Iron Gate, Europe 11 F12 44 42N 22 30 E
Iron Mountain, U.S.A. 42 C3 45 49N 88 4W
Ironton, U.S.A. 42 F6 38 32N 82 41W
Irrawaddy →, Burma 25 D8 15 50N 95 6 E
Irtysh →, Russia 18 C8 61 4N 68 52 E
Ísafjörður, Iceland 6 A2 66 5N 23 9W
Isar →, Germany 10 D7 48 48N 12 57 E
Isère →, France 8 D6 44 59N 4 51 E
Iseyin, Nigeria 30 C2 8 0N 3 36 E
Ishpeming, U.S.A. 42 B4 46 29N 87 40W
İskenderun, Turkey 15 G6 36 32N 36 10 E
Islamabad, Pakistan 23 C4 33 40N 73 10 E
Island Pond, U.S.A. 43 C12 44 49N 71 53W
Ismâ'ilîya, Egypt 29 B11 30 37N 32 18 E
Israel ■, Asia 24 B2 32 0N 34 50 E
Issoire, France 8 D5 45 32N 3 15 E
İstanbul, Turkey 13 D13 41 0N 29 0 E
Istres, France 8 E6 43 31N 4 59 E
Istria, Croatia 10 F7 45 10N 14 0 E
Itaipu Dam, Brazil 47 E4 25 30S 54 30W
Italy ■, Europe 12 C5 42 0N 13 0 E
Ithaca, U.S.A. 42 D9 42 27N 76 30W
Ivanava, Belarus 11 B13 52 7N 25 29 E
Ivano-Frankovsk, Ukraine 11 D13 48 40N 24 40 E
Ivanovo, Russia 14 C7 57 5N 41 0 E
Ivory Coast ■, Africa 28 G3 7 30N 5 0W
Ivujivik, Canada 39 B12 62 24N 77 55W
Iwaki, Japan 19 A7 37 3N 140 55 E
Iwo, Nigeria 30 C2 7 39N 4 9 E
Ixopo, S. Africa 31 C5 30 11S 30 5 E
Izhevsk, Russia 14 C9 56 51N 53 14 E
İzmir, Turkey 13 E12 38 25N 27 8 E

J

Jabalpur, India 23 H7 23 9N 79 58 E
Jackson, Ky., U.S.A. 42 G6 37 33N 83 23W
Jackson, Mich., U.S.A. 42 D5 42 15N 84 24W
Jackson, Miss., U.S.A. 41 D8 32 18N 90 12W
Jacksonville, U.S.A. 41 D10 30 20N 81 39W
Jacobabad, Pakistan 23 E2 28 20N 68 29 E
Jaén, Spain 9 D4 37 44N 3 43W
Jaffna, Sri Lanka 25 E7 9 45N 80 2 E
Jagersfontein, S. Africa 31 B4 29 44S 25 27 E
Jahrom, Iran 24 C4 28 30N 53 31 E
Jaipur, India 23 F5 27 0N 75 50 E
Jakarta, Indonesia 22 D2 6 9S 106 49 E
Jalalabad, Afghan. 23 B3 34 30N 70 29 E
Jalgaon, India 23 J5 21 0N 75 42 E
Jalna, India 23 K5 19 48N 75 38 E
Jalpaiguri, India 23 F12 26 32N 88 46 E
Jamaica ■, W. Indies 44 J16 18 10N 77 30W
Jamalpur, Bangla. 23 G12 24 52N 89 56 E
Jamalpur, India 23 G11 25 18N 86 28 E
Jambi, Indonesia 22 D2 1 38S 103 30 E
James B., Canada 39 C11 51 30N 80 0W

Place names on the yellow-coded large scale map section are to be found in the index at the end of that section

94
INDEX TO WORLD MAPS
Jamestown — Kushtia

Jamestown, *Ky., U.S.A.* 42 G5 36 59N 85 4W
Jamestown, *N.Y., U.S.A.* 42 D8 42 6N 79 14W
Jammu, *India* 23 C5 32 43N 74 54 E
Jammu & Kashmir □, *India* 23 B6 34 25N 77 0 E
Jamnagar, *India* 23 H3 22 30N 70 6 E
Jamshedpur, *India* 23 H11 22 44N 86 12 E
Jaora, *India* 23 H5 23 40N 75 10 E
Japan ■, *Asia* 19 G11 36 0N 136 0 E
Japan, Sea of, *Asia* 19 G11 40 0N 135 0 E
Japurá →, *Brazil* 46 C3 3 8S 65 46W
Jask, *Iran* 24 C4 25 38N 57 45 E
Jaunpur, *India* 23 G9 25 46N 82 44 E
Java, *Indonesia* 22 D3 7 0S 110 0 E
Java Sea, *Indonesia* 22 D2 4 35S 107 15 E
Jedda, *Si. Arabia* 24 C2 21 29N 39 10 E
Jeffersonville, *U.S.A.* 42 F5 38 17N 85 44W
Jelenia Góra, *Poland* 10 C8 50 50N 15 45 E
Jena, *Germany* 10 C6 50 54N 11 35 E
Jerez de la Frontera, *Spain* 9 D2 36 41N 6 7W
Jersey City, *U.S.A.* 43 E10 40 44N 74 4W
Jerusalem, *Israel* 24 B2 31 47N 35 10 E
Jessore, *Bangla.* 23 H12 23 10N 89 10 E
Jhang Maghiana, *Pakistan* 23 D4 31 15N 72 22 E
Jhansi, *India* 23 G7 25 30N 78 36 E
Jhelum, *Pakistan* 23 C4 33 0N 73 45 E
Jhelum →, *Pakistan* 23 D4 31 20N 72 10 E
Jiamusi, *China* 21 B8 46 40N 130 26 E
Jian, *China* 21 D6 27 6N 114 59 E
Jiangsu □, *China* 21 C7 33 0N 120 0 E
Jiangxi □, *China* 21 D6 27 30N 116 0 E
Jihlava →, *Czech Rep.* 11 D9 48 55N 16 36 E
Jilin, *China* 21 B7 43 44N 126 30 E
Jilin □, *China* 21 B7 44 0N 127 0 E
Jima, *Ethiopia* 29 G12 7 40N 36 47 E
Jinan, *China* 21 C6 36 38N 117 1 E
Jinja, *Uganda* 32 D6 0 25N 33 12 E
Jinzhou, *China* 21 B7 41 5N 121 3 E
Jixi, *China* 21 B8 45 20N 130 50 E
João Pessoa, *Brazil* 46 C6 7 10S 34 52W
Jodhpur, *India* 23 F4 26 23N 73 8 E
Johannesburg, *S. Africa* 31 B4 26 10S 28 2 E
Johnson City, *U.S.A.* 43 D10 42 7N 75 58W
Johnstown, *U.S.A.* 42 E8 40 20N 78 55W
Johor Baharu, *Malaysia* 22 C2 1 28N 103 46 E
Joliet, *U.S.A.* 42 E3 41 32N 88 5W
Joliette, *Canada* 43 B11 46 3N 73 24W
Jolo, *Phil.* 22 C4 6 0N 121 0 E
Jönköping, *Sweden* 6 G10 57 45N 14 10 E
Jonquière, *Canada* 43 A12 48 27N 71 14W
Jordan ■, *Asia* 24 B2 31 0N 36 0 E
Jos, *Nigeria* 30 C3 9 53N 8 51 E
Juan de Fuca Str., *Canada* 40 A2 48 15N 124 0W
Juiz de Fora, *Brazil* 46 E5 21 43S 43 19W
Jullundur, *India* 23 D5 31 20N 75 40 E
Junagadh, *India* 23 J3 21 30N 70 30 E
Juneau, *U.S.A.* 38 C6 58 18N 134 25W
Junggar Pendi, *China* 20 B3 44 30N 86 0 E
Jupiter →, *Canada* 43 A16 49 29N 63 37W
Jura, *Europe* 8 C7 46 40N 6 5 E
Jutland, *Denmark* 6 G9 56 25N 9 30 E
Jyväskylä, *Finland* 6 F13 62 14N 25 50 E

K

K2, *Pakistan* 23 B6 35 58N 76 32 E
Kabardino Balkaria □, *Russia* 15 F7 43 30N 43 30 E
Kābul, *Afghan.* 23 B2 34 28N 69 11 E
Kabwe, *Zambia* 33 G5 14 30S 28 29 E
Kachin □, *Burma* 25 C8 26 0N 97 30 E
Kaduna, *Nigeria* 30 B3 10 30N 7 21 E
Kaesong, *N. Korea* 21 C7 37 58N 126 35 E
Kagoshima, *Japan* 19 D2 31 35N 130 33 E
Kai Is., *Indonesia* 22 D5 5 55S 132 45 E
Kaifeng, *China* 21 C6 34 48N 114 21 E
Kaiserslautern, *Germany* 10 D4 49 26N 7 45 E
Kaitaia, *N.Z.* 35 H13 35 8S 173 17 E
Kajaani, *Finland* 6 F13 64 17N 27 46 E
Kakinada, *India* 25 D7 16 57N 82 11 E
Kalaallit Nunaat = Greenland □, *N. Amer.* 48 C4 66 0N 45 0W
Kalahari, *Africa* 31 A3 24 0S 21 30 E
Kalamazoo, *U.S.A.* 42 D5 42 17N 85 35W
Kalamazoo →, *U.S.A.* 42 D4 42 40N 86 10W
Kalemie, *Congo (Zaïre)* 32 F5 5 55S 29 9 E
Kalgoorlie-Boulder, *Australia* 34 G3 30 40S 121 22 E
Kalimantan, *Indonesia* 22 D3 0 0 114 0 E
Kaliningrad, *Russia* 14 D3 54 42N 20 32 E
Kalisz, *Poland* 11 C10 51 45N 18 8 E
Kalkaska, *U.S.A.* 42 C5 44 44N 85 11W
Kalmar, *Sweden* 6 G11 56 40N 16 20 E
Kalmykia □, *Russia* 15 E8 46 5N 46 1 E
Kaluga, *Russia* 14 D6 54 35N 36 10 E
Kama →, *Russia* 14 C9 55 45N 52 0 E
Kamchatka, *Russia* 18 D18 57 0N 160 0 E
Kamina, *Congo (Zaïre)* 32 F5 8 45S 25 0 E
Kamloops, *Canada* 38 C7 50 40N 120 20W
Kampala, *Uganda* 32 D6 0 20N 32 30 E
Kampuchea = Cambodia ■, *Asia* 22 B2 12 15N 105 0 E
Kamyanets-Podilskyy, *Ukraine* 11 D14 48 45N 26 40 E
Kananga, *Congo (Zaïre)* 32 F4 5 55S 22 18 E
Kanawha →, *U.S.A.* 42 F6 38 50N 82 9W
Kanazawa, *Japan* 19 A5 36 30N 136 38 E
Kanchenjunga, *Nepal* 23 F12 27 50N 88 10 E
Kanchipuram, *India* 25 D6 12 52N 79 45 E
Kandy, *Sri Lanka* 25 E7 7 18N 80 43 E
Kane, *U.S.A.* 42 E8 41 40N 78 49W
Kangean Is., *Indonesia* 22 D3 6 55S 115 23 E
Kanin Pen., *Russia* 14 A8 68 0N 45 0 E
Kankakee, *U.S.A.* 42 E4 41 7N 87 52W
Kankakee →, *U.S.A.* 42 E3 41 23N 88 15W
Kankan, *Guinea* 28 F3 10 23N 9 15W
Kano, *Nigeria* 30 B3 12 2N 8 30 E
Kanpur, *India* 23 F8 26 28N 80 20 E
Kansas □, *U.S.A.* 40 C7 38 30N 99 0W
Kansas City, *Kans., U.S.A.* 41 C8 39 7N 94 38W
Kansas City, *Mo., U.S.A.* 41 C8 39 6N 94 35W
Kanye, *Botswana* 31 A4 24 55S 25 28 E
Kaohsiung, *Taiwan* 21 D7 22 35N 120 16 E
Kaolack, *Senegal* 28 F1 14 5N 16 8W
Kaposvár, *Hungary* 11 E9 46 25N 17 47 E
Kapuas →, *Indonesia* 22 D2 0 25S 109 20 E
Kapuas Hulu Ra., *Malaysia* 22 C3 1 30N 113 30 E
Kapuskasing, *Canada* 42 A6 49 25N 82 30W
Kara Bogaz Gol, *Turkmenistan* 15 F9 41 0N 53 30 E
Kara Kum, *Turkmenistan* 18 F8 39 30N 60 0 E
Kara Sea, *Russia* 18 B8 75 0N 70 0 E
Karachi, *Pakistan* 23 G1 24 53N 67 0 E
Karaganda, *Kazakstan* 18 E9 49 50N 73 10 E
Karakoram Ra., *Pakistan* 23 B6 35 30N 77 0 E
Karasburg, *Namibia* 31 B2 28 0S 18 44 E
Karbala, *Iraq* 24 B3 32 36N 44 3 E
Karelia □, *Russia* 14 A5 65 30N 32 30 E
Karimata Is., *Indonesia* 22 D2 1 25S 109 0 E
Karimunjawa Is., *Indonesia* 22 D3 5 50S 110 30 E
Karlskrona, *Sweden* 6 G11 56 10N 15 35 E
Karlsruhe, *Germany* 10 D5 49 0N 8 23 E
Karlstad, *Sweden* 6 G10 59 23N 13 30 E
Karnal, *India* 23 E6 29 42N 77 2 E
Karnataka □, *India* 25 D6 13 15N 77 0 E
Kärnten □, *Austria* 10 E8 46 52N 13 30 E
Karsakpay, *Kazakstan* 18 E8 47 55N 66 40 E
Kasai →, *Congo (Zaïre)* 32 E3 3 30S 16 10 E
Kashan, *Iran* 24 B4 34 5N 51 30 E
Kashi, *China* 20 C2 39 30N 76 2 E
Kassalâ, *Sudan* 29 E12 15 30N 36 0 E
Kassel, *Germany* 10 C5 51 18N 9 26 E
Kasur, *Pakistan* 23 D5 31 5N 74 25 E
Katha, *Burma* 25 C8 24 10N 96 30 E
Katihar, *India* 23 G11 25 34N 87 36 E
Katmandu, *Nepal* 23 F10 27 45N 85 20 E
Katowice, *Poland* 11 C10 50 17N 19 5 E
Katsina, *Nigeria* 30 B3 13 0N 7 32 E
Kattegat, *Denmark* 6 G10 57 0N 11 20 E
Kauai, *U.S.A.* 40 H15 22 3N 159 30W
Kaukauna, *U.S.A.* 42 C3 44 17N 88 17W
Kaunas, *Lithuania* 14 D3 54 54N 23 54 E
Kavála, *Greece* 13 D11 40 57N 24 28 E
Kawagoe, *Japan* 19 B6 35 55N 139 29 E
Kawardha, *India* 23 J8 22 0N 81 17 E
Kawasaki, *Japan* 19 B6 35 35N 139 42 E
Kayes, *Mali* 28 F2 14 25N 11 30W
Kayseri, *Turkey* 15 G6 38 45N 35 30 E
Kazakstan ■, *Asia* 18 E9 50 0N 70 0 E
Kazan, *Russia* 14 C8 55 50N 49 10 E
Kazerun, *Iran* 24 C4 29 38N 51 40 E
Kebnekaise, *Sweden* 6 E11 67 53N 18 33 E
Kecskemét, *Hungary* 11 E10 46 57N 19 42 E
Kediri, *Indonesia* 22 D3 7 51S 112 1 E
Keene, *U.S.A.* 43 D11 42 56N 72 17W
Keetmanshoop, *Namibia* 31 B2 26 35S 18 8 E
Kefallinía, *Greece* 13 E9 38 20N 20 30 E
Keflavík, *Iceland* 6 B2 64 2N 22 35W
Kelang, *Malaysia* 22 C2 3 2N 101 26 E
Kelowna, *Canada* 38 D8 49 50N 119 25W
Kemerovo, *Russia* 18 D10 55 20N 86 5 E
Kemi, *Finland* 6 E12 65 44N 24 34 E
Kemi →, *Finland* 6 E12 65 47N 24 32 E
Kendari, *Indonesia* 22 D4 3 50S 122 30 E
Kenhardt, *S. Africa* 31 B3 29 19S 21 12 E
Kenitra, *Morocco* 28 B3 34 15N 6 40W
Kenosha, *U.S.A.* 42 D4 42 35N 87 49W
Kent, *U.S.A.* 42 E7 41 9N 81 22W
Kenton, *U.S.A.* 42 E6 40 39N 83 37W
Kentucky □, *U.S.A.* 42 G5 37 0N 84 0W
Kentucky →, *U.S.A.* 42 F5 38 41N 85 11W
Kentville, *Canada* 43 C15 45 6N 64 29W
Kenya ■, *Africa* 32 D7 1 0N 38 0 E
Kenya, Mt., *Kenya* 32 E7 0 10S 37 18 E
Kerala □, *India* 25 D6 11 0N 76 15 E
Kerch, *Ukraine* 15 E6 45 20N 36 20 E
Kerinci, *Indonesia* 22 D2 1 40S 101 15 E
Kermadec Trench, *Pac. Oc.* 35 G15 30 30S 176 0W
Kerman, *Iran* 24 B4 30 15N 57 1 E
Kestell, *S. Africa* 31 B4 28 17S 28 42 E
Ketchikan, *U.S.A.* 38 C6 55 21N 131 39W
Kewaunee, *U.S.A.* 42 C4 44 27N 87 31W
Keweenaw B., *U.S.A.* 42 B3 47 0N 88 15W
Keweenaw Pen., *U.S.A.* 42 B3 47 30N 88 0W
Keweenaw Pt., *U.S.A.* 42 B4 47 25N 87 43W
Key West, *U.S.A.* 41 F10 24 33N 81 48W
Keyser, *U.S.A.* 42 F8 39 26N 78 59W
Khabarovsk, *Russia* 18 E15 48 30N 135 5 E
Khairpur, *Pakistan* 23 F2 27 32N 68 49 E
Khamas Country, *Botswana* 31 A4 21 45S 26 30 E
Khandwa, *India* 23 J6 21 49N 76 22 E
Khanewal, *Pakistan* 23 D3 30 20N 71 55 E
Khaniá, *Greece* 13 G11 35 30N 24 4 E
Kharagpur, *India* 23 H11 22 20N 87 25 E
Khargon, *India* 23 J5 21 45N 75 40 E
Kharkov, *Ukraine* 15 E6 49 58N 36 20 E
Khartoum, *Sudan* 29 E11 15 31N 32 35 E
Khaskovo, *Bulgaria* 13 D11 41 56N 25 30 E
Khatanga, *Russia* 18 B12 72 0N 102 20 E
Kherson, *Ukraine* 15 E5 46 35N 32 35 E
Khmelnitskiy, *Ukraine* 11 D14 49 23N 27 0 E
Khorixas, *Namibia* 31 A1 20 16S 14 59 E
Khorramshahr, *Iran* 24 B3 30 29N 48 15 E
Khouribga, *Morocco* 28 B3 32 58N 6 57W
Khulna, *Bangla.* 23 H12 22 45N 89 34 E
Khulna □, *Bangla.* 23 H12 22 25N 89 35 E
Khumago, *Botswana* 31 A3 20 26S 24 32 E
Khushab, *Pakistan* 23 C4 32 20N 72 20 E
Khuzdar, *Pakistan* 23 F1 27 52N 66 30 E
Kicking Horse Pass, *Canada* 38 C8 51 28N 116 16W
Kiel, *Germany* 10 A6 54 19N 10 8 E
Kiel Canal = Nord-Ostsee-Kanal →, *Germany* 10 A5 54 12N 9 32 E
Kielce, *Poland* 11 C11 50 52N 20 42 E
Kieler Bucht, *Germany* 10 A6 54 35N 10 25 E
Kiev, *Ukraine* 11 C16 50 30N 30 28 E
Kigali, *Rwanda* 32 E6 1 59S 30 4 E
Kigoma-Ujiji, *Tanzania* 32 E5 4 55S 29 36 E
Kikwit, *Congo (Zaïre)* 32 E3 5 0S 18 45 E
Kilimanjaro, *Tanzania* 32 E7 3 7S 37 20 E
Kimberley, *S. Africa* 31 B3 28 43S 24 46 E
Kimberley Plateau, *Australia* 34 D4 16 20S 127 0 E
Kincardine, *Canada* 42 C7 44 10N 81 40W
Kindu, *Congo (Zaïre)* 32 E5 2 55S 25 50 E
King William's Town, *S. Africa* 31 C4 32 51S 27 22 E
Kingston, *Canada* 42 C9 44 14N 76 30W
Kingston, *Jamaica* 44 K17 18 0N 76 50W
Kingston, *N.Y., U.S.A.* 43 E10 41 56N 73 59W
Kingston, *Pa., U.S.A.* 43 E10 41 16N 75 54W
Kingston upon Hull, *U.K.* 7 E6 53 45N 0 21W
Kingstown, *St. Vincent* 44 P20 13 10N 61 10W
Kinshasa, *Congo (Zaïre)* 32 E3 4 20S 15 15 E
Kirensk, *Russia* 18 D12 57 50N 107 55 E
Kirgiz Steppe, *Eurasia* 15 D10 50 0N 55 0 E
Kiribati ■, *Pac. Oc.* 36 H10 5 0S 180 0 E
Kirkenes, *Norway* 6 E14 69 40N 30 5 E
Kirkland Lake, *Canada* 42 A7 48 9N 80 2W
Kirkuk, *Iraq* 24 B3 35 30N 44 21 E
Kirkwood, *S. Africa* 31 C4 33 22S 25 15 E
Kirov, *Russia* 14 C8 58 35N 49 40 E
Kirovograd, *Ukraine* 15 E5 48 35N 32 20 E
Kirthar Range, *Pakistan* 23 F1 27 0N 67 0 E
Kiruna, *Sweden* 6 E12 67 52N 20 15 E
Kisangani, *Congo (Zaïre)* 32 D5 0 35N 25 15 E
Kishanganj, *India* 23 F12 26 3N 88 14 E
Kishinev, *Moldova* 11 E15 47 0N 28 50 E
Kisumu, *Kenya* 32 E6 0 3S 34 45 E
Kitakyūshū, *Japan* 19 C2 33 50N 130 50 E
Kitchener, *Canada* 42 D7 43 27N 80 29W
Kíthira, *Greece* 13 F10 36 8N 23 0 E
Kitimat, *Canada* 38 C7 54 3N 128 38W
Kittanning, *U.S.A.* 42 E8 40 49N 79 31W
Kitwe, *Zambia* 33 G5 12 54S 28 13 E
Kivu, L., *Congo (Zaïre)* 32 E5 1 48S 29 0 E
Kladno, *Czech Rep.* 10 C8 50 10N 14 7 E
Klagenfurt, *Austria* 10 E8 46 38N 14 20 E
Klar →, *Sweden* 6 G10 59 23N 13 32 E
Klawer, *S. Africa* 31 C2 31 44S 18 36 E
Klerksdorp, *S. Africa* 31 B4 26 53S 26 38 E
Klipplaat, *S. Africa* 31 C3 33 1S 24 22 E
Klondike, *Canada* 38 B6 64 0N 139 26W
Klyuchevsk Vol., *Russia* 18 D18 55 50N 160 30 E
Knossós, *Greece* 13 G11 35 16N 25 10 E
Knoxville, *U.S.A.* 41 C10 35 58N 83 55W
Knysna, *S. Africa* 31 C3 34 2S 23 2 E
Kōbe, *Japan* 19 B4 34 45N 135 10 E
Koblenz, *Germany* 10 C4 50 21N 7 36 E
Kobroor, *Indonesia* 22 D5 6 10S 134 30 E
Koch Bihar, *India* 23 F12 26 22N 89 29 E
Kodiak I., *U.S.A.* 38 C4 57 30N 152 45W
Koffiefontein, *S. Africa* 31 B4 29 30S 25 0 E
Koforidua, *Ghana* 30 C1 6 3N 0 17W
Koh-i-Bābā, *Afghan.* 23 B1 34 30N 67 0 E
Kohat, *Pakistan* 23 C3 33 40N 71 29 E
Kokchetav, *Kazakstan* 18 D8 53 20N 69 25 E
Kokomo, *U.S.A.* 42 E4 40 29N 86 8W
Kokstad, *S. Africa* 31 C4 30 32S 29 29 E
Kola Pen., *Russia* 14 A6 67 30N 38 0 E
Kolar, *India* 25 D6 13 12N 78 15 E
Kolguyev I., *Russia* 14 A8 69 20N 48 30 E
Kolhapur, *India* 25 D6 16 43N 74 15 E
Kolomna, *Russia* 14 C6 55 8N 38 45 E
Kolwezi, *Congo (Zaïre)* 32 G5 10 40S 25 25 E
Kolyma →, *Russia* 18 C18 69 30N 161 0 E
Kolyma Ra., *Russia* 18 C17 63 0N 157 0 E
Komandorskiye Is., *Russia* 18 D18 55 0N 167 0 E
Komatipoort, *S. Africa* 31 B5 25 25S 31 55 E
Komi □, *Russia* 14 B10 64 0N 55 0 E
Kompong Cham, *Cambodia* 22 B2 12 0N 105 30 E
Kompong Chhnang, *Cambodia* 22 B2 12 20N 104 35 E
Kompong Som, *Cambodia* 22 B2 10 38N 103 30 E
Komsomolets I., *Russia* 18 A11 80 30N 95 0 E
Komsomolsk, *Russia* 18 D15 50 30N 137 0 E
Konin, *Poland* 11 B10 52 12N 18 15 E
Konya, *Turkey* 15 G5 37 52N 32 35 E
Korce, *Albania* 13 D9 40 37N 20 50 E
Korea, North ■, *Asia* 21 C7 40 0N 127 0 E
Korea, South ■, *Asia* 21 C7 36 0N 128 0 E
Korea Strait, *Asia* 21 C7 34 0N 129 30 E
Kōriyama, *Japan* 19 A7 37 24N 140 23 E
Korla, *China* 20 B3 41 45N 86 4 E
Körös →, *Hungary* 11 E11 46 43N 20 12 E
Kortrijk, *Belgium* 10 C2 50 50N 3 17 E
Kos, *Greece* 13 F12 36 50N 27 15 E
Košice, *Slovak Rep.* 11 D11 48 42N 21 15 E
Kosovo □, *Serbia, Yug.* 13 C9 42 30N 21 0 E
Kosti, *Sudan* 29 F11 13 8N 32 43 E
Kostroma, *Russia* 14 C7 57 50N 40 58 E
Koszalin, *Poland* 10 A9 54 11N 16 8 E
Kota, *India* 23 G5 25 14N 75 49 E
Kota Baharu, *Malaysia* 22 C2 6 7N 102 14 E
Kota Kinabalu, *Malaysia* 22 C3 6 0N 116 4 E
Kotka, *Finland* 6 F13 60 28N 26 58 E
Kotri, *Pakistan* 23 G2 25 22N 68 22 E
Kotuy →, *Russia* 18 B12 71 54N 102 6 E
Kounradskiy, *Kazakstan* 18 E9 46 59N 75 0 E
Kra, Isthmus of, *Thailand* 22 B1 10 15N 99 30 E
Kragujevac, *Serbia, Yug.* 13 B9 44 2N 20 56 E
Krajina, *Bos.-H.* 12 B7 44 45N 16 35 E
Kraków, *Poland* 11 C10 50 4N 19 57 E
Krasnodar, *Russia* 15 E6 45 5N 39 0 E
Krasnoturinsk, *Russia* 14 C11 59 46N 60 12 E
Krasnovodsk, *Turkmenistan* 15 F9 40 5N 53 5 E
Krasnoyarsk, *Russia* 18 D11 56 8N 93 0 E
Kratie, *Cambodia* 22 B2 12 32N 106 10 E
Krefeld, *Germany* 10 C4 51 20N 6 32 E
Kremenchug, *Ukraine* 15 E5 49 5N 33 25 E
Krishna →, *India* 25 D7 15 57N 80 59 E
Krishnanagar, *India* 23 H12 23 24N 88 33 E
Kristiansand, *Norway* 6 G9 58 8N 8 1 E
Kristiansund, *Norway* 6 F9 63 7N 7 45 E
Krivoy Rog, *Ukraine* 15 E5 47 51N 33 20 E
Kroonstad, *S. Africa* 31 B4 27 43S 27 19 E
Krosno, *Poland* 11 D11 49 42N 21 46 E
Kruger Nat. Park, *S. Africa* 31 A5 23 30S 31 40 E
Krugersdorp, *S. Africa* 31 B4 26 5S 27 46 E
Kruisfontein, *S. Africa* 31 C3 33 59S 24 43 E
Kruševac, *Serbia, Yug.* 13 C9 43 35N 21 28 E
Kuala Lumpur, *Malaysia* 22 C2 3 9N 101 41 E
Kuala Terengganu, *Malaysia* 22 C2 5 20N 103 8 E
Kualakapuas, *Indonesia* 22 D3 2 55S 114 20 E
Kucing, *Malaysia* 22 C3 1 33N 110 25 E
Kudat, *Malaysia* 22 C3 6 55N 116 55 E
Kugluktuk, *Canada* 38 B8 67 50N 115 5W
Kumanovo, *Macedonia* 13 C9 42 9N 21 42 E
Kumasi, *Ghana* 30 C1 6 41N 1 38W
Kumayri = Gyumri, *Armenia* 15 F7 40 47N 43 50 E
Kumbakonam, *India* 25 D6 10 58N 79 25 E
Kunlun Shan, *Asia* 20 C3 36 0N 86 30 E
Kunming, *China* 20 D5 25 1N 102 41 E
Kuopio, *Finland* 6 F13 62 53N 27 35 E
Kupang, *Indonesia* 22 E4 10 19S 123 39 E
Kür →, *Azerbaijan* 15 G8 39 29N 49 15 E
Kurashiki, *Japan* 19 B3 34 40N 133 50 E
Kurdistan, *Asia* 24 B3 37 20N 43 30 E
Kure, *Japan* 19 B3 34 14N 132 32 E
Kurgan, *Russia* 18 D8 55 26N 65 18 E
Kuril Is., *Russia* 18 E17 45 0N 150 0 E
Kurnool, *India* 25 D6 15 45N 78 0 E
Kursk, *Russia* 14 D6 51 42N 36 11 E
Kuruman, *S. Africa* 31 B3 27 28S 23 28 E
Kuruman →, *S. Africa* 31 B3 26 56S 20 39 E
Kurume, *Japan* 19 C2 33 15N 130 30 E
Kushiro, *Japan* 19 F12 43 0N 144 25 E
Kushtia, *Bangla.* 23 H12 23 55N 89 5 E

Place names on the yellow-coded large scale map section are to be found in the index at the end of that section

Kütahya   **Mandal**

Place names on the yellow-coded large scale map section are to be found in the index at the end of that section

96 INDEX TO WORLD MAPS

Mandale — Nagercoil

Mandale, *Burma* 25 C8 22 0N 96 4 E
Mandi, *India* 23 D6 31 39N 76 58 E
Mandla, *India* 23 H8 22 39N 80 30 E
Mandsaur, *India* 23 G5 24 3N 75 8 E
Mandvi, *India* 23 H2 22 51N 69 22 E
Mangalore, *India* 25 D6 12 55N 74 47 E
Manggar, *Indonesia* 22 D2 2 50S 108 10 E
Mangole, *Indonesia* 22 D4 1 50S 125 55 E
Manila, *Phil.* 22 B4 14 40N 121 3 E
Manila B., *Phil.* 22 B4 14 40N 120 35 E
Manipur □, *India* 25 C8 25 0N 94 0 E
Manistee, *U.S.A.* 42 C4 44 15N 86 19W
Manistee →, *U.S.A.* 42 C4 44 15N 86 21W
Manistique, *U.S.A.* 42 C4 45 57N 86 15W
Manitoba □, *Canada* 38 C10 55 30N 97 0W
Manitou Is., *U.S.A.* 42 C4 45 8N 86 0W
Manitoulin I., *Canada* 42 C6 45 40N 82 30W
Manitowoc, *U.S.A.* 42 C4 44 5N 87 40W
Manizales, *Colombia* 46 B2 5 5N 75 32W
Mannar, *Sri Lanka* 25 E6 9 1N 79 54 E
Mannheim, *Germany* 10 D5 49 29N 8 29 E
Manokwari, *Indonesia* 22 D5 0 54S 134 0 E
Manosque, *France* 8 E6 43 49N 5 47 E
Mansfield, *U.S.A.* 42 E6 40 45N 82 31W
Mantes-la-Jolie, *France* 8 B4 48 58N 1 41 E
Manton, *U.S.A.* 42 C5 44 25N 85 24W
Mántova, *Italy* 12 B4 45 9N 10 48 E
Manzai, *Pakistan* 23 C3 32 12N 70 15 E
Manzhouli, *China* 21 B6 49 35N 117 25 E
Manzini, *Swaziland* 31 B5 26 30S 31 25 E
Maoming, *China* 21 D6 21 50N 110 54 E
Mapam Yumco, *China* 23 D8 30 45N 81 28 E
Maputo, *Mozam.* 31 B5 25 58S 32 32 E
Mar del Plata, *Argentina* 47 F4 38 0S 57 30W
Marabá, *Brazil* 46 C5 5 20S 49 5W
Maracaibo, *Venezuela* 46 A2 10 40N 71 37W
Maracaibo, L., *Venezuela* 46 B2 9 40N 71 30W
Maracay, *Venezuela* 46 A3 10 15N 67 28W
Marajo I., *Brazil* 46 C5 1 0S 49 30W
Marañón →, *Peru* 46 C2 4 30S 73 35W
Marbella, *Spain* 9 D3 36 30N 4 57W
Marche, *France* 8 C4 46 5N 1 20 E
Mardan, *Pakistan* 23 B4 34 20N 72 0 E
Mari El □, *Russia* 14 C8 56 30N 48 0 E
Maribor, *Slovenia* 10 E8 46 36N 15 40 E
Marico →, *Africa* 31 A4 23 35S 26 57 E
Maricourt, *Canada* 39 C12 56 34N 70 49W
Marie-Galante, *Guadeloupe* 45 D12 15 56N 61 16W
Mariental, *Namibia* 31 A2 24 36S 18 0 E
Marietta, *U.S.A.* 42 F7 39 25N 81 27W
Marinette, *U.S.A.* 42 C4 45 6N 87 38W
Marion, *Ind., U.S.A.* 42 E5 40 32N 85 40W
Marion, *Ohio, U.S.A.* 42 E6 40 35N 83 8W
Maritimes, Alpes, *Europe* 10 F4 44 10N 7 10 E
Mariupol, *Ukraine* 15 E6 47 5N 37 31 E
Marmara, Sea of, *Turkey* 13 D13 40 45N 28 15 E
Marmora, *Canada* 42 C9 44 28N 77 41W
Marne →, *France* 8 B5 48 48N 2 24 E
Maroua, *Cameroon* 29 F7 10 40N 14 20 E
Marquesas Is., *Pac. Oc.* 37 H14 9 30S 140 0W
Marquette, *U.S.A.* 42 B4 46 33N 87 24W
Marrakesh, *Morocco* 28 B3 31 9N 8 0W
Marseilles, *France* 8 E6 43 18N 5 23 E
Marshall Is. ■, *Pac. Oc.* 36 G9 9 0N 171 0 E
Martaban, G. of, *Burma* 25 D8 16 5N 96 30 E
Martha's Vineyard, *U.S.A.* 43 E12 41 25N 70 38W
Martigues, *France* 8 E6 43 24N 5 4 E
Martinique □, *W. Indies* 45 E12 14 40N 61 0W
Martinsburg, *U.S.A.* 42 F9 39 27N 77 58W
Martinsville, *U.S.A.* 42 F4 39 26N 86 25W
Marwar, *India* 23 G4 25 43N 73 45 E
Maryland □, *U.S.A.* 42 F9 39 0N 76 30W
Masan, *S. Korea* 21 C7 35 11N 128 32 E
Maseru, *Lesotho* 31 B4 29 18S 27 30 E
Mashhad, *Iran* 24 B4 36 20N 59 35 E
Massachusetts □, *U.S.A.* 43 D11 42 30N 72 0W
Massena, *U.S.A.* 43 C10 44 56N 74 54W
Massif Central, *France* 8 D5 44 55N 3 0 E
Massillon, *U.S.A.* 42 E7 40 48N 81 32W
Masurian Lakes, *Poland* 11 B11 53 50N 21 0 E
Masvingo, *Zimbabwe* 33 J6 20 8S 30 49 E
Matadi, *Congo (Zaïre)* 32 F2 5 52S 13 31 E
Matagami, *Canada* 42 A9 49 45N 77 34W
Matagami, L., *Canada* 42 A9 49 50N 77 40W
Matamoros, *Mexico* 44 B4 25 33N 103 15W
Matane, *Canada* 43 A14 48 50N 67 33W
Mataró, *Spain* 9 B7 41 32N 2 29 E
Matatiele, *S. Africa* 31 C4 30 20S 28 49 E
Matera, *Italy* 12 D7 40 40N 16 36 E
Mathura, *India* 23 F6 27 30N 77 40 E
Mato Grosso □, *Brazil* 46 D4 14 0S 55 0W
Mato Grosso, Plateau of, *Brazil* 46 D4 15 0S 55 0W
Matsue, *Japan* 19 B3 35 25N 133 10 E
Matsuyama, *Japan* 19 C3 33 45N 132 45 E
Mattawa, *Canada* 42 B8 46 20N 78 45W
Mattawamkeag, *U.S.A.* 43 C13 45 32N 68 21W
Matterhorn, *Switz.* 10 F4 45 58N 7 39 E
Maubeuge, *France* 8 A6 50 17N 3 57 E
Maui, *U.S.A.* 40 H16 20 48N 156 20W
Maumee →, *U.S.A.* 42 E6 41 42N 83 28W
Maumere, *Indonesia* 22 D4 8 38S 122 13 E
Maun, *Botswana* 31 A3 20 0S 23 26 E
Mauna Loa, *U.S.A.* 40 J17 19 30N 155 35W
Mauritania ■, *Africa* 28 D3 20 50N 10 0W
Mauritius ■, *Ind. Oc.* 27 J9 20 0S 57 0 E
May Pen, *Jamaica* 44 K16 17 58N 77 15W
Mayfield, *U.S.A.* 42 G3 36 44N 88 38W
Maysville, *U.S.A.* 42 F6 38 39N 83 46W
Mazar-e Sharīf, *Afghan.* 24 B5 36 41N 67 0 E
Mazatlán, *Mexico* 44 C3 23 13N 106 25W
Mbabane, *Swaziland* 31 B5 26 18S 31 6 E
Mbandaka, *Congo (Zaïre)* 32 D3 0 1N 18 18 E
Mbanza Ngungu, *Congo (Zaïre)* 32 F2 5 12S 14 53 E
Mbeya, *Tanzania* 32 F6 8 54S 33 29 E
Mbini □, *Eq. Guin.* 32 D2 1 30N 10 0 E
Mbuji-Mayi, *Congo (Zaïre)* 32 F4 6 9S 23 40 E
Meadville, *U.S.A.* 42 E7 41 39N 80 9W
Meaford, *Canada* 42 C7 44 36N 80 35W
Meaux, *France* 8 B5 48 58N 2 50 E
Mechelen, *Belgium* 10 C3 51 2N 4 29 E
Mecklenburg, *Germany* 10 B6 53 33N 11 40 E
Medan, *Indonesia* 22 C1 3 40N 98 38 E
Medellín, *Colombia* 46 B2 6 15N 75 35W
Medicine Hat, *Canada* 38 D8 50 0N 110 45W
Medina, *Si. Arabia* 24 C2 24 35N 39 52 E
Mediterranean Sea, *Europe* 26 C5 35 0N 15 0 E
Médoc, *France* 8 D3 45 10N 0 50W
Meekatharra, *Australia* 34 F2 26 32S 118 29 E
Meerut, *India* 23 E6 29 1N 77 42 E
Meghalaya □, *India* 23 G13 25 50N 91 0 E
Mei Xian, *China* 21 D6 24 16N 116 6 E
Mekhtar, *Pakistan* 23 D2 30 30N 69 15 E
Meknès, *Morocco* 28 B3 33 57N 5 33W
Mekong →, *Asia* 22 C2 9 30N 106 15 E
Melaka, *Malaysia* 22 C2 2 15N 102 15 E
Melanesia, *Pac. Oc.* 36 H7 4 0S 155 0 E
Melbourne, *Australia* 34 H8 37 50S 145 0 E
Melitopol, *Ukraine* 15 E6 46 50N 35 22 E
Melun, *France* 8 B5 48 32N 2 39 E
Melville I., *Australia* 34 C5 11 30S 131 0 E
Melville Pen., *Canada* 39 B11 68 0N 84 0W
Memphis, *U.S.A.* 41 C9 35 8N 90 3W
Menasha, *U.S.A.* 42 C3 44 13N 88 26W
Mende, *France* 8 D5 44 31N 3 30 E
Mendoza, *Argentina* 47 F3 32 50S 68 52W
Menominee, *U.S.A.* 42 C4 45 6N 87 37W
Menominee →, *U.S.A.* 42 C4 45 6N 87 36W
Menorca, *Spain* 9 C8 40 0N 4 0 E
Mentawai Is., *Indonesia* 22 D1 2 0S 99 0 E
Mérida, *Mexico* 44 C7 20 58N 89 37W
Meriden, *U.S.A.* 43 E11 41 32N 72 48W
Mersin, *Turkey* 15 G5 36 51N 34 36 E
Mesa, *U.S.A.* 40 D4 33 25N 111 50W
Mesopotamia, *Iraq* 24 C3 33 30N 44 0 E
Messina, *Italy* 12 E6 38 11N 15 34 E
Messina, *S. Africa* 31 A5 22 20S 30 5 E
Messina, Str. di, *Italy* 12 F6 38 15N 15 35 E
Metz, *France* 8 B7 49 8N 6 10 E
Meuse →, *Europe* 10 C3 50 45N 5 41 E
Mexicali, *Mexico* 44 A1 32 40N 115 30W
México, *Mexico* 44 D5 19 20N 99 10W
Mexico ■, *Cent. Amer.* 44 C4 25 0N 105 0W
Mexico, G. of, *Cent. Amer.* 44 B7 25 0N 90 0W
Mhow, *India* 23 H5 22 33N 75 50 E
Miami, *U.S.A.* 41 E10 25 47N 80 11W
Mianwali, *Pakistan* 23 C3 32 38N 71 28 E
Michigan □, *U.S.A.* 41 B9 44 0N 85 0W
Michigan, L., *U.S.A.* 42 D4 44 0N 87 0W
Michipicoten I., *Canada* 42 B5 47 40N 85 40W
Micronesia, Federated States of ■, *Pac. Oc.* 36 G7 9 0N 150 0 E
Middelburg, *Eastern Cape, S. Africa* 31 C3 31 30S 25 0 E
Middelburg, *Mpumalanga, S. Africa* 31 B4 25 49S 29 28 E
Middlesbrough, *U.K.* 7 D6 54 35N 1 13W
Middletown, *N.Y., U.S.A.* 43 E10 41 27N 74 25W
Middletown, *Ohio, U.S.A.* 42 F5 39 31N 84 24W
Midi, Canal du →, *France* 8 E4 43 45N 1 21 E
Midland, *Canada* 42 C8 44 45N 79 50W
Midland, *Mich., U.S.A.* 42 D5 43 37N 84 14W
Midland, *Tex., U.S.A.* 40 D6 32 0N 102 3W
Midway Is., *Pac. Oc.* 36 E10 28 13N 177 22W
Midwest, *U.S.A.* 41 B9 42 0N 90 0W
Mieres, *Spain* 9 A3 43 18N 5 48W
Milan, *Italy* 12 B3 45 28N 9 12 E
Mildura, *Australia* 34 G7 34 13S 142 9 E
Milford, *U.S.A.* 43 F10 38 55N 75 26W
Milk →, *U.S.A.* 40 A5 48 4N 106 19W
Millau, *France* 8 D5 44 8N 3 4 E
Millinocket, *U.S.A.* 43 C13 45 39N 68 43W
Millville, *U.S.A.* 43 F10 39 24N 75 2W
Milwaukee, *U.S.A.* 42 D4 43 2N 87 55W
Minas Gerais □, *Brazil* 46 D5 18 50S 46 0W
Minatitlán, *Mexico* 44 D6 17 59N 94 31W
Mindanao, *Phil.* 22 C4 8 0N 125 0 E
Mindoro, *Phil.* 22 B4 13 0N 121 0 E
Mindoro Str., *Phil.* 22 B4 12 30N 120 30 E
Minneapolis, *U.S.A.* 41 B8 44 59N 93 16W
Minnesota □, *U.S.A.* 41 A8 46 0N 94 15W
Minorca = Menorca, *Spain* 9 C8 40 0N 4 0 E
Minsk, *Belarus* 11 B14 53 52N 27 30 E
Miramichi B., *Canada* 43 B15 47 15N 65 0W
Mirpur Khas, *Pakistan* 23 G2 25 30N 69 0 E
Mirzapur, *India* 23 G9 25 10N 82 34 E
Mishawaka, *U.S.A.* 42 E4 41 40N 86 11W
Miskolc, *Hungary* 11 D11 48 7N 20 50 E
Misool, *Indonesia* 22 D5 1 52S 130 10 E
Mississippi □, *U.S.A.* 41 D9 33 0N 90 0W
Mississippi →, *U.S.A.* 41 E9 29 9N 89 15W
Mississippi River Delta, *U.S.A.* 41 E8 29 10N 89 15W
Missouri □, *U.S.A.* 41 C8 38 25N 92 30W
Missouri →, *U.S.A.* 41 C8 38 49N 90 7W
Misurata, *Libya* 29 B8 32 24N 15 3 E
Mitchell →, *Australia* 34 D7 15 12S 141 35 E
Mitumba Mts., *Congo (Zaïre)* 32 F5 7 0S 27 30 E
Miyazaki, *Japan* 19 D2 31 56N 131 30 E
Mizoram □, *India* 25 C8 23 30N 92 40 E
Mjøsa, *Norway* 6 F10 60 40N 11 0 E
Mmabatho, *S. Africa* 31 B4 25 49S 25 30 E
Mobile, *U.S.A.* 41 D9 30 41N 88 3W
Mochudi, *Botswana* 31 A4 24 27S 26 7 E
Módena, *Italy* 12 B4 44 40N 10 55 E
Mogadishu, *Somali Rep.* 27 F8 2 2N 45 25 E
Mogalakwena →, *S. Africa* 31 A4 22 38S 28 40 E
Mogilev, *Belarus* 11 B16 53 55N 30 18 E
Mojave Desert, *U.S.A.* 40 D3 35 0N 116 30W
Moldavia = Moldova ■, *Europe* 11 E15 47 0N 28 0 E
Molde, *Norway* 6 F9 62 45N 7 9 E
Moldova ■, *Europe* 11 E15 47 0N 28 0 E
Molepolole, *Botswana* 31 A4 24 28S 25 28 E
Mollendo, *Peru* 46 D2 17 0S 72 0W
Molokai, *U.S.A.* 40 H16 21 8N 157 0W
Molopo →, *Africa* 31 B3 27 30S 20 13 E
Molteno, *S. Africa* 31 C4 31 22S 26 22 E
Molucca Sea, *Indonesia* 22 D4 2 0S 124 0 E
Moluccas, *Indonesia* 22 D4 1 0S 127 0 E
Mombasa, *Kenya* 32 E7 4 2S 39 43 E
Mona Passage, *W. Indies* 45 D11 18 30N 67 45W
Monaco ■, *Europe* 8 E7 43 46N 7 23 E
Mönchengladbach, *Germany* 10 C4 51 11N 6 27 E
Monclova, *Mexico* 44 B4 26 50N 101 30W
Moncton, *Canada* 43 B15 46 7N 64 51W
Mongolia ■, *Asia* 20 B5 47 0N 103 0 E
Mongu, *Zambia* 33 H4 15 16S 23 12 E
Monroe, *La., U.S.A.* 41 D8 32 30N 92 7W
Monroe, *Mich., U.S.A.* 42 E6 41 55N 83 24W
Monrovia, *Liberia* 28 G2 6 18N 10 47W
Mons, *Belgium* 10 C3 50 27N 3 58 E
Mont-de-Marsan, *France* 8 E3 43 54N 0 31W
Mont-Laurier, *Canada* 43 B10 46 35N 75 30W
Montagu, *S. Africa* 31 C3 33 45S 20 8 E
Montana □, *U.S.A.* 40 A5 47 0N 110 0W
Montargis, *France* 8 C5 47 59N 2 43 E
Montauban, *France* 8 D4 44 2N 1 21 E
Montbéliard, *France* 8 C7 47 31N 6 48 E
Montceau-les-Mines, *France* 8 C6 46 40N 4 23 E
Monte-Carlo, *Monaco* 10 G4 43 46N 7 23 E
Montego Bay, *Jamaica* 44 J16 18 30N 78 0W
Montélimar, *France* 8 D6 44 33N 4 45 E
Montenegro □, *Yugoslavia* 13 C8 42 40N 19 20 E
Montería, *Colombia* 46 B2 8 46N 75 53W
Monterrey, *Mexico* 44 B4 25 40N 100 30W
Montes Claros, *Brazil* 46 D5 16 30S 43 50W
Montevideo, *Uruguay* 47 F4 34 50S 56 11W
Montgomery, *U.S.A.* 41 D9 32 23N 86 19W
Monticello, *U.S.A.* 42 E4 40 45N 86 46W
Montluçon, *France* 8 C5 46 22N 2 36 E
Montmagny, *Canada* 43 B12 46 58N 70 34W
Montpelier, *U.S.A.* 43 C11 44 16N 72 35W
Montpellier, *France* 8 E5 43 37N 3 52 E
Montréal, *Canada* 43 C11 45 31N 73 34W
Montreux, *Switz.* 10 E4 46 26N 6 55 E
Montserrat □, *W. Indies* 44 L19 16 40N 62 10W
Mooi River, *S. Africa* 31 B4 29 13S 29 50 E
Moorreesburg, *S. Africa* 31 C2 33 6S 18 38 E
Moose Jaw, *Canada* 38 C9 50 24N 105 30W
Moosehead L., *U.S.A.* 43 C13 45 38N 69 40W
Mopti, *Mali* 28 F4 14 30N 4 0W
Mora, *Sweden* 6 F10 61 2N 14 38 E
Moradabad, *India* 23 E7 28 50N 78 50 E
Morava →, *Serbia, Yug.* 13 B9 44 36N 21 4 E
Morava →, *Slovak Rep.* 11 D9 48 10N 16 59 E
Mordvinia □, *Russia* 14 D7 54 20N 44 30 E
Morehead, *U.S.A.* 42 F6 38 11N 83 26W
Morelia, *Mexico* 44 D4 19 42N 101 7W
Morena, Sierra, *Spain* 9 C3 38 20N 4 0W
Morgantown, *U.S.A.* 42 F8 39 38N 79 57W
Morlaix, *France* 8 B2 48 36N 3 52W
Moro G., *Phil.* 22 C4 6 30N 123 0 E
Morocco ■, *N. Afr.* 28 B3 32 0N 5 50W
Morogoro, *Tanzania* 32 F7 6 50S 37 40 E
Morotai, *Indonesia* 22 C4 2 10N 128 30 E
Morris, *U.S.A.* 42 E3 41 22N 88 26W
Moscow, *Russia* 14 C6 55 45N 37 35 E
Moselle →, *Europe* 10 C4 50 22N 7 36 E
Moshi, *Tanzania* 32 E7 3 22S 37 18 E
Mosselbaai, *S. Africa* 31 C3 34 11S 22 8 E
Most, *Czech Rep.* 10 C7 50 31N 13 38 E
Mostaganem, *Algeria* 28 A5 35 54N 0 5 E
Mostar, *Bos.-H.* 13 C7 43 22N 17 50 E
Mosul, *Iraq* 24 B3 36 15N 43 5 E
Motihari, *India* 23 F10 26 30N 84 55 E
Moulins, *France* 8 C5 46 35N 3 19 E
Moulmein, *Burma* 25 D8 16 30N 97 40 E
Moundsville, *U.S.A.* 42 F7 39 55N 80 44W
Mount Carmel, *U.S.A.* 42 F4 38 25N 87 46W
Mount Desert I., *U.S.A.* 43 C13 44 21N 68 20W
Mount Gambier, *Australia* 34 H7 37 50S 140 46 E
Mount Isa, *Australia* 34 E6 20 42S 139 26 E
Mount Pleasant, *U.S.A.* 42 D5 43 36N 84 46W
Mount Sterling, *U.S.A.* 42 F6 38 4N 83 56W
Mount Vernon, *N.Y., U.S.A.* 43 E11 40 55N 73 50W
Mount Vernon, *Ohio, U.S.A.* 42 E6 40 23N 82 29W
Mozambique ■, *Africa* 33 H7 19 0S 35 0 E
Mozambique Chan., *Africa* 33 H8 17 30S 42 30 E
Mpumalanga, *S. Africa* 31 B5 29 50S 30 33 E
Muar, *Malaysia* 22 C2 2 3N 102 34 E
Mubarraz, *Si. Arabia* 24 C3 25 30N 49 40 E
Mudanjiang, *China* 21 B7 44 38N 129 30 E
Mufulira, *Zambia* 33 G5 12 32S 28 15 E
Muktsar, *India* 23 D5 30 30N 74 30 E
Mukur, *Afghan.* 23 C1 32 50N 67 42 E
Mulde →, *Germany* 10 C7 51 53N 12 15 E
Mulhacén, *Spain* 9 D4 37 4N 3 20W
Mulhouse, *France* 8 C7 47 40N 7 20 E
Mull, *U.K.* 7 C4 56 25N 5 56W
Muller Ra., *Indonesia* 22 C3 0 30N 113 30 E
Multan, *Pakistan* 23 D3 30 15N 71 36 E
Mumbaī, *India* 25 D6 18 55N 72 50 E
Muna, *Indonesia* 22 D4 5 0S 122 30 E
Muncie, *U.S.A.* 42 E5 40 12N 85 23W
Munger, *India* 23 G11 25 23N 86 30 E
Munich, *Germany* 10 D6 48 8N 11 34 E
Munising, *U.S.A.* 42 B4 46 25N 86 40W
Münster, *Germany* 10 C4 51 58N 7 37 E
Murchison →, *Australia* 34 F1 27 45S 114 0 E
Murcia, *Spain* 9 D5 38 5N 1 10W
Mureş →, *Romania* 11 E11 46 15N 20 13 E
Müritz-see, *Germany* 10 B7 53 25N 12 42 E
Murmansk, *Russia* 14 A5 68 57N 33 10 E
Murray, *U.S.A.* 42 G3 36 37N 88 19W
Murray →, *Australia* 34 H6 35 20S 139 22 E
Murwara, *India* 23 H8 23 46N 80 28 E
Muscat, *Oman* 24 C4 23 37N 58 36 E
Musgrave Ras., *Australia* 34 F5 26 0S 132 0 E
Musi →, *Indonesia* 22 D2 2 20S 104 56 E
Muskegon →, *U.S.A.* 42 D4 43 14N 86 21W
Muskegon Heights, *U.S.A.* 42 D4 43 12N 86 16W
Mustang, *Nepal* 23 E9 29 10N 83 55 E
Mutare, *Zimbabwe* 33 H6 18 58S 32 38 E
Muzaffarnagar, *India* 23 E6 29 26N 77 40 E
Muzaffarpur, *India* 23 F10 26 7N 85 23 E
Mwanza, *Tanzania* 32 E6 2 30S 32 58 E
Mweru, L., *Zambia* 32 F5 9 0S 28 40 E
Myanmar = Burma ■, *Asia* 25 C8 21 0N 96 30 E
Myingyan, *Burma* 25 C8 21 30N 95 20 E
Myitkyina, *Burma* 25 C8 25 24N 97 26 E
Mymensingh, *Bangla.* 23 G13 24 45N 90 24 E
Mysore, *India* 25 D6 12 17N 76 41 E
Mzimkulu →, *S. Africa* 31 C5 30 44S 30 28 E

N

Naab →, *Germany* 10 D6 49 1N 12 2 E
Nadiad, *India* 23 H4 22 41N 72 56 E
Nafud Desert, *Si. Arabia* 24 C3 28 15N 41 0 E
Nagaland □, *India* 25 C8 26 0N 94 30 E
Nagano, *Japan* 19 A6 36 40N 138 10 E
Nagaoka, *Japan* 19 A6 37 27N 138 51 E
Nagasaki, *Japan* 19 C1 32 47N 129 50 E
Nagaur, *India* 23 F4 27 15N 73 45 E
Nagercoil, *India* 25 E6 8 12N 77 26 E

Nagoya   **Oskarshamn**

Place names on the yellow-coded large scale map section are to be found in the index at the end of that section

Place names on the yellow-coded large scale map section are to be found in the index at the end of that section

Queenstown   **Saser**

Place names on the yellow-coded large scale map section are to be found in the index at the end of that section

Saskatchewan   **Szombathely**

Place names on the yellow-coded large scale map section are to be found in the index at the end of that section.

Tabas　　　　　　　　　　　　　　　　　　　　　　　　　　　　　**Vänern**

Place names on the yellow-coded large scale map section are to be found in the index at the end of that section

Vanino

Vanino, Russia ..... 18 E16 48 50N 140 5 E
Vännäs, Sweden ... 6 F11 63 58N 19 48 E
Vannes, France 8 C2 47 40N 2 47W
Vanrhynsdorp,
  S. Africa .... 31 C2 31 36S 18 44 E
Vanua Levu, Fiji ... 35 D14 16 33S 179 15 E
Vanuatu ■, Pac. Oc. 35 D12 15 0S 168 0 E
Varanasi, India .... 23 G9 25 22N 83 0 E
Varanger Fjord,
  Norway .... 6 D13 70 3N 29 25 E
Varberg, Sweden ... 6 G10 57 6N 12 20 E
Varna, Bulgaria ... 13 C12 43 13N 27 56 E
Västerås, Sweden ... 6 G11 59 37N 16 38 E
Västervik, Sweden .. 6 G11 57 43N 16 33 E
Vatican City ■, Europe 12 D5 41 54N 12 27 E
Vatnajökull, Iceland . 6 B5 64 30N 16 48W
Vättern, Sweden ... 6 G10 58 25N 14 30 E
Vega, Norway ...... 6 E10 65 40N 11 55 E
Vellore, India ..... 25 D6 12 57N 79 10 E
Vendée □, France .. 8 C3 46 50N 1 35W
Vendôme, France .. 8 C4 47 47N 1 3 E
Venezuela ■, S. Amer. 46 B3 8 0N 66 0W
Venice, Italy ...... 12 B5 45 27N 12 21 E
Ventoux, Mt., France . 8 D6 44 10N 5 17 E
Veracruz, Mexico .. 44 D5 19 10N 96 10W
Veraval, India ..... 23 J3 20 53N 70 27 E
Vercelli, Italy .... 12 B3 45 19N 8 25 E
Verdun, France ..... 8 B6 49 9N 5 24 E
Vereeniging, S. Africa 31 B4 26 38S 27 57 E
Verkhoyansk, Russia . 18 C15 67 35N 133 25 E
Verkhoyansk Ra.,
  Russia .... 18 C14 66 0N 129 0 E
Vermont □, U.S.A. . 43 D11 44 0N 73 0W
Verona, Italy ...... 12 B4 45 27N 11 0 E
Versailles, France .. 8 B5 48 48N 2 8 E
Verviers, Belgium .. 10 C3 50 37N 5 52 E
Vesoul, France ..... 8 C7 47 40N 6 11 E
Vesterålen, Norway .. 6 E10 68 45N 15 0 E
Vesuvio, Italy ..... 12 D6 40 49N 14 26 E
Veszprém, Hungary . 11 E9 47 8N 17 57 E
Vicenza, Italy ..... 12 B4 45 33N 11 33 E
Vichy, France ...... 8 C5 46 9N 3 26 E
Victoria, Canada .. 38 D7 48 30N 123 25W
Victoria □, Australia . 34 H7 37 0S 144 0 E
Victoria, L., Africa .. 32 E6 1 0S 33 0 E
Victoria de Durango =
  Durango, Mexico .. 44 C4 24 3N 104 39W
Victoria Falls,
  Zimbabwe .... 33 H5 17 58S 25 52 E
Victoria I., Canada .. 38 A8 71 0N 111 0W
Victoria West, S. Africa 31 C3 31 25S 23 4 E
Victoriaville, Canada . 43 B12 46 4N 71 56W
Vienna, Austria ... 10 D9 48 12N 16 22 E
Vienne, France ..... 8 D6 45 31N 4 53 E
Vienne →, France .. 8 C4 47 13N 0 5 E
Vientiane, Laos ... 22 B2 17 58N 102 36 E
Vierzon, France .... 8 C5 47 13N 2 5 E
Vietnam ■, Asia ... 22 B2 19 0N 106 0 E
Vigo, Spain 9 A1 42 12N 8 41W
Vijayawada, India .. 25 D7 16 31N 80 39 E
Vikna, Norway ..... 6 F10 64 55N 10 58 E
Vilaine →, France .. 8 C2 47 30N 2 27W
Vilhelmina, Sweden . 6 F11 64 35N 16 39 E
Villach, Austria ... 10 E7 46 37N 13 51 E
Villahermosa, Mexico 44 D6 17 59N 92 55W
Ville-Marie, Canada . 42 B8 47 20N 79 30W
Villeneuve-sur-Lot,
  France .... 8 D4 44 24N 0 42 E
Vilnius, Lithuania ... 14 D4 54 38N 25 19 E
Vilyuy →, Russia ... 18 C14 64 24N 126 26 E
Vilyuysk, Russia ... 18 C14 63 40N 121 35 E
Viña del Mar, Chile . 47 F2 33 0S 71 30W
Vincennes, U.S.A. .. 42 F4 38 41N 87 32W
Vindhya Ra., India .. 23 H6 22 50N 77 0 E
Vineland, U.S.A. .. 43 F10 39 29N 75 2W
Vinnitsa, Ukraine .. 11 D15 49 15N 28 30 E
Vire, France 8 B3 48 50N 0 53W
Virgin Is. (British) □,
  W. Indies 45 D12 18 30N 64 30W
Virgin Is. (U.S.) □,
  W. Indies 45 D12 18 20N 65 0W
Virginia, S. Africa ... 31 B4 28 8S 26 55 E
Virginia □, U.S.A. .. 42 G8 37 30N 78 45W
Visby, Sweden ..... 6 G11 57 37N 18 18 E
Vishakhapatnam, India 25 D7 17 45N 83 20 E
Vistula →, Poland .. 11 A10 54 22N 18 55 E
Viterbo, Italy ..... 12 C5 42 25N 12 6 E
Viti Levu, Fiji ... 35 D14 17 30S 177 30 E
Vitória, Brazil ... 46 E5 20 20S 40 22W
Vitoria, Spain 9 A4 42 50N 2 41W
Vitsyebsk, Belarus .. 14 C5 55 10N 30 15 E
Vladimir, Russia ... 14 C7 56 15N 40 30 E
Vladikavkaz, Russia . 15 F7 43 0N 44 35 E
Vladivostok, Russia . 18 E15 43 10N 131 53 E
Vlissingen, Neths. .. 10 C2 51 26N 3 34 E
Vlóra, Albania ... 13 D8 40 32N 19 28 E
Vltava →,
  Czech Rep. ...... 10 D8 50 21N 14 30 E
Vogelkop, Indonesia . 22 D5 1 25S 133 0 E
Vogelsberg, Germany 10 C5 50 31N 9 12 E
Vojvodina □,
  Serbia, Yug. ... 13 B9 45 20N 20 0 E
Volga →, Russia ... 15 E8 46 0N 48 30 E
Volga Hts., Russia .. 15 D8 51 0N 46 0 E
Volgograd, Russia .. 15 E7 48 40N 44 25 E
Volksrust, S. Africa . 31 B4 27 24S 29 53 E
Vologda, Russia ... 14 C6 59 10N 39 45 E
Vólos, Greece ..... 13 E10 39 24N 22 59 E
Volta →, Ghana ... 30 C2 5 46N 0 41 E
Volta, L., Ghana ... 30 C2 7 30N 0 15 E

Volzhskiy, Russia ... 15 E7 48 56N 44 46 E
Vorkuta, Russia ... 14 A11 67 48N 64 20 E
Voronezh, Russia ... 14 D6 51 40N 39 10 E
Vosges, France .... 8 B7 48 20N 7 10 E
Vrede, S. Africa ... 31 B4 27 24S 29 6 E
Vredenburg, S. Africa 31 C2 32 56S 18 0 E
Vryburg, S. Africa .. 31 B3 26 55S 24 45 E
Vryheid, S. Africa .. 31 B5 27 45S 30 47 E
Vyatka →, Russia .. 14 C9 55 37N 51 28 E

W

Waal →, Neths. .... 10 C3 51 37N 5 0 E
Wabash, U.S.A. 42 E5 40 48N 85 49W
Wabash →, U.S.A. .. 42 G3 37 48N 88 2 W
Waco, U.S.A. 41 D7 31 33N 97 9W
Wâd Medanî, Sudan . 29 F11 14 28N 33 30 E
Waddington, Mt.,
  Canada 38 C7 51 23N 125 15W
Wagga Wagga,
  Australia .... 34 H8 35 7S 147 24 E
Wah, Pakistan ..... 23 C4 33 45N 72 40 E
Waigeo, Indonesia .. 22 D5 0 20S 130 40 E
Wainganga →, India 23 K7 18 50N 79 55 E
Waingapu, Indonesia 22 D4 9 35S 120 11 E
Wakayama, Japan .. 19 B4 34 15N 135 15 E
Wales □, U.K. 7 E5 52 19N 4 43W
Walgett, Australia .. 34 F8 30 0S 148 5 E
Wallaceburg, Canada 42 D6 42 34N 82 23W
Wallachia = Valahia,
  Romania .... 11 F13 44 35N 25 0 E
Wallis & Futuna, Is.,
  Pac. Oc. 35 C15 13 18S 176 10W
Walvis Bay, Namibia . 31 A1 23 0S 14 28 E
Wanganui, N.Z. ... 35 H14 39 56S 175 3 E
Wapakoneta, U.S.A. . 42 E5 40 34N 84 12W
Warangal, India ... 25 D6 17 58N 79 35 E
Wardha →, India ... 23 K7 19 57N 79 11 E
Warmbad, S. Africa . 31 A4 24 51S 28 19 E
Warrego →, Australia 34 G8 30 24S 145 21 E
Warren, Mich., U.S.A. 42 D6 42 30N 83 0W
Warren, Ohio, U.S.A. 42 E7 41 14N 80 49W
Warren, Pa., U.S.A. . 42 E8 41 51N 79 9W
Warrenton, S. Africa . 31 B3 28 9S 24 47 E
Warrnambool,
  Australia .... 34 H7 38 25S 142 30 E
Warsaw, Poland ... 11 B11 52 13N 21 0 E
Warsaw, U.S.A. 42 E5 41 14N 85 51W
Warta →, Poland .. 10 B8 52 35N 14 39 E
Warwick, U.S.A. ... 43 E12 41 42N 71 28W
Wasatch Ra., U.S.A. . 40 B4 40 30N 111 15W
Washington, D.C.,
  U.S.A. 42 F9 38 54N 77 2W
Washington, Ind.,
  U.S.A. 42 F4 38 40N 87 10W
Washington, Pa.,
  U.S.A. 42 E7 40 10N 80 15W
Washington □, U.S.A. 40 A2 47 30N 120 30W
Washington, Mt.,
  U.S.A. 43 C12 44 16N 71 18W
Washington I., U.S.A. 42 C4 45 23N 86 54W
Waterbury, U.S.A. .. 43 E11 41 33N 73 3W
Waterford, Ireland .. 7 E3 52 15N 7 8W
Waterloo, Canada .. 42 D7 43 30N 80 32W
Watertown, U.S.A. .. 43 D10 43 59N 75 55W
Waterval-Boven,
  S. Africa .... 31 B5 25 40S 30 18 E
Waterville, U.S.A. .. 43 C13 44 33N 69 38W
Watseka, U.S.A. ... 42 E4 40 47N 87 44W
Watubela Is.,
  Indonesia .... 22 D5 4 28S 131 35 E
Waukegan, U.S.A. .. 42 D4 42 22N 87 50W
Waukesha, U.S.A. .. 42 D3 43 1N 88 14W
Wauwatosa, U.S.A. . 42 D4 43 3N 88 0W
Wawa, Canada 42 B5 47 59N 84 47W
Wayne, U.S.A. 42 F6 38 13N 82 27W
Waynesboro, U.S.A. . 42 F8 38 4N 78 53W
Waynesburg, U.S.A. . 42 F7 39 54N 80 11W
Wazirabad, Pakistan . 23 C5 32 30N 74 8 E
Webster Springs,
  U.S.A. 42 F7 38 29N 80 25W
Weddell Sea,
  Antarctica 48 E5 72 30S 40 0W
Weifang, China ... 21 C6 36 44N 119 7 E
Welch, U.S.A. 42 G7 37 26N 81 35W
Welkom, S. Africa .. 31 B4 28 0S 26 46 E
Welland, Canada ... 42 D8 43 0N 79 15W
Wellesley Is., Australia 34 D6 16 42S 139 30 E
Wellington, N.Z. ... 35 J13 41 19S 174 46 E
Wellsboro, U.S.A. .. 42 E9 41 45N 77 18W
Wellsville, U.S.A. .. 42 D9 42 7N 77 57W
Wels, Austria ..... 10 D8 48 9N 14 1 E
Wenzhou, China ... 21 D7 28 0N 120 38 E
Wepener, S. Africa .. 31 B4 29 42S 27 3 E
Weser →, Germany . 10 B5 53 36N 8 28 E
West Bend, U.S.A. .. 42 D3 43 25N 88 11W
West Bengal □, India 23 H11 23 0N 88 0 E
West Beskids, Europe 11 D10 49 30N 19 0 E
West Fjord, Norway . 6 E10 67 55N 14 0 E
West Point, U.S.A. .. 42 G9 37 32N 76 48W
West Pt., Canada ... 43 A15 49 52N 64 40W
West Virginia □,
  U.S.A. 42 F7 38 45N 80 30W
Westbrook, U.S.A. .. 43 D12 43 41N 70 22W
Western Australia □,
  Australia .... 34 F3 25 0S 118 0 E

Western Ghats, India 25 D6 14 0N 75 0 E
Western Sahara ■,
  Africa 28 D2 25 0N 13 0W
Western Samoa ■,
  Pac. Oc. 35 C16 14 0S 172 0W
Westerwald, Germany 10 C4 50 38N 7 56 E
Westminster, U.S.A. . 42 F9 39 34N 76 59W
Weston, U.S.A. 42 F7 39 2N 80 28W
Wetar, Indonesia ... 22 D4 7 30S 126 30 E
Whangarei, N.Z. ... 35 H13 35 43S 174 21 E
Wheeling, U.S.A. ... 42 E7 40 4N 80 43W
White →, U.S.A. ... 42 G3 38 25N 87 45W
White Nile →, Sudan 29 E11 15 38N 32 31 E
White Sea, Russia .. 14 A6 66 30N 38 0 E
Whitefish Point, U.S.A. 42 B5 46 45N 84 59W
Whitehorse, Canada . 38 B6 60 43N 135 3W
Whitewater, U.S.A. .. 42 D3 42 50N 88 44W
Whitney, Mt., U.S.A. . 40 C3 36 35N 118 18W
Whyalla, Australia .. 34 G6 33 2S 137 30 E
Wiarton, Canada ... 42 C7 44 40N 81 10W
Wichita, U.S.A. 41 C7 37 42N 97 20W
Wichita Falls, U.S.A. 40 D7 33 54N 98 30W
Wiener Neustadt,
  Austria .... 10 E9 47 49N 16 16 E
Wiesbaden, Germany 10 C5 50 4N 8 14 E
Wilge →, S. Africa .. 31 B4 27 3S 28 20 E
Wilhelmshaven,
  Germany .... 10 B5 53 31N 8 7 E
Wilkes-Barre, U.S.A. 43 E10 41 15N 75 53W
Willemstad, Neth. Ant. 45 E11 12 5N 69 0W
Williamsburg, U.S.A. 42 G9 37 17N 76 44W
Williamson, U.S.A. .. 42 G6 37 41N 82 17W
Williamsport, U.S.A. 42 E9 41 15N 77 0W
Williston, S. Africa .. 31 C3 31 20S 20 53 E
Willowmore, S. Africa 31 C3 33 15S 23 30 E
Wilmington, Del.,
  U.S.A. 43 F10 39 45N 75 33W
Wilmington, Ohio,
  U.S.A. 42 F6 39 27N 83 50W
Winchester, Ky.,
  U.S.A. 42 G6 38 0N 84 11W
Winchester, Va.,
  U.S.A. 42 F8 39 11N 78 10W
Windhoek, Namibia . 31 A2 22 35S 17 4 E
Windsor, Canada ... 42 D6 42 18N 83 0W
Windward Is.,
  W. Indies 44 P20 13 0N 61 0W
Winnebago, L., U.S.A. 42 D3 44 0N 88 26W
Winnipeg, Canada .. 38 D10 49 54N 97 9W
Winnipeg, L., Canada 38 C10 52 0N 97 0W
Winooski, U.S.A. ... 43 C11 44 29N 73 11W
Winston-Salem, U.S.A. 41 C10 36 6N 80 15W
Winterthur, Switz. .. 10 E5 47 30N 8 44 E
Wisconsin □, U.S.A. 41 B9 44 45N 89 30W
Witbank, S. Africa .. 31 B4 25 51S 29 14 E
Witdraai, S. Africa .. 31 B3 26 58S 20 48 E
Wkra →, Poland ... 11 B11 52 27N 20 44 E
Włocławek, Poland .. 11 B10 52 40N 19 3 E
Wokam, Indonesia .. 22 D5 5 45S 134 28 E
Wolfsburg, Germany . 10 B6 52 25N 10 48 E
Wollongong, Australia 34 G9 34 25S 150 54 E
Wolverhampton, U.K. 7 E5 52 35N 2 7W
Wǒnsan, N. Korea .. 21 C7 39 11N 127 27 E
Woods, L. of the,
  Canada 38 D10 49 15N 94 45W
Woodstock, Canada . 42 D7 43 10N 80 45W
Woonsocket, U.S.A. . 43 E11 42 0N 71 31W
Worcester, S. Africa . 31 C2 33 39S 19 27 E
Worcester, U.S.A. .. 43 D12 42 16N 71 48W
Worms, Germany ... 10 D5 49 37N 8 21 E
Wrangel I., Russia .. 18 B19 71 0N 180 0 E
Wrocław, Poland ... 11 C9 51 5N 17 5 E
Wuhan, China ..... 21 C6 30 31N 114 18 E
Wuhu, China ...... 21 C6 31 22N 118 21 E
Wuppertal, Germany 10 C4 51 16N 7 12 E
Würzburg, Germany . 10 D5 49 46N 9 55 E
Wutongqiao, China . 20 D5 29 22N 103 50 E
Wuxi, China .... 21 C7 31 33N 120 18 E
Wuzhou, China .... 21 D6 23 30N 111 18 E
Wyndham, Australia . 34 D4 15 33S 128 3 E
Wyoming □, U.S.A. . 40 B5 43 0N 107 30W

X

Xau, L., Botswana .. 31 A3 21 15S 24 44 E
Xenia, U.S.A. 42 F6 39 41N 83 56W
Xiaguan, China ... 20 D5 25 32N 100 16 E
Xiamen, China .... 21 D6 24 25N 118 4 E
Xi'an, China ...... 21 C5 34 15N 109 0 E
Xiangfan, China ... 21 C6 32 2N 112 8 E
Xiangtan, China ... 21 D6 27 51N 112 54 E
Xingu →, Brazil ... 46 C4 1 30S 51 53W
Xining, China ..... 20 C5 36 34N 101 40 E
Xuzhou, China .... 21 C6 34 18N 117 10 E

Y

Yablonovyy Ra.,
  Russia .... 18 D13 53 0N 114 0 E
Yakutsk, Russia ... 18 C14 62 5N 129 50 E
Yamagata, Japan .. 19 A7 38 15N 140 15 E
Yambol, Bulgaria .. 13 C12 42 30N 26 36 E
Yamdena, Indonesia . 22 D5 7 45S 131 20 E

Zwolle

Yamethin, Burma .. 25 C8 20 29N 96 18 E
Yamuna →, India .. 23 G8 25 30N 81 53 E
Yangtze Kiang →,
  China .... 21 C7 31 48N 121 10 E
Yanji, China ...... 21 B7 42 59N 129 30 E
Yantai, China ..... 21 C7 37 34N 121 22 E
Yaoundé, Cameroon . 30 D4 3 50N 11 35 E
Yapen, Indonesia .. 22 D5 1 50S 136 0 E
Yarkhun →, Pakistan 23 A4 36 17N 72 30 E
Yarmouth, Canada .. 43 D14 43 50N 66 7W
Yaroslavl, Russia .. 14 C6 57 35N 39 55 E
Yatsushiro, Japan .. 19 C2 32 30N 130 40 E
Yazd, Iran .... 24 B4 31 55N 54 27 E
Yekaterinburg, Russia 14 C11 56 50N 60 30 E
Yellow Sea, China .. 21 C7 35 0N 123 0 E
Yellowknife, Canada . 38 B8 62 27N 114 29W
Yellowstone →,
  U.S.A. 40 A6 47 59N 103 59W
Yellowstone National
  Park, U.S.A. 40 B5 44 40N 110 30W
Yemen ■, Asia .... 24 D3 15 0N 44 0 E
Yenbo, Si. Arabia .. 24 C2 24 0N 38 5 E
Yenisey →, Russia .. 18 B10 71 50N 82 40 E
Yeniseysk, Russia .. 18 D11 58 27N 92 13 E
Yeola, India ...... 23 J5 20 2N 74 30 E
Yerevan, Armenia .. 15 F7 40 10N 44 31 E
Yeu, I. d', France .. 8 C2 46 42N 2 20W
Yibin, China ...... 20 D5 28 45N 104 32 E
Yichang, China .... 21 C6 30 40N 111 20 E
Yining, China ..... 20 B3 43 58N 81 10 E
Yogyakarta, Indonesia 22 D3 7 49S 110 22 E
Yokkaichi, Japan .. 19 B5 34 55N 136 38 E
Yokohama, Japan .. 19 B6 35 27N 139 28 E
Yokosuka, Japan .. 19 B6 35 20N 139 40 E
Yonkers, U.S.A. ... 43 E11 40 56N 73 54W
Yonne →, France .. 8 B5 48 23N 2 58 E
York, U.K. 7 E6 53 58N 1 6W
York, U.S.A. 42 F9 39 58N 76 44W
Yosemite National
  Park, U.S.A. 40 C3 37 45N 119 40W
Yoshkar Ola, Russia . 14 C8 56 38N 47 55 E
Youngstown, U.S.A. . 42 E7 41 6N 80 39W
Yuan Jiang →, China 21 D6 28 55N 111 50 E
Yucatan, Mexico ... 44 D7 19 30N 89 0W
Yucatan Str.,
  Caribbean 44 C7 22 0N 86 30W
Yugoslavia ■, Europe 13 B9 44 0N 20 0 E
Yukon →, U.S.A. .. 38 B3 62 32N 163 54W
Yukon Territory □,
  Canada 38 B6 63 0N 135 0W
Yunnan □, China .. 20 D5 25 0N 102 0 E
Yuzhno-Sakhalinsk,
  Russia .... 18 E16 46 58N 142 45 E
Yvetot, France ..... 8 B4 49 37N 0 44 E

Z

Zabrze, Poland .... 11 C10 50 18N 18 50 E
Zagreb, Croatia ... 10 F9 45 50N 16 0 E
Zagros Mts., Iran .. 24 B3 33 45N 48 5 E
Zahedan, Iran ..... 24 C5 29 30N 60 50 E
Zaïre = Congo, Dem.
  Rep. of the ■, Africa 32 E4 3 0S 23 0 E
Zaïre →, Africa ... 32 F2 6 4S 12 24 E
Zákinthos, Greece .. 13 F9 37 47N 20 57 E
Zambezi →, Africa . 33 H7 18 35S 36 20 E
Zambia ■, Africa .. 33 G5 15 0S 28 0 E
Zamboanga, Phil. .. 22 C4 6 59N 122 3 E
Zamora, Spain 9 B3 41 30N 5 45W
Zamość, Poland ... 11 C12 50 43N 23 15 E
Zanesville, U.S.A. .. 42 F6 39 56N 82 1W
Zanjan, Iran ...... 24 B3 36 40N 48 35 E
Zanzibar, Tanzania . 32 F7 6 12S 39 12 E
Zaporozhye, Ukraine 15 E6 47 50N 35 10 E
Zaragoza, Spain ... 9 B5 41 39N 0 53W
Zaria, Nigeria .... 30 B3 11 0N 7 40 E
Zaskar Mts., India .. 23 C6 33 15N 77 30 E
Zeebrugge, Belgium . 10 C2 51 19N 3 12 E
Zeerust, S. Africa .. 31 B4 25 31S 26 4 E
Zenica, Bos.-H. ... 13 B7 44 10N 17 57 E
Zhangjiakou, China . 21 B6 40 48N 114 55 E
Zhangzhou, China .. 21 D6 24 30N 117 35 E
Zhanjiang, China .. 21 D6 21 15N 110 20 E
Zhejiang □, China .. 21 D7 29 0N 120 0 E
Zhengzhou, China .. 21 C6 34 45N 113 34 E
Zhigansk, Russia .. 18 C14 66 48N 123 27 E
Zhitomir, Ukraine .. 11 C15 50 20N 28 40 E
Zibo, China .... 21 C6 36 47N 118 3 E
Zielona Góra, Poland 10 C8 51 57N 15 31 E
Zigong, China ..... 20 D5 29 15N 104 48 E
Ziguinchor, Senegal . 28 F1 12 35N 16 20W
Žilina, Slovak Rep. . 11 D10 49 12N 18 42 E
Zimbabwe ■, Africa 33 H5 19 0S 30 0 E
Zion National Park,
  U.S.A. 40 C4 37 15N 113 5W
Zlatoust, Russia ... 14 C10 55 10N 59 40 E
Zlin, Czech Rep. ... 11 D9 49 14N 17 40 E
Zonguldak, Turkey . 15 F5 41 28N 31 50 E
Zrenjanin, Serbia, Yug. 13 B9 45 22N 20 23 E
Zug, Switz. .... 10 E5 47 10N 8 31 E
Zunyi, China ...... 20 D5 27 42N 106 53 E
Zürich, Switz. ..... 10 E5 47 22N 8 32 E
Zwickau, Germany . 10 C7 50 44N 12 30 E
Zwolle, Neths. .... 10 B4 52 31N 6 6 E

Place names on the yellow-coded large scale map section are to be found in the index at the end of that section